*Diversity in the Power Elite*

RICHARD L. ZWEIGENHAFT
AND G. WILLIAM DOMHOFF

# *Diversity in the Power Elite*

HAVE WOMEN AND MINORITIES
REACHED THE TOP?

*Yale University Press*
*New Haven & London*

Set in Sabon type by Keystone Typesetting, Inc.
Printed in the United States of America.

Library of Congress Cataloging-in-Publication Data
Zweigenhaft, Richard L
  Diversity in the power elite : have women and minorities reached the top? /
Richard L Zweigenhaft and G. William Domhoff.
      p.      cm.
  Includes bibliographical references and index.
  ISBN 0-300-07236-8 (alk. paper)
  1. Elite (Social sciences) — United States.   2. Power (Social sciences) —
United States.   3. Pluralism (Social sciences) — United States.   4. Minorities —
United States.   5. Women civic leaders — United States.   I. Domhoff,
G. William.   II. Title.
HN90.E4Z94   1998
305.5'2'0973 — dc21                                                    97-17541

A catalogue record for this book is available from the British Library.

The paper in this book meets the guidelines for permanence and durability of the Committee on Production Guidelines for Book Longevity of the Council on Library Resources.

10  9  8  7  6  5  4  3  2  1

# Contents

# Preface

This is the third in a trilogy of books we have written together on diversity in the power elite. The first, *Jews in the Protestant Establishment,* published in 1982, was a study of Jews in the American corporate elite. It showed that class is more important than ethnicity at the highest levels of the social structure. The second, *Blacks in the White Establishment? A Study of Race and Class in America,* published in 1991, traced the careers of African Americans who had attended elite boarding schools and universities in their youth. It concluded that race remained more important than class in the lives of these highly successful men and women.

Now, in this third book, we examine the extent to which the power elite described by C. Wright Mills in 1956 — a power elite that was exclusively white, male and almost entirely Christian — has become diversified in terms of gender, ethnicity, race, sexual orientation and social class. To the extent that the power elite has become diversified, we explore why this has happened, who has and has not become part of the power elite, and what the implications are for understanding the workings of the power elite.

In this book, as in the previous two, we have tried to blend our appreciation of the two disciplines of sociology and psychology. We have explored both structural processes (often considered part of stratification) and more personal processes related to identity formation (often considered part of personality and social psychology). We think of our work as "social psychological" in the broadest, and we believe best, sense of the term.

In venturing forth on a project that cuts across so many specializations and sensitive issues, we are especially grateful to the many colleagues and friends who gave us guidance throughout our research and writing. We want to thank Deborah Woo and Catherine Lew for the important background information they provided us through interviews and reports that gave us the basis for writing the chapter on Asian Americans, and to thank Woo for her careful reading of that chapter. Tom Pettigrew read most of the manuscript and gave us valuable feedback and much-appreciated encouragement. In addition, the following people read portions of the manuscript, and we wish to thank them for their helpful and honest comments: Edna Bonacich, John D'Emilio, Joe Feagin, Aida Hurtado, Jeffrey Janowitz, John Kitsuse, Wendy Mink, Laura O'Toole, Vânia Penha-Lopes, Martha Julia Sellers, Steve Sellers, Lynda Woodworth, and Lisa Young. We also thank Steve Wright, whose experimental work on the effects of placing tokens in power groups sensitized us to the ironic effects of tokenism in tending to demobilize excluded groups. We are most grateful to Richard Alba for his thorough and thoughtful reading of the entire manuscript, and to Gladys Topkis, our wonderful editor at Yale, for her enthusiastic support, her helpful comments, and her gentle but firm guidance. We also wish to thank Dan Heaton for his adroit manuscript editing, Maritza Almeida for her patient guidance on when and where to use accents in Chapter 4, and Lynda Woodworth of Catalyst, Peter Garrett of Directorship, and Charles Moskos of Northwestern University for their generous sharing of data.

The younger-but-senior author, Richie Zweigenhaft, received various forms of assistance from Guilford College. In particular, he wishes to express appreciation for a sabbatical leave in the fall of 1995, and for various research grants from the Office of the Academic Dean and the Faculty Development Program. He would also like to thank all of the librarians at Guilford for their help on this project, most especially, Betty Place, as well as the following Guilford students or former students for their research assistance: Cari Boram, Katharine Cannon, Michael Hamilton, Damara Luce, Patty Perez, Michael Peterson, Jennifer Simms, and Sonora Stein. In addition, he would like to express deep appreciation and affection for the members of the psychology department — they have provided both collegiality and friendship for many years. We would also like to thank Jessica Hasson, a student at the University of California, Santa Cruz, for helping us with the study of photographs of Latino corporate directors described in Chapter 4.

# Introduction:
## Has the Power Elite Gone Multicultural?

Injustices based on race, gender, ethnicity, and sexual orientation have been the most emotional and contested issues in American society since the end of the 1960s, far exceeding concerns with social class, and rivaled only by conflicts about abortion. These issues are now subsumed under the umbrella terms *diversity* and *multiculturalism,* and they have been written about extensively from the perspectives of both the aggrieved and those at the middle and lower levels of the social ladder who resist any changes.

In this book we look at multiculturalism from a new angle: we examine its impact on the small group at the top of American society that we call the power elite — those who own and manage large banks and corporations, finance the political campaigns of conservative Democrats and virtually all Republicans at the state and national levels, and serve in government as appointed officials and military leaders. We ask whether the decades of pressure from civil rights groups, feminists, and gay and lesbian rights activists has resulted in a more culturally diverse power elite. If it has, what effects has this new diversity had on the functioning of the power elite and on its relation to the rest of society?

We also compare our findings on the power elite with those from our parallel study of Congress to see whether there are differences in social background, education, and party affiliation for minorities and women in these two realms of power. We explore the possibility that elected officials come from a wider range of occupational and income backgrounds than members of the power elite. In addition, we ask whether either of the major political parties has been more active than the other in advancing the careers of women and minorities.

According to many commentators, the higher circles in the United States had indeed become multicultural by the late 1980s and early 1990s. Some went even further, saying that the old power elite had been pushed aside entirely. The demise of the "old" power elite was the theme of such books as Nelson Aldrich's *Old Money* and Robert Christopher's *Crashing the Gates,* the latter emphasizing the rise of ethnic minorities.[1] There have also been wide-eyed articles in mainstream magazines, such as one in the late 1980s in *U.S. News and World Report* entitled "The New American Establishment," which celebrated a new diversity at the top, claiming that "new kinds of men and women" have "taken control of institutions that influence important aspects of American life." School and club ties are no longer important, the article announced; the new role of women was highlighted with a picture of some of the "wise women" who had joined the "wise men" who dominated the old establishment.[2]

Then, in July 1995, *Newsweek* ran a cover story on "The Rise of the Overclass," featuring a gallery of one hundred high-tech, media, and Wall Street stars, women as well as men, minorities as well as whites, who supposedly come from all rungs of the social ladder.[3] The term *overclass* was relatively new, but the argument — that the power elite was dead, superseded by a diverse meritocratic elite — was not.

We are wary about these claims announcing the arrival of new elites because they never have been documented systematically. Moreover, they are suspect because similar claims have been made repeatedly in American history and have been proved incorrect each time. In popular books and magazines from the 1830s, 1920s, and 1950s, the leading commentators of the day assert that there used to be a tightly knit and cohesive governing group in the United States, but not any longer. A closer look at the supposedly new era several decades later has invariably shown that the new power group was primarily the old one after all, with a few additions and alterations here and there.[4]

1. Nelson W. Aldrich Jr., *Old Money: The Mythology of America's Upper Class* (New York: Knopf, 1988); Robert C. Christopher, *Crashing the Gates: The De-WASPing of America's Power Elite* (New York: Simon and Schuster, 1989).

2. "The New American Establishment," *U.S. News and World Report,* February 8, 1988, pp. 39, 45–46.

3. "The Rise of the Overclass," *Newsweek,* July 31, 1995, pp. 32–46.

4. Edward Pessen, *Riches, Class, and Power Before the Civil War* (Lexington, Mass.: D. C. Heath, 1973); Edward Pessen, ed., *Three Centuries of Social Mobility in America* (Lexington, Mass.: D. C. Heath, 1974).

Since the 1870s the refrain about the new diversity of the governing circles has been closely intertwined with a staple of American culture created by Horatio Alger Jr., whose name has become synonymous with upward mobility in America. Born in 1832 to a patrician family — Alger's father was a Harvard graduate, a Unitarian minister, and a Massachusetts state senator — Alger graduated from Harvard at the age of nineteen. There followed a series of unsuccessful efforts to establish himself in various careers. Finally, in 1864 Alger was hired as a Unitarian minister in Brewster, Massachusetts. Fifteen months later, he was dismissed from this position for homosexual acts with boys in the congregation.

Alger returned to New York, where he soon began to spend a great deal of time at the Newsboys' Lodging House, founded in 1853 for footloose youngsters between the ages of twelve and sixteen and home to many youths who had been mustered out of the Union Army after serving as drummer boys. At the Newsboys' Lodging House Alger found his literary niche and his subsequent claim to fame: writing books in which poor boys make good. His books sold by the hundreds of thousands in the last third of the nineteenth century, and by 1910 they were enjoying annual sales of more than one million in paperback.[5]

The deck is not stacked against the poor, according to Horatio Alger. When they simply show a bit of gumption, work hard, and thereby catch a break or two, they can become part of the American elite. The persistence of this theme, reinforced by the annual Horatio Alger Awards to such well-known personalities as Ronald Reagan, Bob Hope, and Billy Graham (who might not have been so eager to accept them if they had known of Alger's shadowed past), suggests that we may be dealing once again with a cultural myth. In its early versions, of course, the story concerned the great opportunities available for poor white boys willing to work their way to the top. More recently, the story has featured black Horatio Algers who started in the ghetto, Latino Horatio Algers who started in the barrio, Asian-American Horatio Algers whose parents were immigrants, and female Horatio Algers who seem to have no class backgrounds — all of whom now sit on the boards of the country's largest corporations.

But is any of this true? Can anecdotes and self-serving autobiographical accounts about diversity, meritocracy, and upward social mobility survive a more systematic analysis? Have very many women and previously excluded minorities made it to the top? Has class lost its importance in shaping life chances?

5. See Richard M. Huber, *The American Idea of Success* (New York: McGraw Hill, 1971), 44–46; Gary Scharnhorst, *Horatio Alger, Jr.* (Boston: Twayne, 1980), 24, 29, 141.

In this book we address these and related questions within the framework provided by the iconoclastic sociologist C. Wright Mills in his hard-hitting classic *The Power Elite,* published in 1956 when the media were in the midst of what Mills called the Great American Celebration. In spite of the Depression of the 1930s, Americans had pulled together to win World War II, and the country was both prosperous at home and influential abroad. Most of all, according to enthusiasts, the United States had become a relatively classless and pluralistic society, where power belonged to the people through their political parties and public opinion. Some groups certainly had more power than others, but no group or class had too much. The New Deal and World War II had forever transformed the corporate-based power structure of earlier decades.

Mills challenged this celebration of pluralism by studying the social backgrounds and career paths of the people who occupied the highest positions in what he saw as the three major institutional hierarchies in postwar America — the corporations, the executive branch of the federal government, and the military. He found that almost all the members of this leadership group, which he called the power elite, were white Christian males who came from "at most, the upper third of the income and occupational pyramids," despite the many Horatio Algeresque claims to the contrary.[6] A majority came from an even narrower stratum, the 11 percent of U.S. families headed by businesspeople or highly educated professionals like physicians and lawyers. Mills concluded that power in the United States in the 1950s was just about as concentrated as it had been since the rise of the large corporations, although he stressed that the New Deal and World War II had given political appointees and military chieftains more authority than they had exercised previously.

It is our purpose, therefore, to take a detailed look at the social, educational, and occupational backgrounds of the leaders of these three institutional hierarchies to see whether they have become more diverse in terms of gender, race, ethnicity, and sexual orientation, and also in terms of socioeconomic origins. Unlike Mills, we think the power elite is more than a set of institutional leaders. It is also the leadership group for the small upper class of owners and managers of large income-producing properties, the 1 percent of Americans who in 1992 possessed 37.2% of all net worth.[7] But that theoretical difference is not of great moment here. The important commonality is the great wealth and power embodied in these institutional hierarchies and the people who lead them.

6. C. Wright Mills, *The Power Elite* (New York: Oxford University Press, 1956), 279. For Mills's specific findings, see 104–105, 128–129, 180–181, 393–394, and 400–401.
7. Edward N. Wolff, *Top Heavy* (New York: New Press, 1996), 67.

We first study the directors and chief executive officers of the largest banks and corporations, as determined by annual rankings compiled by *Fortune* magazine. The use of *Fortune* rankings is now standard practice in studies of corporate size and power. Over the years, *Fortune* has changed the number of corporations on its annual list and the way it groups them. For example, the separate listings by business sector in the past, like "life insurance companies," "diversified financial companies," and "service companies," have been combined into one overall list, primarily because many large businesses are now in more than one of the traditional sectors. Generally speaking, we use the *Fortune* list or lists available for the time period under consideration.

Second, again following Mills, we focus on the appointees to the president's cabinet when we turn to the "political directorate," his general term for top-level officials in the executive branch of the federal government. We also have included the director of the Central Intelligence Agency in one chapter because of the increased importance of that agency since Mills wrote. In chapters concerning groups that have not had anyone in presidential cabinets, we profile the highest-level appointees as of 1995. Third, and rounding out our portrait of the power elite, we examine the same top positions in the military — generals and admirals — that formed the basis for Mills's look at the military elite.

As noted at the outset of this introduction, we also study Congress. In the case of senators, we do the same kind of background studies that we do for members of the power elite. For members of the House of Representatives, we concern ourselves only with party affiliation for most groups. We include findings on women and minority senators and representatives for two reasons. First, this allows us to see whether there is more diversity in the electoral system than in the power elite. Second, we do not think — as Mills did — that Congress should be relegated to the "middle level" of power. To the contrary, we believe that Congress is an integral part of the power structure in America.

Until the 1980s, most northern Republicans and most southern Democrats supported the power elite on the labor, welfare, and business regulation issues critical to it, whereas a majority of Democrats outside of the South were sympathetic to a coalition of liberals, minorities, and labor. Due to the Voting Rights Act of 1965 and the gradual industrialization of the South since World War II, southern conservatives have moved steadily into the Republican Party. At the same time, many moderate Republicans outside the South have been defeated by Democrats, leading to a situation where the two major power coalitions are increasingly housed almost exclusively in just one of the two dominant political parties. We therefore can use party preference to gauge whether women and minorities in the power elite differ from women and minorities elected to Congress in terms of how liberal or conservative they are.

In addition to studying the extent to which women and minorities have risen in the system, we focus on whether they have followed different avenues to the top than their predecessors did, and on any special roles they may play. Are they in the innermost circles of the power elite, or are they more likely to serve as buffers and go-betweens? Do they go just so far and no farther? What obstacles does each group face?

We also examine whether or not the presence of women and minorities affects the power elite itself. Do those women and minorities who become part of the power elite influence it in a more liberal direction, or do they end up endorsing traditional conservative positions, such as opposition to trade unions, taxes, and government regulation of business? In addition, in the final chapter we consider the possibility that the diversity forced on the power elite has had the ironic effect of strengthening it, at least in the short run, by providing it with people who can reach out to the previously excluded groups and by showing that the American system can deliver on its most important promise, an equal opportunity for every individual.

These are not simple issues, and the answers to some of the questions we ask vary greatly depending on which previously disadvantaged group we are talking about. Nonetheless, in the course of our research, a few general patterns emerged that we examine throughout the text and then tie together in the final chapter. Six general points may help readers to see the patterns develop as we embark upon a narrative in the next six chapters that focuses on specific issues related to entry into the power elite by Jews, women, blacks, Latinos, Asian Americans, and, finally, gays and lesbians.

1. The power elite now shows considerable diversity, at least as compared with its state in the 1950s, but its core group continues to be wealthy white Christian males, most of whom are still from the upper third of the social ladder. They have been filtered through a handful of elite schools in law, business, public policy, and international relations.

2. In spite of the increased diversity of the power elite, high social origins continue to be a distinct advantage in making it to the top. There are relatively few rags-to-riches stories in the groups we studied, and those we did find tended to come through the electoral process, usually within the Democratic Party. In general, it still takes at least three generations to rise from the bottom to the top in the United States.

3. The new diversity within the power elite is transcended by common values and a sense of hard-earned class privilege. The newcomers to the power elite have found ways to signal that they are willing to join the game as it has always been played, assuring the old guard that they will call for no

more than relatively minor adjustments, if that. There are few liberals and fewer crusaders in the power elite, despite its new multiculturalism. Class backgrounds, current roles, and future aspirations are more powerful in shaping behavior in the power elite than gender, ethnicity, or race.

4. Not all the groups we studied have been equally successful in contributing to the new diversity in the power elite. Women, blacks, Latinos, Asian Americans, and openly homosexual men and women are all underrepresented, but to varying degrees and with different rates of increasing representation. We will explore the reasons for these differences in our final chapter.

5. Although the corporate, political, and military elites accepted diversity only in response to pressure from minority activists and feminists, these elites have benefited from the presence of new members. Some serve either a buffer or a liaison function with such groups and institutions as consumers, angry neighborhoods, government agencies, and wealthy foreign entrepreneurs.

6. There is greater diversity in Congress than in the power elite, and the majority of the female and minority elected officals are Democrats.

We begin with the story of how Jews, over the course of the twentieth century, have become fully participating members of the power elite. As one of the most discriminated against of the white ethnic immigrant groups, Jews have been studied in great detail. Their assimilation into the highest circles can serve as a benchmark.

Although anti-Catholicism nearly reached the levels of anti-Semitism in some contexts early in the twentieth century, we do not use the acceptance of Catholics into the power elite as a benchmark for several reasons. Discrimination against Jews, unlike discrimination against Catholics, had cultural and racist overtones that went far beyond religious differences. Moreover, the exclusion of Jews was more complete than was the exclusion of Catholics, and the acceptance of Catholics into the establishment occurred earlier than did the acceptance of Jews. In 1954 when he published his classic work *The Nature of Prejudice*, Gordon Allport was still concerned about anti-Catholicism.[8] By the late 1950s, however, anti-Catholicism had declined dramatically, a condition that was confirmed by the election of the Irish Catholic John F. Kennedy as president in 1960. As E. Digby Baltzell pointed out in *The Protestant Establishment*, Kennedy's election "marked a definite trend toward a

8. Gordon W. Allport, *The Nature of Prejudice* (Garden City, N.Y.: Doubleday, 1954; Anchor abr. ed., 1958), 224–226, 239.

representative establishment as far as the Catholic community is concerned."[9] In clear contrast, Jews still faced considerable discrimination at that time, both in and out of the establishment.

Still, we recognize that the changed situation for Jews does not provide a perfect basis for comparison with the experiences of women and minorities. For one thing, Jews accounted for only 3.3 percent of the population in 1950, at a time when 10 percent of the population was black — and they make up only about 2 percent now, when blacks constitute nearly 14 percent and Latinos 10 percent. For another, many Jews, more than is generally realized, came to the United States with economic or educational advantages, especially those who became major corporate figures.[10]

Following the chapter on Jews (Chapter 2) are empirically based chapters on women (Chapter 3), blacks (Chapter 4), Latinos (Chapter 5), and Asian Americans (Chapter 6) in the power elite. We also have included a chapter on gay men and lesbians (Chapter 7), in which we faced challenging research issues. We know that there are Jews, women, blacks, Latinos, and Asian Americans in the power elite, but, unless they have chosen to be public about their sexual orientation, we can only assume that some of those in the power elite are gay. From our perspective the relevant issue is not how many in the power elite are gay or who they are, but whether or not those who are gay feel comfortable in acknowledging this publicly. Given the dependence of the researcher upon self-disclosure by gay men and lesbians, sexual orientation is a more difficult topic to study than gender or race, so the data we draw upon to address this issue are not as systematic as they are in other chapters. Nevertheless, the findings we draw upon, most of which are based on studies by gay and lesbian researchers, provide a solid basis for our conclusion that as yet there is little or no tolerance for diversity of sexual orientation within the power elite.

Because people have more than one identity and therefore are not solely women or black or homosexual, overlaps and cross-weavings in our presentation are inevitable. We have organized our findings into chapters that focus on a single identity at a time. When relevant, however, we attempt to address the complexity that can emerge when two or more of a person's identities seem to matter in his or her career.

Although our range of groups is a wide one, we have not tried to be com-

9. E. Digby Baltzell, *The Protestant Establishment: Aristocracy and Caste in America* (New York: Random House, 1964; New Haven: Yale University Press, 1987), 83.

10. See Stephen Steinberg, *The Ethnic Myth: Race, Ethnicity, and Class in America* (New York: Atheneum, 1981); Richard L. Zweigenhaft and G. William Domhoff, *Jews in the Protestant Establishment* (New York: Praeger, 1982).

pletely inclusive. First, we have not analyzed the fortunes of recent immigrant groups that have fewer than a million members in the United States. These include immigrants from India and Thailand, refugees from Cambodia and Vietnam, and immigrants from small Pacific Islands and various countries in Africa. They have not been here long enough to establish a clear pattern, and there is less information available on them than there is on the groups that we have chosen to write about. Further, we see little evidence that any of them are represented in the highest levels of the American power structure.

Second, we have not dealt with the diverse group of tribes that are variously called American Indians or Native Americans. There are several reasons for this decision. To begin with, as of the 1990 census there were only 1.96 million American Indians — less than 1 percent of the population — and 59 percent of those who are married are married to non-Indians.[11] Moreover, those who are exclusively Native Americans in their heritage live separately from one another in small culturally distinct groups in every part of the United States. Finally, 21 percent of those who identify themselves as members of one or another Native American group live on reservations apart from the rest of American society, which means that they are not likely to become part of the power elite or be elected to Congress.[12] We do, however, see the subjugated position of Native Americans who are on reservations as one component of the theoretical argument we shall present in the final chapter about why some minority groups are more successful than others at making their way into the ranks of the power elite.

11. Karl Eschbach, "The Enduring and Vanishing American Indian: American Indian Population Growth and Intermarriage in 1990," *Ethnic and Racial Studies* 18, no. 1 (1995), 89–108. There were only 377,000 American Indians in 1950, before the new social movements made an Indian identity both respectable and useful. Many of those who now identify themselves as Native Americans have only one grandparent or great-grandparent who was Indian.

12. See Mary B. Davis, ed., *Native America in the Twentieth Century: An Encyclopedia* (New York: Garland, 1994). The most visible Native American in an important position in American society is Ben Nighthorse Campbell, who was elected to the U.S. Senate as a Democrat in 1992 and then switched to the Republican Party shortly thereafter. Campbell's father was part Apache, part Pueblo Indian, and part Cheyenne. His mother was a Portuguese immigrant. Following his father's advice, as a boy and as a young man Ben Campbell did not acknowledge his Native American heritage. Not until the mid-1960s, when he was in his thirties, did he decide to investigate his Indian background. In 1980, at the age of forty-seven, he became a member of the Northern Cheyenne tribe and adopted the middle name Nighthorse (*Current Biography* [1994], 86–90).

# Jews in the Power Elite

Most Jewish immigrants came to America because they perceived it as the land of opportunity, but many also came to escape religious persecution. It has been well documented that Jews in the United States have been extremely successful, and, as we shall demonstrate, in the past few decades they have achieved full representation, even overrepresentation, in the power elite and Congress. But the America that most Jewish immigrants encountered was not as free of anti-Semitism as it is now: the successful assimilation of Jews into the highest circles of power is all the more noteworthy because of the widespread religious discrimination that persisted until well after the publication of Mills's *The Power Elite* in 1956.

When the centimillionaire Laurence Tisch was growing up in the 1940s, an ambitious young Jewish man was making a mistake if he went to work for one of the large corporations — unless it was a company that had been founded by Jews. Discrimination against Jews in the corporate world was such that he might be hired, if he didn't look or act "too Jewish," but he would not rise very high in the company. After Tisch and his brother Robert parlayed a moderately successful family business into one of the largest diversified financial corporations in America, worth billions, Tisch told us in a 1980 interview that "the Jews are better off not being in these big corporations because all they'll do is get bogged down."[1] A few years later, he bought CBS.

Similarly, very few Jews had been elected to high political office before the 1970s, even though Stephen Isaacs's book *Jews and American Politics,* published in 1974, presented extensive evidence that Jews were more involved in the political process than any other group of Americans. His criteria included voter turnout, work on political campaigns, fund raising, political polling, and political commentary. "In America," Isaacs wrote, "Jews stand out in every political area save one: holding elective office."[2] By the 1990s, however, far more Jews had been elected to the Senate and the House than would be expected on the basis of their representation in the population at large, even from districts with a relative handful of Jewish voters.

Nor was the military free of discrimination against Jews. Leonard Kaplan was one of 955 entering members of the class of 1922 at the U.S. Naval Academy. When the members of each class arrived at Annapolis in those days, each was required to write his name, hometown, date and place of birth, religion, and father's occupation in a register. Kaplan was one of seventeen midshipmen who wrote that their religion was "Jewish" or "Hebrew."[3]

Kaplan's experience at the Naval Academy consisted of four years of vicious and abominable treatment by his classmates. In the lingo of the day, he was "sent to Coventry" — no one spoke to him or even acknowledged his presence. He lived alone for four years. When the yearbook appeared at the end of his senior year, it included a crude cartoon of him, a derogatory biographical sketch (claiming, for example, that he was "born in the township of Zion, county of Cork, State of Ignorance"), and his name was omitted from the index; moreover, unlike all the other pages in the yearbook, the page about him was perforated so that it could be torn out and discarded with ease.[4] In 1995, the head of the CIA and the top admiral in the navy were both Jewish, and the fact was virtually ignored by the media.

Anti-Semitism at the Naval Academy was part of a broader pattern of prejudice and discrimination against Jews in the United States in the 1920s.

1. Personal interview by Richard Zweigenhaft with Laurence Tisch, New York, July 23, 1980.

2. Stephen D. Isaacs, *Jews and American Politics* (Garden City, N.Y.: Doubleday, 1974), 10.

3. Norman Polmar and Thomas B. Allen, *Rickover: Controversy and Genius* (New York: Simon and Schuster, 1982), 39–40.

4. Not all Jewish midshipmen at the Naval Academy in the early 1920s were "sent to Coventry," but various forms of hazing were widespread, and no one escaped it completely. Two members of the class of 1923 who may have been Jewish (one was named

Henry Ford, one of the most influential and respected Americans (one survey of college students found that he was rated the third "greatest man of all time," right after Napoleon and Jesus Christ), was virulently anti-Semitic. His public statements and his publications earned him the attention of many who hated Jews and presumably helped to persuade others to do so. In fact, Adolf Hitler periodically expressed his admiration for Ford, stating that "we look to Ford as the leader of the growing Fascist party in America" and "I regard Henry Ford as my inspiration."[5] Throughout the 1920s, many Jews refused to purchase Ford automobiles.[6]

Nor were the most prestigious colleges and universities free of discrimination against Jews, either in their hiring or in their admissions policies. In 1922 the president of Harvard urged the university to adopt a quota system to solve "the Jewish problem." A similar stance by the president of Columbia University cut the percentage of Jews at Columbia from 40 percent to 20 percent within two years. Many medical schools and other professional schools joined a growing number of undergraduate colleges in restricting access to Jewish students. Jewish academicians had a difficult time obtaining positions or attaining tenure at these schools.[7]

Anti-Semitism is not dead in the United States, but study after study indicates that it has diminished dramatically since World War II, and Jews have ended up more successful than any other white immigrant group. As Seymour Martin Lipset and Earl Raab write, Jews are "the best educated, the most middle-class, and, ultimately, the most affluent ethnoreligious group in the country. No other immigrant group has evinced such rapid and dramatic success."[8]

---

Seltzer and the other Wetherstine, but neither listed himself as Jewish on arrival) attempted suicide as a result of the vicious hazing they experienced. This led to a congressional investigation (ibid., 51–52, 55–57).

5. Albert Lee, *Henry Ford and the Jews* (New York: Stein and Day, 1980), 3, 46.

6. Stanley Feldstein, *The Land That I Show You* (Garden City, N.Y.: Anchor, 1978), 224–227.

7. E. Digby Baltzell, *The Protestant Establishment: Aristocracy and Caste in America* (New York: Random House, 1964; New Haven: Yale University Press, 1987), 210–211; M. G. Synnott, *The Half-Opened Door: Discrimination at Harvard, Yale, and Princeton, 1900–1970* (Westport, Conn.: Greenwood, 1979), 14–17; Dan A. Oren, *Joining the Club: A History of Jews and Yale* (New Haven: Yale University Press, 1985); Susanne Klingenstein, *Jews in the American Academy, 1900–1940* (New Haven: Yale University Press, 1991).

8. Seymour Martin Lipset and Earl Raab, *Jews and the New American Scene* (Cambridge: Harvard University Press, 1995), 27.

But Jews are not merely "the most middle-class" and the most affluent white immigrant group. They have become full-fledged members of the power elite, which makes it useful to look at the dramatic change Jews have experienced for clues to understanding the prejudice and obstacles that face women and minorities when they demand entry into the higher levels of society. First, however, there is a tricky preliminary question that must be addressed.

### So Who's Jewish Anyhow?

As a girl, Dianne Goldman had a double exposure to religion: her mother was Catholic and her father was Jewish. She attended Catholic schools, graduating in 1951 from the Convent of the Sacred Heart High School in San Francisco. As she recalls her upbringing, "I was brought up supposedly with some Catholic religion and some Jewish, and I was to choose. I went to a convent and I went to a temple at the same time, but I don't think that works very well."[9] Dianne Goldman was married three times, to Jewish men named Jack Berman, Bertram Feinstein, and Richard Blum.[10] She goes by the surname of her second husband. But is Dianne Feinstein, United States senator from California, Jewish?

Richard Darman held a series of high-level government jobs during the Reagan and Bush administrations, including director of the Office of Management and Budget. His grandfather had been president of his synagogue, his father the founder and president of another synagogue. Darman himself was raised as a Jew and had a bar mitzvah. But Darman married a Gentile woman and became an Episcopalian.[11] Is Darman Jewish?

Whether Dianne Feinstein or Richard Darman is Jewish depends on whom you ask and what definition is used. It is no easy question. Indeed, the noted anthropologist Melville Herskovits claimed that "of all human groupings, there is none wherein the problem of definition has proved to be more difficult than for the Jews."[12] Defining who is Jewish may not be the most difficult of

9. "Dianne Feinstein," *Current Biography* (1979), 128.

10. Jerry Roberts, *Dianne Feinstein: Never Let Them See You Cry* (San Francisco: HarperCollins West, 1994).

11. Marjorie Williams, "The Long and the Short of Richard G. Darman," *Washington Post Magazine*, July 29, 1990, pp. 10–15, 25–33. Williams writes, "Darman grew touchy when asked about his grandfather and his religion, explaining that his background is 'complex,' including Jewish and Catholic forebears. He is, he said, 'a mongrel and currently a practicing Episcopalian'" (p. 25). See also Barry Rubin, *Assimilation and Its Discontents* (New York: Knopf, 1995), 218.

12. Melville Herskovits, "Who Are the Jews?" in Abraham Chapman, ed., *Jewish-American Literature: An Anthology* (New York: New American Library), 473.

"all human groupings" — as we shall see in subsequent chapters, defining who is black, Hispanic, or Asian American is no easy task either — but it is certainly a matter of considerable complexity.

At different times, in different places, and with different political agendas, different criteria have been applied to determine whether or not someone is Jewish. In general, four major definitions have prevailed. The first and most traditional is based on the body of Jewish religious law called the *halacha;* it states that a person is Jewish if he or she was born to a Jewish mother or has followed a prescribed set of procedures to convert to Judaism. A second way to define Jewishness is based not on birth or conversion but on conviction. According to this definition, people are Jewish if they consider themselves Jewish. This includes those whose mothers were Jewish and who see them-selves as Jewish, those whose fathers were Jewish and who see themselves as Jewish, and those who have converted. A third way to define Jewishness is based on an ancestral tabulation, according to which a person who has one Jewish parent (like Dianne Feinstein) is "half-Jewish," a person who has one Jewish grandparent is "one-fourth Jewish," and so on. A fourth definition of Jewishness, somewhat similar to our second, is based on membership in such Jewish institutions as synagogues or Jewish clubs. Such membership not only implies that one's self-identity includes being Jewish, but it also suggests some willingness for Jewish affiliations to be part of one's public identity.

In this chapter, we will generally draw on the second definition — if Dianne Feinstein thinks of herself as Jewish and Richard Darman thinks of himself as Episcopalian, those self-definitions are fine with us. But we will also pay atten-tion to the third definition — whether one's parents or grandparents were Jew-ish. If, for example, a member of the political, corporate, or military elite had a parent or grandparent who was Jewish but was not told about this, or knew it and denied it, this situation is revealing, for it demonstrates just how powerful the pressures were to assimilate. It is, for example, one thing to say that the influential journalist Walter Lippmann did not consider himself Jewish; it is quite another thing to say that he was born to wealthy and well-assimilated Jewish parents but would not join any Jewish organizations or even speak before any Jewish groups, and that he refused to accept an award from the Jewish Academy of Arts and Sciences.[13]

13. Ronald Steel, *Walter Lippmann and the American Century* (Boston: Little, Brown, 1980), 195. For a fascinating account of how Steel came to realize that Lippmann's Jewish background was the source of great personal anguish and should be an important component of his biography, see Ronald Steel, "Living With Walter Lippmann," in Wil-liam Zinsser, ed., *Extraordinary Lives: The Art and Craft of American Biography* (Bos-ton: Houghton Mifflin, 1986), 121–160.

We will also pay attention to the definition based on the religion of one's parents and grandparents because it has often been used by others to decide whether a person is Jewish, and in some situations other people's definitions of who we are take precedence over our own. As Laurence Tisch put it, "When Hitler came around he didn't ask questions whether you were or you weren't — it wasn't what you said, it was what he said."[14] Similarly, if the senior executives at a corporation did not want Jews in their midst, it was likely to be their definition of who was or was not Jewish that mattered. So, in order to understand why the power elite has been willing to accept more Jews into its ranks, we have to understand whom they have perceived as Jewish — and why this is apparently no longer of such concern to them.

## Jews in the Power Elite from the Era of C. Wright Mills to the Present

Americans have always believed that their society is different. It has no social classes. Anyone, through hard work, can be upwardly mobile. Even eminent historians have contributed to this belief. In portrayals of corporate leaders and the very rich, they have stressed examples of men who had gone from rags to riches, just as in the stories that Horatio Alger wrote. From this focus the historians have proceeded to broad generalizations based on a small number of biographies. For example, in *Political and Social Growth of the American People*, Arthur Schlesinger Sr., claimed that business leaders arose "in most cases from obscure origins, and unhindered by moral scruples, they were fired by a passionate will to succeed."[15]

But systematic studies showed otherwise. When William Miller of the Harvard University Research Center in Entrepreneurial History studied the backgrounds of 190 men who were business leaders between 1901 and 1910 — individuals "at the apex of some of the mightiest organizations the world up to then had seen" — he found that very few had come from impoverished backgrounds or even from working-class or foreign origins. In fact, 79 percent had fathers who were businessmen or professionals; only 12 percent had fathers who were farmers, and only 2 percent had fathers who were "workers." As Miller concluded: "American historians . . . stress this elite's typically lower-class, foreign, or farm *origins* and speculate on the forces that impelled men upward from such insalubrious environs. Yet poor immigrant boys and poor

14. Tisch interview; see also Richard L. Zweigenhaft and G. William Domhoff, *Jews in the Protestant Establishment* (New York: Praeger, 1982), 102.

15. Arthur M. Schlesinger Sr., *Political and Social Growth of the American People, 1865–1940* (New York: Macmillan, 1941), 129.

farm boys together actually make up no more than 3 percent of the business leaders who are the subject of this essay. . . . Poor immigrant and poor farm boys who become business leaders have always been more conspicuous in American history books than in American history."[16]

In another study of the backgrounds of business leaders — this one looked at the highest-ranking businessmen in 1900, 1925, and 1950 — Mabel Newcomer, chairwoman of the economics department at Vassar, also found that they tended to come from the upper levels of the class structure. Fully 55.7 percent of the fathers of the 1950 executives had been business executives (seven times the proportion of business executives in the U.S. population at the time the executives were born), and another 17.8 percent were professionals (six times the proportion of professional men in the population). When she divided the families of the 1950 executives into three classes and defined the lowest of the three as "poor," by which she meant those families that had not been able to contribute to their children's education beyond high school, she found that only 12.1 percent came from poor families. (The figure was virtually the same for the men who were top executives in 1900.)[17]

When C. Wright Mills examined the backgrounds of the "very rich" in 1900, 1925, and 1950, he found no support for the prevailing myth that most were the sons of immigrants who had pulled themselves up by their own bootstraps. Instead, the data led Mills to the following characterization: "American-born, city-bred, eastern-originated, the very rich have been from families of higher class status, and, like other members of the new and old upper classes of local society . . . they have been Protestants. Moreover, about half have been Episcopalians, and a fourth, Presbyterians."[18]

The "very rich" identified by Mills were not exactly the same people who occupied positions in the political, corporate, and military elites, but there was, Mills found, considerable overlap, especially between the very rich and the corporate elite. When he looked separately at the men who made up the political, corporate, and military elites, he found that in each case most were Protestant and that they were especially likely to be Episcopalians and Presbyterians. For example, Mills wrote that the members of the corporate elite in 1950 were "predominately Protestant and more likely, in comparison with the proportions at large, to be Episcopalians or Presbyterians than Baptists or

16. William Miller, "American Historians and the Business Elite," in William Miller, ed., *Men in Business* (New York: Harper and Row, 1962), 309–328.

17. Mabel Newcomer, *The Big Business Executive: The Factors That Made Him, 1900–1950* (New York: Columbia University Press, 1955), 55, 62–63.

18. C. Wright Mills, *The Power Elite* (New York: Oxford University Press, 1956), 106.

Methodists. The Jews and Catholics among them are fewer than among the population at large."[19]

The very rich and corporate elite also shared one other characteristic that is not mentioned by Mills because of his purposeful neglect of political parties: they were, and still are, overwhelmingly Republicans. The relatively few exceptions were wealthy southern whites, who at the time had a major role in the Democratic Party through its congressional delegation, and those Catholics and Jews who were Democrats due to the prejudices of the Protestant rich.

Mills did not focus on anti-Semitism, but eight years later, in *The Protestant Establishment,* Baltzell did. He did not use the term "power elite," for, unlike Mills, he believed that America had the potential to form a true aristocracy, which he chose to call an "establishment," based in part on class background but also in part on merit. Those born and bred to the upper class, Baltzell believed, could and should provide enlightened leadership for the entire society, but only if they were willing to accept new blood into their privileged ranks. "In a free society," Baltzell wrote, "while an establishment will always be dominated by the upper-class members, it also must be constantly rejuvenated by members of the elite who are in the process of acquiring upper-class status."[20] Baltzell, himself a product of an upper-class background and thus a person with an inside view, saw a battle within the establishment. On one hand were those who advocated allowing the best and most assimilated members of the lower classes to enter the clubs and social circles of the upper class, not only because it was the right and egalitarian thing to do but because it strengthened the existing order; this was the American "aristocracy" that Baltzell advocated. On the other hand were those whose prejudices against those beneath them in the class hierarchy led them to maintain the barriers. Their "caste" view, Baltzell believed, weakened the elite, making it ultimately unable to provide the leadership or expect the following that America needed.

## Jews in the Corporate Elite

On December 14, 1973, readers of *The Wall Street Journal* awoke to the following headline: "Boss-to-Be at DuPont Is an Immigrant's Son Who Climbed Hard Way." This was news, indeed, for the boss-to-be was not merely an immigrant and had not merely climbed the hard way but was Irving Shapiro, a Jew who had been named chairman of the board and chief executive officer of one of the oldest and largest corporations in America. Never before

19. Ibid., 127–128.
20. Baltzell, *Protestant Establishment,* 8.

had a Jew achieved such a prominent position in a corporation that had not been founded or purchased by Jews. Shapiro assumed that his appointment was a harbinger of things to come and that the barriers that had prevented Jews from rising to the top in the corporate world were finally coming down. As he explained in an interview shortly before his retirement in 1981: "That's really been the great dividend from my position. All kinds of people have moved up in banks and other corporations simply on the premise that there is no longer a barrier."[21]

In order to show just how many doors to the corporate elite have opened for Jews, we shall look at the presence of Jews in the higher circles of the corporate world throughout the twentieth century, paying special attention to their career pathways and to how their presence affected their identities as Jews.

### THE OVERREPRESENTATION OF JEWS IN THE CORPORATE ELITE

For the most part, the religious makeup of the corporate elite changed very little throughout the first half of the twentieth century, though there is evidence of a slight increase in the percentage of Jews during that time. In his study of the backgrounds of business leaders between 1901 and 1910, Miller found that 90 percent were Protestant, 7 percent were Catholic, and 3 percent were Jewish.[22] In her study of the backgrounds of presidents and chairmen of the largest companies in 1900, 1925, and 1950, Newcomer found that the percentage of Jews in the corporate elite was 3.4 percent at the turn of the century and had risen to 4.3 percent in 1925 and 4.6 percent by 1950. Jews were "heavily concentrated in the merchandising, entertainment, and mass communications fields," but very few were to be found in "heavy industry or public utilities, and none at all among the railroad executives." Moreover, she estimated that 40 percent of the Jews in her 1950 sample had "organized their own enterprises."[23]

A number of studies of the postwar era reveal that the percentage of Jews in the corporate elite continued to climb. Although these studies used different samples and methods, all looked at the ethnic backgrounds of *Fortune*-level corporate directors. The results are compelling in their consistent finding that Jews have been increasingly overrepresented.

In 1972, as part of the American Leadership Study by the Bureau of Applied Social Research at Columbia University, a sample of directors of *Fortune*-level

21. Personal interview by Richard Zweigenhaft with Irving Shapiro, Wilmington, Del., February 23, 1981.

22. Miller, "American Historians," 324.

23. Newcomer, *Big Business Executive,* 46–49.

companies and "holders of large fortunes" were interviewed. Although Jews constituted only about 3 percent of the national population at that time, 6.9 percent of these business leaders and affluent men were Jewish.[24] These findings mirrored those of a 1976 survey conducted by *Fortune,* which showed that 7 percent of the chief executive officers of 800 American corporations were Jewish.[25] At about the same time, Frederick Sturdivant and Roy Adler examined the backgrounds of 444 executives from 247 major American corporations. They found that 6 percent of their sample was Jewish.[26]

In a series of systematic studies performed in the late 1970s, and in interviews with thirty Jewish corporate directors conducted in 1980 and 1981, we found that Jews were well represented in the corporate elite but were more likely to be in small *Fortune*-level companies rather than large ones. We also found that they had traveled different pathways in getting to the corporate elite than had their Gentile counterparts. Whereas Gentile executives were most likely to have advanced through the managerial ranks of the corporation, the Jewish directors were most likely to have joined the boards as outsiders with expertise in such areas as investment banking, corporate law, or public relations — unless they had risen through the ranks of companies owned or founded by Jews.[27]

It is both noteworthy and informative that many of these Jewish directors had attained skills in areas that subsequently became necessary to the corporations. Rather than merely figuring out ways to gain entry into the corridors of corporate power, or waiting until the doors opened enough to let them in, many pursued less traditional areas, areas open to Jews, and the skills they developed later served as their entrée. In *A Certain People,* Charles Silberman describes the same pattern in prominent law firms and in the legal departments of large corporations in the postwar years. Both the corporations and law firms discovered that they needed lawyers who knew how to negotiate with trade unions and interpret the increasingly arcane tax laws.[28]

By the mid-1980s, studies indicated that the percentage of Jews in senior executive positions had climbed a bit higher. In a 1986 survey of the CEOs of

24. Richard D. Alba and Gwen Moore, "Ethnicity in the American Elite," *American Sociological Review* 47 (1982), 373–383.

25. Charles G. Burck, "A Group Profile of the Fortune 500 Chief Executive," *Fortune,* May 1976, pp. 174–175.

26. Frederick D. Sturdivant and Roy D. Adler, "Executive Origins: Still a Gray Flannel World," *Harvard Business Review,* November–December 1976, pp. 125–133.

27. See Zweigenhaft and Domhoff, *Jews in the Protestant Establishment,* 25–46.

28. Charles E. Silberman, *A Certain People: American Jews and Their Lives Today* (New York: Summit, 1985), 96–97.

Fortune 500 and Service 500 companies, modeled after Newcomer's 1955 study, *Fortune* found that 7.6 percent identified themselves as Jewish.[29] That same year, in a survey of 4,350 senior executives just below the chief-executive level, Korn-Ferry, an executive search firm, found that 7.4 percent were Jewish. More dramatic was the finding that 13 percent of those under the age of 40 were Jewish.[30]

As part of his dissertation on persistence and change in the power elite, Ralph Pyle looked at the backgrounds of large samples of individuals listed in the 1950 and 1992 editions of *Who's Who in America*. When he examined the religious affiliations of those who were chief executive officers, directors, or vice presidents of Fortune 500 or Service 500 companies, he found that in 1992 Episcopalians were 7.96 times as likely to be represented as their church membership figures would suggest (down from 8.42 times as likely in 1950); Presbyterians were 3.08 times as likely (down from 4.31 times as likely in 1950); and Jews were 2.76 times as likely (up from .76 times as likely in 1950). Episcopalians and Presbyterians were thus still very much overrepresented among corporate directors, though they had lost a little ground since 1950, but Jews had moved from being underrepresented in 1950 to being overrepresented in 1992.[31]

Pyle's systematic findings provide the most compelling evidence that the percentage of Jews in the corporate elite has increased since the 1950s. They do not, however, tell us whether Jews are less likely to be on the largest *Fortune*-level boards and more likely to be on the smaller ones, because his data are based on relatively small samples.

We therefore pursued this question by applying a very different technique, one that we also employ in the chapters on Latinos and Asian Americans. For

29. Maggie McComus, "Atop the Fortune 500: A Survey of the C.E.O.," *Fortune*, April 28, 1986, pp. 26–31. In 1956, in addition to its list of the top five hundred industrial corporations, *Fortune* began to publish a list of nonindustrial companies. By 1983 that list had become the Service 500, with companies grouped in several categories (banks, diversified services, life insurance, etc.). In 1995, because of the considerable blurring of lines that had been caused by mergers and acquisitions, *Fortune* decided to combine the industrial and service companies into a single list. See Thomas A. Stewart, "A New 500 for the New Economy," *Fortune*, May 15, 1995, p. 166.

30. Robert A. Bennett, "No Longer a WASP Preserve," *New York Times*, June 29, 1986.

31. Ralph E. Pyle, "Persistence and Change in the Establishment: Religion, Education and Gender Among America's Elite, 1950 and 1992," Ph.D. diss., Purdue University, 1995, p. 143; see also Ralph E. Pyle, *Persistence and Change in the Protestant Establishment* (Westport, Conn.: Praeger, 1996), 62.

years, demographers have used the distinctive names within racial and ethnic groups to estimate the size of various populations. As early as 1942, Samuel Kohs compiled a list of those names that appeared most frequently in the files of the Los Angeles Federation, an umbrella group for Jewish congregations and organizations in the Los Angeles area. Kohs found that the 106 most common surnames in those files accounted for about 16 percent of the names on various other Jewish Federation lists and that thirty-five names accounted for about 12 percent of the names on most lists. Various other researchers have since used his list of thirty-five names, or variations of it, and have found that the proportion of Jews with these distinctively Jewish names has remained relatively constant over time. Moreover, no meaningful differences in attitudes or behaviors have been found between Jews with distinctive and nondistinctive names.[32]

To determine the number of Jews on boards at the top and bottom of the *Fortune* list, we looked up each of the top 100 companies and each of the companies ranked between number 401 and number 500 for 1975, 1985, and 1995 in the corresponding editions of the *Standard and Poor's Directory,* which includes all the names of the men and women who sit on boards of directors. For each, we counted names that appear on the list of distinctive Jewish names. The results can be seen in table 1.1.

If we are correct in our assumption that the distinctive Jewish name (DJN) technique can be applied to corporate directors, then these figures suggest,

---

32. Harold S. Himmelfarb, R. Michael Loar, and Susan H. Mott, "Sampling by Ethnic Surnames: The Case of American Jews," *Public Opinion Quarterly* 47 (1983), 247–260. They conclude that the distinctive Jewish name (DJN) technique is particularly useful for those who are interested "in explanatory rather than descriptive studies (i.e., studies which are interested in explaining patterns rather than making accurate estimates of population characteristics") (254).

The thirty-five distinctive Jewish names are Berman, Bernstein, Caplan, Cohen, Cohn, Epstein, Feldman, Friedman, Ginsberg, Gold, Goldberg, Goldman, Goldstein, Greenberg, Grossman, Horowitz, Kahn, Kaplan, Katz, Levin, Levine, Levinson, Rosen, Rosenbaum, Rosenbloom, Rosenthal, Rothman, Rubin, Samuels, Shapiro, Siegel, Silverman, Weinberg, Weiner, and Weinstein.

Ira Rosenwaike, in "Surnames Among American Jews," *Names* 38 (1990), 31–38, demonstrates not only that many Jews have names that are not at all distinctively Jewish, such as Gordon and Miller, but that even among those people with distinctive Jewish names, like Cohen, a small percentage are not Jewish. His data, based on a 1982 survey of 1.2 million American men and women, conducted by the American Cancer Society, indicate that about 89 percent of those with the names on the thirty-five-name DJN list are Jewish. Even taking this into account, the estimates that we will present of the number of Jewish directors on *Fortune*-500 boards are still substantially higher than the percentage of Jews in the larger population.

Table 1.1
*Corporate Directors with Distinctive Jewish Names*

| | Rank of Companies | |
| --- | --- | --- |
| | 1–100 | 401–500 |
| 1975 | 11 | 14 |
| 1985 | 8 | 9 |
| 1995 | 17 | 5 |

first, that the total number of Jews with distinctive Jewish names on Fortune 500 boards has not increased since 1975 (in fact, there is a slight decrease); second, the presence of people with distinctive Jewish names on the boards of the biggest companies (the top 100) has increased, while the number on the boards of the smaller companies (numbers 401–500) has decreased; and, third, if it is the case that the number of Jews with these thirty-five distinctive Jewish names represents about 12 percent of the total number of Jews in the population under study, then the number of Jews on the 200 *Fortune* boards we looked at was about 210 in 1975, 140 in 1985, and 185 in 1995. These figures represent 6.6 percent, 4.3 percent, and 7.7 percent, respectively, of the total number of directors of the corporations studied in those years.[33]

The data based on distinctive Jewish names provide only an estimate of the percentage of Jews on corporate boards. Still, as can be seen in table 1.2, these findings, along with other findings reported in this section, demonstrate that as the percentage of Jews in America declined steadily in the twentieth century, the percentage of Jews on corporate boards increased. Jews are most certainly overrepresented in the corporate elite.

DO JEWS IN THE CORPORATE ELITE STAY JEWISH?

As we have indicated, the various waves of Jewish immigrants to America felt strong pressure to assimilate into the dominant Gentile culture. Many immigrants thus worked at becoming "more American" and "less Jewish." "More American" typically meant learning to speak English without an accent, dressing the way people in the new country dressed, and generally learn-

33. These percentages are based on an average board size of sixteen in 1975 and 1985 and fourteen in 1995. See Murray Weidenbaum, "The Evolving Corporate Board," *Society,* March–April 1995, p. 12. The fluctuations in the figures in table 1.1 could reflect different companies moving in or out of the top 100 or bottom 100 of the Fortune 500. Even if this is the case, the numbers still demonstrate overrepresentation of Jews on corporate boards throughout this period.

Table 1.2
*Jews in the Corporate Elite*

|        | % Jews in Corporate Elite | % Jews in Population[a] |
|--------|---------------------------|------------------------|
| 1900   | 3.4[b]                    |                        |
| 1925   | 4.3[b]                    | 3.4                    |
| 1950   | 4.6[b]                    | 3.3                    |
| 1972   | 6.9[c]                    | 2.9                    |
| 1976   | 7.0[d]                    | 2.7                    |
| 1976   | 6.0[e]                    | 2.7                    |
| 1986   | 7.6[f]                    | 2.5                    |
| 1986   | 7.4[g]                    | 2.5                    |
| 1995   | 7.7[h]                    | 2.3                    |

[a]The figures in this column are from *The American Jewish Yearbook* and *The Encyclopedia Judaica*; before 1925 the estimates included only those Jews who were members of Jewish congregations, so no figure appears for 1900.
[b]Newcomer, *Big Business Executive.*
[c]Alba and Moore, "Ethnicity in the American Elite."
[d]Burck, "Group Profile."
[e]Sturdivant and Adler, "Executive Origins."
[f]McComus, "Atop the Fortune 500."
[g]Bennett, "No Longer a WASP Preserve."
[h]DJN technique.

ing the cultural mores. "Less Jewish" sometimes meant decreased involvement in synagogues and other Jewish organizations, changing one's name, or having one's nose "fixed."[34]

Intermarriage patterns provide the best indicator of the extent to which American Jews have been able and willing to assimilate. Milton Gordon considers intermarriage "the keystone in the arch of assimilation"; more recently, Lipset and Raab call it "the definitive evidence of diminished group cohesion."[35] Until the middle of the century, marriages between Jews and non-Jews were the exception rather than the rule.

In a classic study, sociologist Ruby Jo Reeves Kennedy looked at the records of more than eight thousand marriages in New Haven, Connecticut, between 1870 and 1940. She found that there had been a loosening of what she called "strict endogamy": by the end of the period, more Protestants of different denominations married one another than was the case earlier, and

34. Rubin, *Assimilation and Its Discontents,* 64.

35. Milton Gordon, *Assimilation in American Life* (New York: Oxford University Press, 1964), 81; Lipset and Raab, *Jews and the New American Scene,* 53.

more Irish-American Catholics married Italian-American Catholics. But there had also been a strong persistence of "religious endogamy": as of 1940, the rates of in-group marriage were 80 percent for Protestants, 84 percent for Catholics, and 94 percent for Jews. Kennedy therefore proposed that the idea of America as a "melting pot" should be replaced by an alternative image, that of the "triple melting pot." Even after updating her study to include data from 1950, Kennedy argued that "cultural lines may fade, but religious barriers are holding fast."[36]

Those religious barriers eventually broke down. Richard Alba's extensive research led him to conclude that "the well-known triple-melting pot thesis . . . does not seem to be holding up," and its breakdown, though demonstrable for all non-Hispanic white Americans, is "best illustrated by the marriage patterns of Jews."[37] One study of Jews who married between 1966 and 1972 revealed that 32 percent married outside the faith.[38] By the late 1980s, that figure was more than 55 percent.[39] Almost all those who marry non-Jews remain Jewish, but only one-seventh of their spouses convert to Judaism. Slightly less than a third of the children in these mixed marriages are brought up Jewish, and only about 10 percent of them marry Jews. As Lipset and Raab conclude: "The cycle is downward. There is some reason to give credence to the sour joke: 'What do you call the grandchildren of intermarried Jews? Christians!'"[40]

In the context of this larger pattern of assimilation, we have found that Jews who have been successful in the corporate world have been even more likely than other Jews to assimilate, and they have done so in ways that have allowed them to fit comfortably into the power elite. For Jews at the top of the class hierarchy, class has come to supercede religious identity.[41]

In an interview study of graduates of the Harvard Business School, we asked

---

36. Ruby Jo Reeves Kennedy, "Single or Triple Melting Pot? Intermarriage Trends in New Haven, 1870–1940," *American Journal of Sociology* 49, no. 4 (1944), 331–339; Ruby Jo Reeves Kennedy, "Single or Triple Melting Pot? Intermarriage in New Haven, 1870–1950," *American Journal of Sociology* 58, no. 1 (1952), 56–59.

37. Richard Alba, *Ethnic Identity: The Transformation of White America* (New Haven: Yale University Press, 1991), 14.

38. Steven M. Cohen, "The Coming Shrinkage of American Jewry: A Review of Recent Research," in J. Zimmerman and B. Trainin, eds., *Renascence or Oblivion: Proceedings of a Conference on Jewish Population, 1978* (New York: Federation of Jewish Philanthropies), 1–25.

39. Lipset and Raab cite an NJPS survey that found that for the five-year period prior to 1990, the figure was 57 percent (*Jews and the New American Scene*, 45).

40. Lipset and Raab, *Jews and the New American Scene*, 72–73.

41. See Zweigenhaft and Domhoff, *Jews in the Protestant Establishment*, chapter 5, "Identity and Class in the Corporate Elite," 89–111.

both Jewish and Gentile managers about how Jews had been treated in their companies. For the most part, the respondents indicated that Jews had done well, but some were convinced that certain kinds of Jews were more likely to be successful than others. As one of the Jewish respondents put it, "If an individual is perceived as quite Jewish, into Jewish social events, it may have a negative impact. Those who have moved faster in this company are the less visible Jews." Another told us that one of his Jewish colleagues had never visited Israel because of his fear that it would have "political ramifications."[42]

The most candid comments came from one of the Gentile interviewees, who acknowledged his own prejudices as he explained his view of how things worked at his company: "If you really want to know the way I feel, I think at the top levels being Jewish will hurt a person's chances. But it depends on how he plays his cards. This one man I know is so polished, such an upper-class person, there's no way to know he's Jewish. I'll admit I'm prejudiced. There are certain aspects of Jewish people I don't like — they're pushy, they're loud, especially those damn New York bastards. Christ, I'm so sick of hearing about Israel. My friend is fine, however. He's an upper-class type person, the kind who could make it to the top."[43]

Given this portrayal of the corporate world, we were not surprised when we found — both in a series of systematic studies comparing Jews who were and were not corporate directors, and in the interviews we conducted with Jewish directors — that Jews in the corporate elite are less likely to see Jewishness as a salient part of their identity than are other Jews. Moreover, we found that this was particularly true of those corporate directors whose parents or grand-parents had also been in the corporate elite, and that there were no differences in this regard between German Jews and the handful of Eastern European Jews who came from wealthy backgrounds. This was true not only in terms of marriage patterns but in their interest in Israel, the likelihood of their having visited Israel, and the ways they chose to reveal (or not reveal) their Jewish identity in books like *Who's Who in America*.[44]

Those corporate directors we interviewed who were the first in their fam-ily to make it into the corporate elite — men like Laurence Tisch and Irving Shapiro — were still very much involved in and committed to Jewish issues. They had married Jews, for example, and they had been to Israel many times. Those, however, who were the second or third generation in their families to

---

42. Richard L. Zweigenhaft, *Who Gets to the Top? Executive Suite Discrimination in the Eighties* (New York: Institute of Human Relations, 1984), 14–15.

43. Zweigenhaft, *Who Gets to the Top?* 12.

44. Zweigenhaft and Domhoff, *Jews in the Protestant Establishment*, 89–111.

have been among America's economic elite — men like Joseph Frederick Cullman III, who was then chairman of the board and CEO at Philip Morris; and William Wishnick, chairman of the board and CEO at Witco Chemical, a company started by his father — had married non-Jews and were less likely to have visited Israel. We asked those we interviewed what being Jewish meant to them. The responses of the second- and third-generation members of the corporate elite were revealing. The most telling came from one man who paused and then admitted, "It really doesn't mean anything."[45]

Our research and the work of others indicate that over the past forty years Jews have been successful in the corporate world, and they have steadily increased their presence in the corporate elite. The doors that opened at DuPont for Irving Shapiro did portend the ascent of other Jews to leadership in non-Jewish companies. It did not turn heads — it certainly did not warrant shocked front page headlines in the *Wall Street Journal* — when Richard Rosenberg, the Jewish son of a clothing salesman, became chairman and CEO at the Bank of America, or when the Walt Disney Company, founded by a man who had refused to hire Jews, picked as its CEO and chairman Michael Eisner, a Jew from a wealthy New York family, to save it from the threat of a hostile takeover.[46]

At the same time, however, because of the general pressures and inducements to assimilate, being Jewish is likely to become progressively less important to these successful Jews and less important still to their children and their grandchildren. The pattern of socialization into the power elite ensures that the people who enter the higher circles do not differ significantly from those who are already there. Those who can "fit in" best are most likely to get there, and this means — at least in corporations not founded or owned by Jews — that those who put less public emphasis on their Jewishness are most likely to make it to the top. So, ironically, forty years after Mills wrote his book, more Jews

---

45. Ibid., 110

46. See Carrie Dolan, "BankAmerica's Rosenberg Will Succeed Clausen as Chief; Dividend Lifted 66%," *Wall Street Journal,* February 6, 1990. This article does not mention Rosenberg's religion, nor was it mentioned in the much briefer announcement of his appointment in the *New York Times.* Rosenberg does, however, include that he is Jewish in his *Who's Who in America* biographical sketch. The information on Eisner is from *Current Biography* (1987), 154–157.

As for Disney's anti-Semitism, Leonard Mosley provides numerous examples in his biography, *Disney's World* (New York: Stein and Day, 1985). For example, when a young animator named David Swift announced that he had been offered a better job at Columbia Pictures, Disney's send-off was hostile. "He called me in, finally," Swift said later, "and putting on a phony Jewish accent, he said, 'Okay, Davy Boy, off you go to work with those Jews. It's where you belong, with those Jews.'" (207).

are in the corporate elite, but the longer they have been there the less likely are they to be Jewish in any meaningful sense. Whether these same patterns will reappear for other excluded groups is a key question that we explore throughout this book.

## Jews in the Cabinet

When we looked at the cabinets of each president since Eisenhower, we found that Jews have held 13 of the 209 cabinet positions (6.2 percent).[47] These men (all have been men) are listed in table 1.3. With the exception of Ronald Reagan and George Bush, who included no Jews among the 52 people they appointed to their cabinets, each presidential cabinet since 1956 has included at least one Jewish person. Notably, 10 of the 81 cabinet appointments under Democratic presidents have been Jewish (12.3 percent), but only 3 of the 128 appointments under Republican presidents (2.3 percent).[48]

Each of these men married at least once, and each has at least one child (the average number of children is 2.5). Eight married Jewish women, but six married non-Jews. The marriages to non-Jews reflect the frequency of intermarriage found among Jews and especially among successful Jewish businessmen: Cohen married a Unitarian; Kissinger's second marriage was to an Epis-

47. This is higher than the percentage of Jews in presidential cabinets from 1897 through 1972. In her study of presidential cabinets during those years, Beth Mintz found that of the 166 people whose religion she could identify, six were Jewish. Jews, therefore, represented 3.6 percent of the total, a figure that was slightly higher than the percentage of Jews in the larger population at that time. Two were in the cabinets of Republican presidents (Oscar S. Straus, secretary of commerce and labor, 1906–1909; and Lewis L. Strauss, secretary of commerce, 1958–59), and four were in the cabinets of Democratic presidents (Henry Morganthau Jr., secretary of the treasury, 1934–1945; Arthur J. Goldberg, secretary of labor, 1961–1962; Abraham A. Ribicoff, secretary of health, education, and welfare, 1961–1962; and Wilbur J. Cohen, secretary of health, education and welfare, 1968–1969). Beth Mintz, "The President's Cabinet, 1897–1972: A Contribution to the Power Structure Debate," in "New Directions in Power Structure Research," a special issue of *Insurgent Sociologist* 5, no. 3 (1975), 131–148.

48. For this analysis, we have included only cabinet positions, not such "cabinet-level" positions as ambassador to the United Nations or secretary for veterans affairs, even though those who hold cabinet-level positions typically attend cabinet meetings. Nor have we included Madeline Albright, secretary of state during Clinton's second term. Albright was raised as a Catholic and later became an Episcopalian. Shortly after her confirmation as secretary of state she learned that her parents had converted to Catholicism from Judaism, and that three of her grandparents had died in the Holocaust. Her history adds another dimension to the difficult question of who is Jewish. Steven Erlanger, "Albright Grateful for Her Parents' Painful Choices," *New York Times*, April 5, 1997.

Table 1.3
*Jews in the Cabinet, 1956–1997*

|  | President | Years | Position |
|---|---|---|---|
| Lewis Strauss | Eisenhower | 1958–59 | Commerce |
| Arthur Goldberg | Kennedy | 1961–62 | Labor |
| Abraham Ribicoff | Kennedy | 1961–62 | Health, Education, and Welfare |
| Wilbur Cohen | Johnson | 1968–69 | Health, Education, and Welfare |
| Henry Kissinger | Nixon | 1973–74 | State |
|  | Ford | 1974–77 | State |
| Edward Levi | Ford | 1975–77 | Attorney General |
| Michael Blumenthal | Carter | 1977–79 | Treasury |
| Harold Brown | Carter | 1977–81 | Defense |
| Philip Klutznick | Carter | 1980–81 | Commerce |
| Neil Goldschmidt | Carter | 1979–81 | Transportation |
| Robert Reich | Clinton | 1993–97 | Labor |
| Dan Glickman | Clinton | 1995– | Agriculture |
| Robert Rubin | Clinton | 1995– | Treasury |

copalian; Michael Blumenthal married a Presbyterian and, according to a profile in *Current Biography,* "he was baptized as a Presbyterian about the time of his marriage"; Harold Brown married an Episcopalian and, according to the profile in *Current Biography,* written in 1977, he and his wife "now consider themselves 'unchurched' "; Goldschmidt married twice, both times to non-Jews; and Reich met his wife, who is not Jewish, when he was a Rhodes Scholar in England.[49]

These men are highly educated—almost all hold law degrees or Ph.D.'s. One of the two exceptions is Strauss, who completed high school but, despite an early interest in physics, never attended college. The other exception, Wilbur Cohen, received a bachelor's degree in economics from the University of Wisconsin in 1934. He then accepted a job as a research assistant to one of his professors, who had been appointed to a government position by Roosevelt to help formulate the Social Security Act. After twenty years in government service, Cohen became professor of public welfare administration at the University of Michigan.

Most of these men came from comfortable circumstances, backgrounds

49. "Michael Blumenthal," *Current Biography* (1977), 77; "Harold Brown," *Current Biography* (1977), 89. We were unable to determine whether Robert Rubin's wife, who was born Judith Oxenberg, is Jewish.

that would be considered middle class or upper middle class. Two — Kissinger and Blumenthal — were born in Germany and suffered the hardships of dislocation (especially Blumenthal, who spent the war years in Shanghai, two of them in a Japanese internment camp), but both families were solidly middle class. The parents of both Arthur Goldberg and Abraham Ribicoff were immigrants who had to struggle to make ends meet — Goldberg's father, who died when Arthur, the youngest of eight children, was three, drove a horse and buggy around Chicago selling produce to hotels, and Ribicoff's father worked in a factory.

## Jews in the Military Elite

Although Jews fought on both sides during the Civil War, by the late nineteenth century it was often claimed that Jews avoided or were incapable of military service. Mark Twain, for example, wrote that the Jew "is charged with a disinclination patriotically to stand by the flag as a soldier. By his make and his ways he is substantially a foreigner and even the angels dislike foreigners."[50]

In response to such claims, in 1896 a group of seventy-eight Jewish veterans of the Union Army met in New York City and formed the Hebrew Union Veterans, a precursor to the Jewish War Veterans, an organization dedicated to "uphold the fair name of the Jew and fight his battles wherever unjustly assailed" and "to gather and preserve the records of patriotic service performed by men of Jewish faith."[51] In 1984, the Jewish War Veterans opened the National Museum of Jewish History in Washington.

As we have seen, by the 1920s, when virulent anti-Semitism was widespread in the United States, Jews in the military were no more free from its effects than other Jews. Some Jews, though, managed to rise through the military ranks. One of Leonard Kaplan's fellow midshipmen in the class of 1922 at the Naval Academy was Hyman Rickover. Rickover, like Kaplan, wrote "Hebrew" next to his name when he arrived in Annapolis in the fall of 1918. Unlike Kaplan, however, Rickover was not "sent to Coventry." Although he was seen as a "loner" and a "grind," he maintained cordial relationships with his classmates. He was a competent student (he finished 106th in a class of 539), but it is unlikely that anyone would have predicted that he would become one of the most important military figures of the twentieth century.

50. Gloria R. Mosesson, *The Jewish War Veterans Story* (Washington, D.C.: The Jewish War Veterans of America, 1971), 17. In a subsequent article, in response to pressure from veterans' groups, Twain retracted these statements.

51. Mosesson, *Jewish War Veterans Story,* 19.

Rickover was born in 1898 in a village north of Warsaw, Poland, and came to America as a small child, the son of a tailor. After spending his youth in Chicago, he was nominated to attend the Naval Academy by his Congressman, Adolph Sabath, like himself an immigrant and a Jew. Rickover's career was long and distinguished. He served in the navy for more than sixty years, including thirty years in charge of the navy's nuclear power program, becoming known as the "father of the atomic submarine." His career was rife with controversy. In July 1951 he was passed over by the navy board for promotion to rear admiral, and a year later he was passed over again. Navy regulations did not permit a third try, and he would ordinarily have had to retire in mid-1953. But a massive lobbying campaign outside the military created support for Rickover in Congress and the media, and he was promoted to rear admiral in July 1953. Twenty years later, when he was in his mid-seventies, he became an admiral.

The opposition within the navy to promoting Rickover in the early 1950s may or may not have been based on his Jewish background. It is difficult to know for certain, for the navy boards that turned him down two years in a row held their meetings in secret. The reasons given publicly, of course, had nothing to do with his religious origins. But many of Rickover's supporters suspected that religion was a factor, and there can be no doubt that some admirals made anti-Semitic comments when speaking of Rickover. One admiral referred to him as "that little Jew," and another said of him, "When they circumcised him they threw the wrong end away."[52]

Ironically, Rickover had long since ceased thinking of himself as Jewish. In 1931, he married Ruth Masters, an Episcopalian, and left his Judaism behind. In fact, shortly after his marriage, he wrote a letter to his parents telling them of his decision to become an Episcopalian; his biographers wrote that he "lived for years without their forgiveness." Not only did he tell people that he was an Episcopalian, but when called upon to testify before congressional committees about nuclear power, he was prone to interlace his comments with references to Jesus.[53]

Forty years after Rickover's controversial promotion, there are Jews in the seniormost levels of the military establishment. What is most striking is not merely their presence but the absence of any surprise that they are there. For many in the military, whether or not one is Jewish is simply no longer an issue. According to James Zimble, former surgeon general of the navy, who retired as a vice admiral (a two-star rank) and who at the time of our interview with

52. Polmar and Allen, *Rickover*, 192, 194.
53. Ibid., 80, 637.

him was president of the Uniformed Services University of the Health Sciences: "I have neither been victim of nor witnessed any anti-Semitism in the military. I know there are still redneck holdouts in the Deep South and elsewhere, but the military has gotten beyond that."[54]

Zimble's claims about the treatment of Jews in the military were echoed by others with whom we spoke, including Arnold Resnicoff, one of the two highest ranking rabbis in the navy. As a rabbi who has been in the navy for more than twenty years, he should be aware of serious episodes of anti-Semitism in that branch of the military. In response to our question, he said: "There is no institution — and I believe this with all my heart, I'm not just giving you some company line — that fights prejudice, anti-Semitism, racism, as much as the military. Acts of overt anti-Semitism are extremely rare, and they are punished immediately. In all my years in the military, I have seen very few cases of anti-Semitism. Those were acts by individuals, and the institution reacted swiftly and forcefully."[55]

Those we spoke with asserted that the military fights prejudice not only against Jews but also against blacks, Latinos, and, as one of them put it, "even women." They acknowledge that discrimination against homosexuals remains another, more difficult matter. We will return to this issue in Chapter 6. For now, let us consider recent appointments of two Jewish men that suggest strongly that Zimble and Resnicoff are correct in their assertion that being Jewish is not an issue with regard to to promotion in the military, even promotion to the very highest levels of the military establishment.

Jeremy Michael Boorda, who became the top-ranking naval officer in March 1994, turned out to be Jewish, though most people were unaware of that until it was mentioned in a long magazine profile of him that appeared in the *Washingtonian*. Boorda's parents, Herman and Gertrude Boorda, ran a dress shop in a small town in Illinois fifty miles south of Chicago. Their marriage was not a happy one, and there was so much tension in the home that Mike ran off and joined the navy in the middle of his junior year of high school.

Almost forty years later, married to a non-Jew, the father of three children, Boorda became, as far as we can tell, the only Jewish four-star admiral in history, and the first Jewish member of the Joint Chiefs of Staff. At the time of

54. Personal interview by Richard Zweigenhaft with Dr. James Zimble, Bethesda, Md., August 25, 1995.

55. Phone interview by Richard Zweigenhaft with Rabbi Arnold Resnicoff, August 25, 1995.

his appointment no one seemed to pay any attention to Boorda's Jewish background. In part this may reflect the bureaucratic conformity demanded by the military. C. Wright Mills noted that the military isolates its members, breaks down their previously acquired tastes and values, and thus creates "a highly uniform type." The warlords, more than others in the power elite, according to Mills, thus come to "resemble one another, internally and externally."[56] In fact, in a celebrated case in the 1980s, the Supreme Court ruled that a military man did not have the right to wear a yarmulke. Such Jewish visibility, even as part of one's religious obligations, was deemed an inappropriate disruption of the uniformity of appearance required by the military.[57]

It is possible that no one paid attention to Boorda's Jewish background because of his own choice to assimilate. He ran away from a troubled and unhappy home, he married a non-Jewish woman, and even some of those who thought they knew him well were surprised to discover that he was Jewish.[58] But in our view, the most important reason that no one paid attention to Boorda's Jewish background was that, as Zimble and Resnicoff believe, being Jewish is no longer an issue in the military.[59]

The promotion of another Jewish man to a position of power in the defense establishment provides additional evidence that being Jewish is no longer an impediment to one's career. In March 1995, President Clinton persuaded John Deutch, who had turned him down once before, to accept the nomination as director of the CIA. Deutch was born in Belgium in 1938, just thirteen months before the beginning of World War II. His family was able to escape the subsequent Nazi occupation by going first to Paris, then to Lisbon, and then,

56. Mills, *Power Elite*, 195.

57. Goldman *v.* Weinberger, 475, US503, 1986.

58. According to Retired Vice-Admiral Bernard M. ("Bud") Kauderer, about a year before the *Washingtonian* article appeared, Boorda was going through a receiving line that included Admiral Sumner Shapiro, the former director of naval intelligence, and a Jew. When he got to Shapiro in the line, Boorda leaned over to him and whispered, "You know, Shap, I'm one of you." Kauderer told us: "This was the first inkling we had that he was Jewish. It was a source of amazement to us." Phone interview by Richard Zweigenhaft, October 27, 1995.

59. In a tragic end to a brilliant career, Boorda — the first man in the history of the navy to rise from sailor to four-star general — committed suicide in May 1996. By the time he committed suicide, Boorda had lost the support of many senior officers in the navy, in large part because of the way he handled a controversy involving Admiral Stanley Arthur, the vice-chief of naval operations. There is no evidence that Boorda's being Jewish had anything to do with the lack of support from the navy's "old guard." See Peter J. Boyer, "Admiral Boorda's War," *New Yorker*, September 16, 1996, pp. 68–86.

in 1940, to the United States. Deutch's father, a chemical engineer who helped invent the process for making synthetic rubber, became deputy director of the government's synthetic rubber program during the war. Deutch's mother, the daughter of diamond merchants, had a doctorate in ancient studies and spoke ten languages. Deutch attended the prominent Sidwell Friends School and received a B.A. from Amherst and a Ph.D. in physical chemistry from the Massachusetts Institute of Technology. He first came to work at the Pentagon in 1961 at the age of twenty-two, as one of the "whiz kids" who worked under Robert McNamara during the Kennedy administration. He left the Pentagon in 1966 to teach chemistry, first at Princeton and then at MIT. As the *New York Times* put it, since that time "he has rotated between posts at MIT and increasingly powerful positions in Democratic administrations."[60]

As was true for Boorda at the time of his appointment, Deutch's religious background received virtually no mention in the press. Although a *New York Times* profile mentioned that "he and his family fled Belgium for France and eventually came to the United States," it did not state explicitly that he, or they, were Jewish. But Deutch is Jewish, as are both of the women he has married. Both are from prominent German-Jewish families in the Washington area, and both were fellow students of his at Sidwell Friends.[61]

For a Jew to head the CIA is even more stunning a sign of acceptance than for a Jew to sit on the Joint Chiefs of Staff, for the CIA has historically been led by Christian men of impeccable upper-class credentials.[62] But Boorda's presence on the Joint Chiefs was a milestone as well, for the Joint Chiefs also has

60. Tim Weiner, "Reluctant Helmsman for a Troubled Agency: John Mark Deutch," *New York Times,* March 11, 1995. In addition to his work at MIT and for the government, Deutch has also served corporations as both board member and consultant. In a lengthy profile of Deutch titled "Mission Impossible" in the *Washingtonian* (December, 1995), Nick Kotz notes that in 1992 Deutch's salary at MIT had been $207,000, but he had earned more than $600,000 from consulting and director's fees at twenty corporations, mostly defense contractors like Martin Marietta and TRW (134).

61. In his cover article for *Parade* magazine, titled "Is He the CIA's Last, Best Hope?" (November 19, 1995), Peter Maas makes no mention of Deutch's Jewish background. Nor is there any mention of Deutch's having attended an elite prep school: Deutch and his wife, we are told, went "to the same high school" (5). In a long article in the *New York Times Magazine* entitled "The C.I.A.'s Most Important Mission: Itself" (December 10, 1995), Tim Weiner did include information about Deutch's Jewish background (84). Kotz's *Washingtonian* article mentions that Deutch's family was Jewish and that his father was on the board of directors of the Washington Hebrew Congregation (66).

62. See, for example, Burton Hersh, *The Old Boys: The American Elite and the Origins of the CIA* (New York: Scribners, 1992).

been a Gentile preserve, albeit less socially exclusive than the CIA. For a time during the Reagan presidency the Joint Chiefs held "prayer breakfasts," led by one of Boorda's predecessors, the devout Roman Catholic four-star admiral James Watkins.[63]

Jews have thus made it to the top of the military elite. In addition to Secretary of Defense Harold Brown, Admiral Boorda, and CIA Director Deutch, numerous Jews have achieved the rank of two stars or higher. (In 1995 there were 248,238 officers in all the branches of the military, but only 456 with the equivalent of a two-star rank or higher; therefore, the officers with at least that represent 0.2 percent of all officers.[64]) Being Jewish in the military of the 1990s is dramatically different from being Jewish at the Naval Academy of the early 1920s.

## Jews in Congress

### THE SENATE

Between 1844 and 1913, six men of Jewish background served in the U.S. Senate.[65] Then, for the next thirty-six years there were no Jews, until Herbert Lehman — having served as governor of New York for ten years and lost a Senate race in 1946 — won a special election in 1949 after the incumbent resigned.

Table 1.4 lists the Jews elected to the Senate since 1950. As the table shows, three Jewish men were elected in the second half of the 1950s: Richard Neuberger of Oregon in 1955; Jacob Javits of New York in 1956 (replacing Lehman, who, at the age of 78, declined to run for a second full term); and Ernest Gruening of Alaska in 1958. By 1992, there were ten Jews in the Senate.[66] Howard Metzenbaum retired in 1994, but in 1996 Ron Wyden, a Jewish Democrat, defeated his Mormon Republican opponent to win the Oregon

63. Richard Halloran, "Navy's Chief Discusses Morality and Weapons," *New York Times*, May 6, 1983.

64. "Distribution of Active Duty Forces by Service, Rank, Sex, and Ethnic Group," May 31, 1995, Washington, D.C.: Department of Defense.

65. They were David Levy, Florida, 1844–1860; Judah Benjamin, Louisiana, 1852–1860; Benjamin Franklin Jonas, Louisiana, 1879–1885; Joseph Simon, Oregon, 1897–1903; Isidor Rayner, Maryland, 1905–1912; and Simon Guggenheim, Colorado, 1907–1913. See Eli N. Evans, *Judah P. Benjamin: The Jewish Confederate* (New York: Free Press, 1988), xx, 32, 47–48, 399; Isaacs, *Jews and American Politics*, 235.

66. *Congressional Quarterly*, November 7, 1992, p. 9. As various writers have noted, ten Jews are enough for a *minyan* — the requirement for public prayer services.

Table 1.4
*Senators of Jewish Descent Since 1956*

| | | |
|---|---|---|
| Herbert Lehman | D-N.Y. | 1949–1956 |
| Richard Neuberger | D-Ore. | 1955–1960 |
| Jacob Javits | R-N.Y. | 1957–1980 |
| Ernest Gruening | D-Ala. | 1959–1969 |
| Abraham Ribicoff | D-Conn. | 1963–1981 |
| Howard Metzenbaum | D-Ohio | 1975–1994 |
| Rudy Boschwitz | R-Minn. | 1979–1990 |
| Herb Kohl | D-Wis. | 1979– |
| Carl Levin | D-Mich. | 1979– |
| Arlen Specter | R-Pa. | 1981– |
| Frank Lautenberg | D-N.J. | 1983– |
| Joseph Lieberman | D-Conn. | 1989– |
| Paul Wellstone | D-Minn. | 1991– |
| Barbara Boxer | D-Calif. | 1993– |
| Russell Feingold | D-Wis. | 1993– |
| Dianne Feinstein | D-Calif. | 1993– |
| Ron Wyden | D-Ore. | 1997– |

Senate seat vacated by Robert Packwood.[67] The list does not include William Cohen of Maine, whose father was Jewish.[68]

As was true for the Jews in presidential cabinets, there is a notable distinction between the two major political parties — thirteen of sixteen Jewish senators have been Democrats. But Democrat or Republican, the steady increase in the number of Jewish senators not only means that the percentage is considerably higher than the percentage of Jews in the general population: it also reflects a sea change in the political role played by Jews in America, who were once limited to behind-the-scenes roles.[69]

67. Timothy Egan, "2 Rivals, Worlds Apart, Vie for Packwood's Seat," *New York Times,* January 16, 1996; Timothy Egan, "Oregon's Mail-In Senator," *New York Times,* February 4, 1996.

68. Cohen's father was Jewish and his mother was, as he describes her, "Irish, Protestant, and proud." Because his father wanted him to have a Jewish upbringing, Cohen began to prepare for his bar mitzvah when he was seven, and only at the age of twelve did he discover that he would have to undergo a special conversion ceremony because his mother was not Jewish. He refused to do so and became a Unitarian. William S. Cohen, *Roll Call: One Year in the United States Senate* (New York: Simon and Schuster, 1981), 60–62.

69. Isaacs, *Jews and American Politics,* 10.

Jews who have been elected to the Senate differ dramatically from one another in the degree to which they have been involved in Judaism. At one pole is Ernest Gruening, whose father was a prominent surgeon with a summer home in Rockport, Massachusetts. Ernest went to Hotchkiss and then to Harvard, first as an undergraduate and then as a medical student. Isaacs reports that Gruening "never paid the slightest attention to things Jewish," and there is no mention of his Jewish heritage in his lengthy autobiography.[70]

At the other pole is Joseph Lieberman, an Orthodox Jew married to a woman named Hadassah, a man who, in accordance with the regulations of his faith, does not use electrical appliances or ride elevators on the Sabbath. It is indeed a sign of change that someone committed to the practice of Orthodox Judaism could in 1988 be elected to the Senate.

Although commitment to orthodoxy is now acceptable, it is neither required nor expected. Indeed, one of the more consequential episodes in the political life of two Jews in the Senate took place in the Minnesota senatorial election of 1990. The Democratic nominee was Paul Wellstone, a liberal activist and professor of political science at Carleton College, who had never held political office and whose father had emigrated from Russia in 1914. (His mother was born in the United States, but her parents were Russian Jewish immigrants.) The Republican nominee and incumbent was Rudy Boschwitz, who was born in Berlin in 1930 and fled to America with his family when he was very young. Boschwitz was heavily favored, not only because he was the incumbent, and not only because Wellstone was so inexperienced, but because his campaign was much more heavily financed — Boschwitz raised seven times as much money as Wellstone.

But Wellstone ran an extremely effective and resourceful campaign, drawing on more than ten thousand volunteers, many of whom had been his students. Boschwitz, meanwhile, made a series of blunders, the worst of which was described by two Minnesota journalists as "one of the most memorable pratfalls ever witnessed in Minnesota politics."[71] He sent a letter to Jewish voters one week before the election to remind them of his own Jewish heritage and support for Israel and to denounce Wellstone for raising his children as non-Jews and for having "no connection whatsoever with the Jewish community or our communal life." This attack backfired, for it seemed to confirm

<hr />

70. Ibid., 202; Ernest Gruening, *Many Battles: The Autobiography of Ernest Gruening* (New York: Liveright, 1973).

71. Dennis J. McGrath and Dane Smith, *Professor Wellstone Goes to Washington: The Inside Story of a Grassroots U.S. Senate Campaign* (Minneapolis: University of Minnesota Press, 1995), 253.

Wellstone's claims that Boschwitz had been running a negative campaign.[72] By 1990, then, a Senate seat from a state with few Jewish residents could be contested by two Jews, and could be decided in part by an apparent perception among voters — including Jewish voters — that it was inappropriate for one candidate to criticize the other for the way he chose to live his life as a Jew.

The seventeen Jewish senators are similar to others in the power elite in a number of ways. Except for Herb Kohl, all have been married, some more than once. Of the six marriages by the five Jewish men elected to the Senate between 1949 and 1963, half were to non-Jews (Gruening's wife, Neuberger's wife, and Javits's first wife). In contrast, the thirteen Jewish men and women elected to the Senate after 1963 have married fourteen times, and only two of these marriages have been to non-Jews. Although the national trend has revealed an increasing likelihood of marrying outside the faith, the more recently elected Jewish senators have been more, not less, likely to marry Jewish partners. This, too, suggests that the pressures for Jewish politicians to assimilate may have decreased over time.

All of the Jewish senators earned at least a bachelor's degree, and two-thirds have gone on to earn higher degrees (nine received law degrees, one an M.B.A., one a medical degree, and one a Ph.D.). They differ from Jews in the corporate community and the executive branch of government, however, in that they come from a broader range of socioeconomic backgrounds. Some, like Javits, Ribicoff, and Lautenberg, were second-generation Americans who grew up in real poverty. Others, like Neuberger, Metzenbaum, Lieberman, and Boxer, had parents who owned small businesses. And some, like Lehman, Gruening, Kohl, and Feinstein, grew up in very comfortable economic settings. By the time they ran for the Senate, many had become millionaires.[73]

THE HOUSE

There has been a similarly dramatic increase in the number of Jews elected to the House of Representatives. In 1975, there were only ten Jewish members of the House, most of whom were elected in Jewish districts in New York. By 1993 there were thirty-three Jewish men and women in the House, and they served districts scattered across the country, including many with fewer than 1 percent Jewish voters. Only five were Republicans, and one,

72. Ibid., 253. See also Brent Staples, "Dirty Political Ads, Reconsidered," New York Times, November 11, 1990; "Ousted Senator Apologizes for Letter to Jews," New York Times, November 10, 1990.

73. Among the millionaires: Lehman, Metzenbaum, Kohl, Lautenberg, and Feinstein. See R. W. Apple Jr., "Never Mind the Log Cabin," New York Times, October 16, 1994.

Bernie Sanders of Vermont, was a socialist who ran as an independent; twenty-seven were Democrats. All but one were pro-choice, almost all supported gun control, and all but one voted for the Civil Rights Act of 1992. After the 1994 elections, when Republicans took control of Congress, the number of Jews in the House dropped to twenty-four, and the number of Jewish Democrats in the House dropped to nineteen; in 1997 the number of Jews in the House increased by one, to twenty-five (twenty-one Democrats, three Republicans, and Sanders).[74]

The clear evidence of representation, or overrepresentation, of Jews in the corporate, cabinet, and military elites reflects a dramatic reversal of the discrimination experienced by Jews in these arenas earlier in the century. Although Jews may still be underrepresented in some business sectors within the corporate community, the data we have examined reveal that Jews are over-represented overall in the corporate elite. Jews are also now overrepresented in both the Senate and the House, where they tend to be Democrats. These findings lead to the important question: how have Jews been able to become part of what was formerly a Christian power elite and Congress?

There are a number of reasons, each of which might provide a basis of comparison in subsequent chapters as we consider the experiences of women and other minorities. First, Jews have had both the ability and the willingness to assimilate into what Alba has called the emerging ethnic category of "European Americans." Almost all Jews are white,[75] and virtually all Jews who have moved into the power elite are white. The ethnic prejudice against Jews therefore was not accompanied by the added feature of race that African Americans, Asian Americans, and others of color have had to contend with. This may have made it easier for Jews to assimilate generally and, more specifically, to be accepted by those in the power elite. And this, we believe, is reflected by the dramatic increase in intermarriages between Jews and Gentiles.

A second factor is the strong cultural emphasis among Jews on academic success and the resulting overrepresentation of Jews among college graduates and among the graduates of the best colleges and universities in America. Mythology to the contrary, having a degree from a prestigious college is a valuable stepping stone to positions in the power elite and Congress. To the

74. *Congressional Quarterly,* November 7, 1992, p. 9; November 12, 1994, p. 11; and January 4, 1997, p. 29; Michael Hoffman, "More Jews in Congress: Does it Make a Difference?" *Moment,* February 1993, pp. 32–39.

75. Almost all, but not all. There are almost one hundred thousand African Americans who are Jewish. See Bernard J. Wolfson, "The Soul of Judaism," *Emerge,* September 1995, pp. 42–46.

degree that women and minorities graduate from the best schools, we should see them in the power elite and in Congress.

Related to the emphasis on academic success is the fact that many Jews came to America with experience as employers or shopkeepers in their own communities.[76] Some of them or their children had achieved financial success before doors began to open for them, primarily in retailing but also in fields like investment banking. It became difficult to exclude members of the Jewish community when they had the financial wherewithal to buy their way into the corporate elite. Once in, they were asked to join other boards as outside directors. And over time, especially with the various waves of mergers and acquisitions that make it difficult to know whether or not a company was founded or is owned by Jews, they have simply become part of the corporate elite. Similarly, because Jews were well educated, politically active, and had acquired all kinds of valuable expertise, as they became a potent group economically, more and more they began to appear in presidential cabinets and, by the 1990s, in Congress.

Richard Alba refers to Jews as "the outstanding instance of a group that is managing to swim to some degree against the assimilatory tide."[77] This may be true when Jews are compared with other white non-Hispanic ethnic groups who are melding into European-American homogeneity. But we have seen that Jews who have made it to the power elite have been likely to assimilate. In contrast to this pattern, we found that recent Jewish senators were less likely than former Jewish senators to have married Gentiles.

A number of variables, then, seem to be important in understanding the successful entry by Jews into the power elite. They are white, and those who rise the highest are likely to have been born in relatively privileged circumstances. They have excellent educational credentials. There is also a variable we haven't mentioned — time. Second- and third-generation American Jews tend to have become fully acculturated, and non-Jewish whites seem to have become more accepting of them. In the chapters that follow we shall focus on various factors — class background, education, and color, as well as whether one was born in the United States (or one's parents were) — to assess the importance of these variables in understanding why members of other groups do or do not gain entry into the power elite and Congress.

76. Stephen Steinberg, *The Ethnic Myth: Race, Ethnicity and Class* (New York: Atheneum, 1981), 93–103.
77. Alba, *Ethnic Identity,* 309.

# 2

## Women in the Power Elite

The power elite depicted by C. Wright Mills was, without doubt, an exclusively male preserve. On the opening page of *The Power Elite* — a book with no preface, no introduction, no acknowledgments, just a direct plunge into the opening chapter — Mills stated clearly that "the power elite is composed of men whose positions enable them to transcend the ordinary environments of ordinary men and women."[1] Although there were some women in the corporate, political, and military worlds, very few were in or near the higher circles that constituted the power elite. Are they there now? If so, how substantial and how visible is their presence? When did they arrive, and how did they get there? What are their future prospects? Do they fare better in Congress? These are some of the questions we will address in this chapter.

### Women in the Corporate Elite

In a chapter entitled "The Chief Executives," Mills described the men who owned and ran the largest corporations in the United States: "Large owners and executives in their self-financing corporations hold the keys of economic power. Not the politicians of the visible government, but the chief

1. C. Wright Mills, *The Power Elite* (New York: Oxford University Press, 1956), 3–4.

executives who sit in the political directorate, by fact and proxy, hold the power and the means of defending the privileges of their corporate world. If they do not reign, they do govern at many of the vital points of everyday life in America, and no powers effectively and consistently countervail against them, nor have they as corporate-made men developed any effectively restraining conscience."[2]

Who were these "corporate-made men" who occupied the "top two or three command posts" in each of the largest "hundred or so corporations"? As we indicated in the previous chapter, when Mills systematically studied their backgrounds, the evidence showed clearly that they were not "country boys who have made good in the city" or the Horatio Alger types of popular myth; nor were they immigrants or even the sons of immigrants. Instead, Mills wrote, these executives, "today as in the past, were born with a big advantage: they managed to have fathers on at least upper middle-class levels of occupation and income; they are Protestant, white, and American-born. These factors of origin led directly to their second big advantage: they are well-educated in the formal sense of college and post-college schooling."[3]

It went without saying that these "typical executives" were men. Although there were a handful of women on the boards of the top corporations, they were wives or daughters in family-controlled companies, or presidents of prestigious women's colleges, and they were unlikely to sit in one of the few most important positions (the top two or three "command posts"). Mills virtually ignored women in the corporate elite because there were so few of them. His failure to make an issue of the absence of women in the corporate elite is evidence that he, too, was a product of his time. If Mills had seen this as an issue of importance, there can be no doubt that he would have addressed it. It was, for Mills as for most others, a given.

Mills died in 1962, a year before the publication of Betty Friedan's influential *The Feminine Mystique* and a few years before the rise of feminism on university campuses. By the 1970s, women had entered the corporate world in far greater numbers than ever before. Indeed, according to the sociologist Jerry A. Jacobs, "the increasing representation of women among the ranks of managers in organizations in the U.S. is perhaps the most dramatic shift in the sex composition of an occupation since clerical work became a female-dominated field in the late nineteenth century."[4] The progress of women in the

2. Ibid., 125.
3. Ibid., 129.
4. Jerry A. Jacobs, "Women's Entry into Management: Trends in Earnings, Authority, and Values Among Salaried Managers," *Administrative Science Quarterly* 37 (1992), 282–301.

highest levels of management was of interest to many. Journalists and academics asked with some frequency whether or not women had made it into the corporate elite, and, if not, why not?

In 1978 *Fortune* magazine presented the results of a systematic study of women on boards of directors of the 1,300 companies that made up the Fortune 500, the Fortune second 500, and the six lists of the top 50 retailers, utilities, banks, life insurance companies, transportation companies, and diversified financial companies. Drawing on the proxy-statement lists, which, as required by law, include the names and salaries of the three highest-paid officers and any board members who earned more than $40,000 in the previous year, they found that 10 of the 6,400 people identified were women, representing "a measly 0.16 percent." Nor did the presence of ten women in those corporate ranks represent progress: a similar study five years earlier had "turned up" eleven women.[5]

Mills's focus, as we have noted, was on the top two or three positions in the top "hundred or so" corporations. By this rather stringent standard, only one person in the 1978 survey came close to qualifying for membership in the corporate elite: Katharine Graham was the chief executive officer of the *Washington Post* (though it was ranked only number 435 on the *Fortune* list in 1978, so it wasn't exactly in the top "hundred or so"). As *Fortune* put it, Graham was "catapulted from housewife to president of the company after her husband's suicide in 1963."[6] This was hyperbole, however, because Graham was not just a "housewife" before her husband's death. Educated at Vassar and the University of Chicago, the daughter of the multimillionaire former owner of the paper, and an experienced journalist herself, she found that her main challenge was being catapulted into a position that had always been held by a male, not being catapulted from the role of housewife.[7]

In 1962, Felice Schwartz founded Catalyst, a nonprofit agency specializing in women's job issues. Over the years, Catalyst developed a dual mission: to assist women in business and the professions to achieve their maximum potential, and to help employers capitalize on the abilities of their female

5. Wyndham Robertson, "The Top Women in Big Business," *Fortune,* July 17, 1978, pp. 58–63.

6. Ibid.

7. Graham's father was Jewish, though she did not discover this until she enrolled at Vassar. She, like her parents, was married in a Lutheran ceremony, and she does not consider herself Jewish. See Howard Bray, *The Pillars of the Post: The Making of a News Empire in Washington* (New York: Norton, 1980), 211; Carol Felsenthal, *Power, Privilege, and the Post: The Katharine Graham Story* (New York: Putnam, 1993), 68, 98, 334, 443. Katharine Graham, *Personal History* (New York: Knopf, 1997), 52–53.

employees.[8] In 1977, responding to requests from some major corporations, Catalyst began its Corporate Board Resource. This program was designed to draw on Catalyst's database of women of achievement "to help board chairmen carefully select and recruit female directors."[9] By the late 1970s, then, Catalyst was systematically monitoring the progress of women on boards and simultaneously working with boards to increase the presence of women.

Using a slightly broader sample than *Fortune* did in 1973 and 1978 — one that included all directors of the top 1,300 companies, not just those who had earned $40,000 or more that year — Catalyst found that in 1977 there were 46 women on boards. By 1984, that figure had climbed to 367, 2.3 percent of all directors in the study.[10]

Starting in 1993 Catalyst began to publish an annual "Census of Female Board Directors" based on the top 1,000 companies — the Fortune 500 and the Fortune Service 500 — as a way of calling attention to how few women sit on corporate boards. As Sheila Wellington, president of Catalyst, wrote in *Directorship Newsletter:* "Hardly had the ink dried on the *1993 Census* before more corporations were calling to alert us to the fact that they'd added a woman to their boards. For months, we fielded calls relaying names of female additions to boards. The day we began the 1994 count, the fax began a steady six-week hum, with company after company telling of their new women directors."[11] Clearly by 1994 "company after company" felt the need to demonstrate that they had included women on their boards.

As can be seen in table 2.1, by the mid-1990s the number of women on boards had climbed steadily, and there were indications that the trend was continuing. Fifty-eight percent of the Fortune 1,000 companies had at least one woman on their boards in 1994, and 20 percent had at least two; all of the

8. Felice Schwartz has shown the ability to help found programs that have real and lasting power. In 1947, just two years after graduating from Smith College, Schwartz founded the National Scholarship Service and Fund for Negro Students (NSSFNS). She left NSSFNS in 1952 but remained on the board for twenty years. NSSFNS was a forerunner and partial model for other programs that provide scholarships for young black students, including the A Better Chance Program. Phone interview by Richard Zweigenhaft with Felice Schwartz, August 7, 1986.

9. "Women on Corporate Boards: The Challenge of Change," Catalyst, 1993, p. 4.

10. "You've Come a Long Way, Baby — But Not as Far as You Thought," *Business Week,* October 1, 1984, p. 126.

11. Sheila Wellington, "Women on Corporate Boards: The Challenge of Change," *Directorship Newsletter,* December 1994. Directorship describes itself as a "data-based firm specializing in corporate governance." In business since 1975, the company uses proxy statements to provide detailed information to its clients (mostly corporations, but also magazines and researchers) on more than seven thousand directors.

Table 2.1
*Women on Corporate Boards in the 1990s*

|  | 1992 | 1993 | 1994 |
|---|---|---|---|
| Directorships held by women at Fortune 1000 companies | 664 (5.7%) | 721 (6.2%) | 814 (6.9%) |
| Number of women holding directorships | a | 500 | 570 |
| Companies with at least one woman on the board | 49% | 52% | 58% |
| Companies with two or more women on the board | 15% | 17% | 20% |

*Source:* Catalyst.
aCatalyst did not tabulate this figure for its 1992 report.

ten most profitable companies had at least one woman director, and five of the ten had two or more. A few boards had more than three women.[12]

In 1995 *Fortune* published a new version of its list, one that merged the companies that had formerly been on the Fortune 500 and Service 500 lists. Catalyst's 1995 report was based only on the Fortune 500, not the entire 1000, and it then recreated lists for 1994 and 1993 by looking at old data only for those companies that still appeared on the 1995 list. (Some had been bumped off by Fortune Service 500 companies formerly on the Service 500 list.) Because larger companies are more likely than smaller companies to include women on their boards, this had the effect of slightly increasing the percentages in the Catalyst report. The share of seats held by women on Fortune 500 companies rose from 6.2 percent to 6.3 percent for the revised analysis based on 1993, and from 6.9 percent to 8.7 percent for the revised analysis based on 1994; for 1995, the figure was up to 9.5 percent. In 1996, Catalyst's annual report indicated that for the first time the figure exceeded 10 percent, though the rate of increase had declined.[13]

12. The following boards had three or more women: American Electric Power, Avon, Baxter International, Central Fidelity Banks, Dayton Hudson, Federal National Mortgage Association, Gannett, Great Atlantic and Pacific Tea, Hasbro, Hershey Foods, Johnson & Johnson, Knight-Ridder, Kroger, Levi Strauss, Long Island Lighting, Longview Fibre, New York Times, Ogden, Principal Mutual Life Insurance, Rochester Community Savings Bank, Rubbermaid, Stanhome, Student Loan Marketing Association, TIAA, U.S. West.

13. See "1995 Catalyst Census: Female Board Directors of the *Fortune* 500," Catalyst; Judith H. Dobrzynski, "Women Pass Milestone in the Board Room," *New York Times,* December 12, 1996.

Table 2.2
*Women on Boards, 1992–1995*

|  | 1992 | 1993 | 1994 | 1995 |
|---|---|---|---|---|
| Directorships held by women at publicly held Fortune 1000 companies | 587 (6.1%) | 647 (6.7%) | 727 (7.6%) | 837 (8.6%) |
| Number of women holding directorships | 408 (5.6%) | 444 (6.1%) | 500 (6.9%) | 556 (7.9%) |

*Source:* Directorship.

In October 1996, Catalyst published a study based on a census of the 1995 annual reports and proxy statements of the five hundred largest companies. Although 9.5 percent of the corporate directors were women, only 1.9 percent of the top five earners at these companies—and only 2.4 percent of those holding the titles of chairman, chief executive, vice chairman, president, chief operating officer, or executive vice president—were women. In the words of Wellington, "the numbers are pathetic" and the picture remains "dismal."[14]

Directorship, a publishing, research, and consulting firm that specializes in corporate governance, has monitored the presence of women on *Fortune*-level boards. Unlike Catalyst, Directorship is a for-profit company, and unlike Catalyst, since 1992 it has also kept track of the number of African Americans, Latinos, Asian Americans, and "foreigners" on *Fortune*-level boards. Directorship bases its data on the proxy statements of all Fortune 1000 firms that are publicly held (819 corporations in 1994). Table 2.2 summarizes the Directorship data on women for 1992–1995.

The figures are quite similar to those from Catalyst. The Catalyst data indicate that the percentage of seats held by women increased from 5.7 percent in 1992 to 6.9 percent in 1994; the Directorship data show an increase from 6.1 percent to 7.6 percent. This slight difference seems to suggest that publicly held companies are a bit more likely than privately held ones to have women on their boards. In both tables, when we divide the number of seats held by women by the number of women holding those seats, each woman on a Fortune 1000 board holds an average of 1.4 to 1.5 seats. (During those same years, the men on Fortune 1000 boards held, on average, about 1.3 seats.)

14. "Catalyst Census of Women Corporate Officers and Top Earners as of February 28, 1996," Catalyst, 1996, pp. 6–9. For the quotations by Sheila Wellington, see Judith H. Dobrzynski, "Study Finds Few Women in 5 Highest Company Jobs," *New York Times,* October 18, 1996.

Who are these women, and how did they come to be corporate directors? Do they come from similar or different backgrounds from the white, Protestant, American-born sons of businessmen and professionals who constituted the corporate elite in 1956? What role do they play on the corporate boards — are they tokens, or have they assumed positions of importance equal to those of their male counterparts on their boards?

Three studies help answer these questions. The first was performed in 1977 by Burson-Marsteller, a public relations and advertising firm, for a client. The second is a 1986 Ph.D. dissertation by Beth Ghiloni. The third and most recent study was done by Catalyst in 1991. Although their methods and samples differed, together these studies suggest some patterns and some changes over time in the characteristics of women on corporate boards.

The Burson-Marsteller study was based on interviews with women who sat on the boards of Fortune 500 companies, the fifty largest banks, or the fifty largest retail organizations. After eliminating those who had been on those boards for less than a year and those who were the wives or daughters of company founders, the researchers contacted seventy-five women, thirty-one of whom agreed to be interviewed.

These women were highly educated. Thirty-nine percent held Ph.D.'s and another 16 percent held law degrees. Only 16 percent had not attained an undergraduate degree. As might be predicted from their level of academic achievement, many had risen to the top of their fields in education and law, but few had attained leadership roles in corporations before being asked to join a corporate board. The study included no information about marital status, race, or class background.[15]

As part of her dissertation, Ghiloni studied the backgrounds of women who sat on Fortune 1000 boards in 1983. She identified 338 women occupying 508 directorships (figures that are similar to the Catalyst data for that period). She, too, found that women directors were "an exceptionally well-educated group": 53 percent held postgraduate degrees (27 percent had Ph.D.'s and the others had M.A.'s, M.B.A.'s, law degrees, or M.D.'s). These women directors, she noted, were more highly educated than male directors; in a comparable study of male directors, Michael Useem and Jerome Karabel found that 44 percent held postgraduate degrees.[16]

15. Burson-Marstellar, *Study of Women Directors* (New York, 1977), cited in "Women on Corporate Boards," Catalyst, 65.

16. Beth W. Ghiloni, "New Women of Power: An Examination of the Ruling Class Model of Domination," Ph.D. diss., University of California, Santa Cruz, 1986, pp. 137–141. See Michael Useem and Jerome Karabel, "Pathways to Top Corporate Management," *American Sociological Review* 51 (1986), 184–199.

Ghiloni did not estimate the percentage of female board members who were from upper-middle-class backgrounds, but she did estimate the percentage who were from the upper class. Using attendance at exclusive prep schools, listing in the *Social Register,* or membership in an exclusive club as evidence of membership in the social upper class, and using ownership of large amounts of stock in a *Fortune*-level firm as evidence of membership in the economic upper class, she concluded that 33 percent of her sample were from either the economic or the social upper class or both. This figure is similar to overall findings for samples of predominantly male directors for 1963 by Domhoff and for 1970 by Dye.[17]

Ghiloni identified four routes that women directors had taken to the corporate boards. The first, and most frequently traveled, was the "business route." About 40 percent of those she studied classified themselves as businesswomen, but they had traveled different paths than the businessmen who sat on boards. Whereas the men had typically spent fifteen to twenty years moving up the ranks of a large corporation, the women were more likely to have been heads of non-*Fortune*-level companies. Many referred to themselves as "consultants," which, as Ghiloni noted, "may mean anything from consulting on one project for a charitable organization once a year to actually owning and operating a large-scale consulting agency in a major city."[18] Some women directors had risen through the ranks of a single corporation to the level of vice president and had then been asked to join boards of firms other than the ones in which they held executive positions — they became outside directors even though they did not sit on the boards of their own firms. Notably, only 3.8 percent of the entire 1983 population of women directors (that is, only thirteen women) were inside directors, and half of these were members of families that owned the firms on whose boards they sat.[19] Clearly, then, most women directors in the early 1980s did not take the usual business pathways to the top.

The "academic path" was the second–most frequently traveled route to the corporate board, taken by 23 percent of the women Ghiloni studied. Many were or had been university presidents, vice presidents, or deans. Six presidents of the "seven sister" schools (Barnard, Bryn Mawr, Mount Holyoke,

17. Ghiloni, "New Women of Power," 122–136; G. William Domhoff, *Who Rules America?* (Englewood Cliffs, N.J.: Prentice Hall, 1967), 51, 57; Thomas R. Dye, *Who's Running America? The Carter Years,* 2d ed. (Englewood Cliffs, N.J.: Prentice Hall, 1979), 169–170.

18. Ghiloni, "New Women of Power," 156.

19. Ibid., 154–155.

Radcliffe, Smith, Vassar, and Wellesley) were among the thirty-eight women college presidents who at that time sat on *Fortune*-level boards.[20]

The "volunteer career" was the third–most frequently traveled path to the corporate board — 19 percent had used this route. These women were especially likely to be members of the social upper class, to have attended one of the seven sister schools, and to have been in the Junior League, an exclusive service organization for women. Their experiences at the head of various nonprofit charitable and cultural organizations often put them in contact with directors and executives from the corporate world who sat on their boards of trustees. This, in turn, gave the women volunteers entrée to the corporate boards.[21]

Finally, a legal career provided the fourth–most frequently traveled pathway to the corporate board — nine percent of the women directors were lawyers. The lawyers were the least likely of those Ghiloni studied to have come from upper-class backgrounds ("only" 20 percent qualified as upper class by Ghiloni's criteria), and only a few had gone to prestigious law schools.[22]

Ghiloni also found that slightly more than a quarter (27 percent) of the 1983 female directors sat on two or more boards; only 18 percent of male directors at that time sat on two or more boards. Notably, almost every African-American woman in her sample of 338 — there were 14, or 4 percent — sat on more than one board.[23] Obviously, a woman on a corporate board is likely to be asked on another corporate board, and an African-American woman is even more likely to receive multiple invitations.

Ghiloni found that the Service 500 companies were slightly more likely to have women on their boards than the companies in the Fortune 500 (55 percent of the Service 500 companies had at least one woman on the board, compared with 45 percent of the Fortune 500). Within the Service 500, women were most likely to be on the boards of banks and utilities (70 percent in each) and least likely to be on the boards of diversified financial companies (30 percent) and transportation companies (22 percent). Within the Fortune 500, they tended to be concentrated in the larger rather than the smaller companies: 73 percent of the one hundred largest industrial corporations had at least one woman on their boards, but only 13 percent of the companies ranked between number 401 and number 500 had at least one woman on their boards.[24]

20. Ibid., 157.
21. Ibid., 159–162.
22. Ibid., 163–164.
23. Ibid., 120.
24. Ibid., 118–119.

The Catalyst study was based on a questionnaire sent in the summer of 1991 to all 394 female directors of Fortune 500 and Fortune Service 500 companies. The response rate was 41 percent, or 162 surveys. When possible, the researchers also drew on information available in annual reports and proxy statements.

The average age of the women directors in 1991 was fifty-six, a bit younger than that of the men who sat on boards that year (average age, fifty-nine). Eighty-five percent had been married; 9 percent were divorced and 6 percent widowed. Almost three-fourths (74 percent) had children, with the older directors having had more children. The racial makeup of the women directors was similar to that found in Ghiloni's study: 90 percent were white, 6 percent were African American, and 3 percent were Hispanic.[25]

The women surveyed in 1991, like those surveyed in 1977 and 1983, were highly educated. One-fourth had attended women's colleges, and all but "one or two" of the women's schools they attended were seven sister schools. Catalyst did not report the number with Ph.D.'s or law degrees but did indicate that the "area of significant experience" for 16 percent of the respondents was law, and that 49 percent were primarily involved with education. Cross-tabulations looking at age and work experience indicated that the older directors were much more likely to have had their major work experience in academia, and the younger directors were much more likely to have had their major work experience in corporations or in companies they had founded.

THE PRESSURE TO ASSIMILATE

Obviously a woman cannot pass as a man in the same way that a Jewish man can pass as a Gentile. A woman in the corporate world may have to find other ways to show that she is "one of the boys" even while struggling to maintain her sense of femininity.

This can put her in no-win situations. In the early 1970s, Cecily Cannan Selby, the national executive director of the Girl Scouts of America, became the first woman to sit on the board of Avon. One of the first meetings she attended was a dinner meeting, and the atmosphere was rather tense. After the meal, one of the men offered her a cigar. "When I accepted," she recalls, "I could feel them all relax."[26]

Rosabeth Moss Kanter has suggested that the need to reduce uncertainty in large and impersonal institutions leads to the strong emphases on conformity

25. "Women on Corporate Boards," Catalyst, 12–20.

26. "Women on Board: Survey Indicates Inroads into the Male-Dominated Business World," *Los Angeles Times,* April 19, 1995.

in behavior and homogeneity in background. "It is the uncertainty quotient," she wrote, "that causes management to become so socially restricting; to develop tight inner circles excluding social strangers; to keep control in the hands of socially homogenous peers; to stress conformity and insist upon a diffuse, unbounded loyalty; and to prefer ease of communication and thus social certainty over the strains of dealing with people who are 'different.' "[27]

A few years after Kanter's book appeared, when we interviewed black and white Jewish and Gentile men and women who had M.B.A.'s from Harvard and were in (or had been in) the corporate world, this theme emerged again and again. Notably, the Jewish women we interviewed agreed that being a woman posed more of a hurdle than being Jewish. A number of them, however, explained that this did not mean that their Jewishness was completely without significance. As one put it, "It's not irrelevant. It's part of the total package. Ultimately, in the fishbowl-type environment you're in, they scrutinize you carefully. It's part of the question of whether you fit the mold. Are you like me or not? If too much doesn't fit, it impacts you negatively." Another explained, "It's the whole package. I heard secondhand from someone as to how I would be perceived as a pushy Jewish broad who went and got an M.B.A. Both elements, being Jewish and being a woman, together with having the M.B.A., were combined to create a stereotype. I had to work against that stereotype from the first day." Another summed the situation up by saying, "Anything that makes you different is more likely to be a factor at senior levels because it's so much more homogeneous there."[28]

In 1990, Elizabeth Dole, then secretary of labor, initiated a department-level investigation into the question of whether or not there was a "glass ceiling" blocking women and minorities from the highest ranks of U.S. corporations. When the report was issued by the Federal Glass Ceiling Commission in 1995, comments by the white male managers who had been interviewed and surveyed supported the earlier claims that upper management was willing to accept women and minorities only if they were not too different. As one manager explained, "What's important is comfort, chemistry, relationships, and collaborations. That's what makes a shop work. When we find minorities and women who think like we do, we snatch them up."[29]

27. Rosabeth Moss Kanter, *Men and Women of the Corporation* (New York: Basic, 1977), 49.

28. Richard L. Zweigenhaft, *Who Gets to the Top? Executive Suite Discrimination in the Eighties* (New York: Institute of Human Relations, 1984), 17.

29. *Good For Business: Making Full Use of the Nation's Human Capital* (Washington, D.C.: U.S. Government Printing Office, 1995), 28.

Terry Miyamoto, an Asian-American labor relations executive at U.S. West, Inc., a telecommunications company that ranked number 62 on the Fortune 500 list in 1995, uses the term "comfort zone" to make the same point about "chemistry" and reducing "uncertainty": "You need to build relationships," she said, "and you need to be pretty savvy. And for a woman or a person of color at this company, you have to put in more effort to get into this comfort zone."[30]

Much has been made of the fact that men have traditionally been socialized to play competitive team sports and women have not. In *The Managerial Woman*, Margaret Hennig and Anne Jardim argue that the experience of having participated in competitive team sports has provided men with many advantages in the corporate world. Playing on sports teams teaches boys such things as how to develop their individual skills in the context of helping the team to win, how to develop cooperative goal-oriented relationships with teammates, how to focus on winning, and how to deal with losing. "The experience of most little girls," they wrote, "has no parallel."[31] Although the opportunities for young women to participate in competitive sports have increased dramatically in recent years, including team sports like basketball and soccer, few such opportunities were available when most women now in higher management in U.S. corporations were young.

Just as football is often identified as the classic competitive and aggressive team sport that prepares men for the rough and tumble (and hierarchical) world of the corporation, an individual sport—golf—is the more convivial but still competitive game that allows boys to play together, shoot the breeze, and do business. As Marcia Chambers shows in *The Unplayable Lie*, the golf course, and especially the country club, can be as segregated by sex as the football field. Few clubs bar women, but some clubs do not allow women to vote, sit on their governing boards, or play golf on weekend mornings.[32]

Many women managers are convinced that their careers suffer because of discrimination against them by golf clubs. In a study of executives who manage "corporate-government affairs," Denise Benoit Scott found that the women in such positions "share meals with staff members and other government relations officials but never play golf." In contrast, men in such positions

30. Peter T. Kilborn, "A Leg Up on Ladder, but Still Far From Top," *New York Times,* June 16, 1995.

31. Margaret Hennig and Anne Jardim, *The Managerial Woman* (New York: Pocket, 1976), 45.

32. Marcia Chambers, *The Unplayable Lie: The Untold Story of Women and Discrimination in American Golf* (New York: Golf Digest/Pocket, 1995). See also Marcia Chambers, "For Women, the Country Club is the Big Handicap," *New York Times,* May 14, 1995.

"play golf with a broad range of people in business and government, including legislators and top corporate executives." As one of the women she interviewed put it: "I wish I played golf. I think golf is the key. If you want to make it, you have to play golf."[33]

Similarly, when the editors of *Executive Female* magazine surveyed the top fifty women in line-management positions (in sales, marketing, production, and general management with a direct impact on the company's bottom line), they asked them why more women had not made it to the "upper reaches of corporate America." The most frequently identified problem was the "comfort factor"—that the men atop their corporations wanted others around them with whom they were comfortable, and that generally meant other men similar to themselves. One of the other most frequently identified problems, not unrelated to the comfort factor, was the exclusion from "the social networks—the clubs, the golf course—where the informal networking that is so important to moving up the ladder often takes place."[34]

Based on the interviews they conducted for *Members of the Club*, Dawn-Marie Driscoll and Carol Goldberg also conclude that there is an important connection between golf and business. Both Driscoll and Goldberg have held directorships on major corporate boards. They establish their insider status at the beginning of their book: "We are both insiders. We always have been and probably always will be." In a section entitled "The Link That Counts," they explain how they came to realize the importance of golf: "We heard so many stories about golf that we began to pay more attention to the interaction between golf and business. We realized the importance of golf had been right in front of our eyes all the time, but because neither of us played golf, we had missed it as an issue for executive women. But golf is central to many business circles."[35]

A few months before Bill Clinton was elected president, his future secretary of energy had some pertinent comments about the importance of fitting into corporate culture and the relevance of playing golf. "Without losing your own

33. Denise Benoit Scott, "The Power of Connections in Corporate-Government Affairs: A Gendered Perspective," paper presented at the American Sociological Association Meetings, Los Angeles, 1994, p. 16.

34. Basia Hellwic, "Executive Female's Breakthrough 50," *Executive Female,* September–October 1992, p. 46.

35. Dawn-Marie Driscoll and Carol R. Goldberg, *Members of the Club: The Coming of Age of Executive Women* (New York: Free Press, 1993), 163. See also Janet Lever, "Sex Differences in the Games Children Play," *Social Problems* 23 (1976), 478–487; Janet Lever, "Sex Differences in the Complexity of Children's Play and Games," *American Sociological Review* 43 (1978), 471–483; Kathryn Ann Farr, "Dominance Bonding Through the Good Old Boy Sociability Group," *Sex Roles* 18 (1988), 259–277.

personality," said Hazel O'Leary, then an executive vice president at Northern States Power in Minnesota, "it's important to be part of the prevailing corporate culture. At this company, it's golf. I've resisted learning to play golf all my life, but I finally had to admit I was missing something that way." She took up golf.[36]

There is evidence that the golf anxiety expressed by women executives has its counterpart in the attitudes held by male executives: in its 1995 report, the Federal Glass Ceiling Commission found that many white male executives "fretted" that minorities and women did not know how to play golf.[37]

Whether or not playing golf is necessary to fit in, it is clear that women who make it into the corporate elite must assimilate sufficiently into the predominantly male culture to make it into the comfort zone. As Kathleen Jamieson points out, however, this, can place them in a double bind. On the one hand, women in the corporate world are expected to be competitive and tough-minded — but not too competitive or tough-minded, or they risk being called ballbusters. On the other hand, women in the corporate world are expected to be feminine enough to be seen as attractive and caring — but not too feminine, lest their appearance and behavior be seen as inappropriate or as an indication that they are tender-minded.[38]

But there are other age-old factors that help smooth the way into the comfort zone for some women: family connections. In 1980, when we interviewed multimillionaire Jay Pritzker for *Jews in the Protestant Establishment,* we asked him about his extremely successful and wealthy family. By the 1980s, the Pritzkers' businesses included the Hyatt hotels, Braniff Airlines, McCall's magazine, casinos, cable television systems, vast tracts of real estate, and hundreds of thousands of acres of timberland. At the time of our interview, various male members of the next generation had entered the family businesses, but none of the women. Although we talked about where his children and nieces and nephews had attended high school, whether or not they had married Jews, and the fact that some of the sons had joined the family business, no mention was made of the daughters doing so.[39]

36. Anne B. Fisher, "When Will Women Get to the Top?" *Fortune,* September 21, 1992, pp. 44–56. Quotation appears on p. 56.

37. Lena Williams, "Not Just a White Man's Game," *New York Times,* November 9, 1995.

38. Kathleen Hall Jamieson, *Beyond the Double Bind: Women and Leadership* (New York: Oxford University Press, 1995), 120–145.

39. Personal interview by Richard Zweigenhaft with Jay Pritzker, Chicago, October 20, 1980. See also "The Hustling Pritzkers," *Business Week,* May 5, 1975, pp. 55–62; "Billionaire Philanthropist A. N. Pritzker Dies," *Washington Post,* February 9, 1986.

Penny Pritzker, Jay's niece, was at that time a twenty-year-old senior at Harvard. After graduating in 1981 with a degree in economics, she went to Stanford, where by 1985 she had earned both an LL.B. and an M.B.A. By 1992 she was head of Classic Residence by Hyatt, a chain of upscale homes for the elderly, and chairman (the term she then preferred) of Coast-to-Coast Financial Savings and Loan, which managed over $1 billion in assets.

Penny Pritzker may or may not play golf—with her abilities, the expertise she has developed in both law and business, and her family connections, she clearly does not need golf. But she is an athlete, and her athleticism as much as her degrees from Stanford reveal characteristics of the next generation of women heading toward the highest levels of the corporate world. In the late 1980s she participated in an "ironman" triathlon in Hawaii, which included a 2½-mile swim, a 112-mile bicycle ride, and a 26-mile run.[40]

Indeed, it is not unusual to discover that women executives have athletic interests formerly held only by men and that they are described in terms formerly applied to men. Consider the following description in *USA Today* of Judy Lewent when she was named chief financial officer of Merck and Company (number 59 on the 1995 *Fortune* list): "Judy C. Lewent plays tennis like a pro, swims like a shark and performs her job as chief financial officer of Merck & Co. with military precision. Her boss, senior VP Francis H. Spiegel, Jr., says, 'She would have been a hell of a Marine. She's lean, mean and determined.... Her idea of a perfect vacation: two hours of tennis each day followed by 50 to 60 laps in the pool and an hour's walk on the beach. Competitiveness seems to define her life."[41]

The men who sit on *Fortune*-level boards, even if they do not have daughters or nieces who have entered the family business, are likely to have women in their family who have alerted them to the realities of sex discrimination. A 1994 Catalyst survey of CEOs found that some men attributed their increased efforts to name women to their boards to the vigilance of their wives and daughters. As one put it, "I have a wife of forty years, three daughters, and

40. "Penny's Ante," *Forbes*, November 13, 1989, 352. Penny Pritzker is just one of a number of nieces and daughters who may emerge at the top of some of America's largest corporations and financial institutions. Another is Abigail Johnson, born in 1961, with a B.A. from Hobart and William Smith College and an M.B.A. from Harvard, who manages one of the portfolios of Fidelity Investments, a company owned by FMR Corp. In 1994 her father, Edward C. "Ned" Johnson III, gave her a voting stake in FMR equal to his own and put her on the board. According to *Business Week*, "It's looking increasingly likely that Abby . . . will eventually succeed him as chairman of the nation's largest mutual-fund firm." "The Daughter Also Rises," *Business Week*, July 17, 1995, pp. 82–83.

41. Julia Lawlor, "Cracks in 'Glass Ceiling,'" *USA Today*, June 1, 1990.

four granddaughters, all of whom are scrutinizing my performance." Others said that their increased sensitivity resulted from women in their families having experienced discrimination in their careers. Another board member said that his wife and three daughters were "in the work force facing this and that," which, in turn, led him "to think and reflect on our own company."[42]

If the reminders and questions do not come from within the family, they come from outside it. In April 1987, *Business Week* ran an article on "The First-Rate Careers of the Second-Generation Tisches." The article noted that the two brothers who built Loew's into a "$19 billion empire" had seven children between them, six boys and a girl. It went on to detail the increasingly important role the sons were playing in the company. A few weeks later, a letter to the editor from a reader in Waukesha, Wisconsin, inquired: "Didn't you forget the female Tisch offspring? She was never mentioned, even in passing."[43]

Some women, then, have attained the needed skills and, like generations of men before them, have used their family connections. Others, without the good fortune of such connections, have benefited from the increased sensitivity on the part of senior managers whose wives, daughters, and granddaughters have helped to educate them.

Aside from wanting their companies to appear diverse (especially if they cater to a diverse clientele) and wanting to mollify their female relatives, is there something more that drives corporations to include women in higher management and on their boards? We think there is. It has to do with the use of women to create a "buffer zone."

As part of his analysis of the transition from a pure patriarchal system, in which all power is held by males, to modern capitalism, Michael Mann proposes that "a kind of compromise between patriarchy and a more gendered stratification hierarchy has emerged," both in the households and in the marketplace. In this compromise, women now occupy buffer zones between the men of their own class and the men in the classes below. This phenomenon appears at every point in the class hierarchy. Women who are part-time and unskilled manual laborers in low-income jobs, for example, serve as a buffer between the mostly male unemployed below them and the mostly male skilled manual workers above them. Secretaries and other white-collar women interact with the blue-collar workers who do maintenance jobs and deliver packages for the male managers. Women are the nurses and paralegals for physicians and

---

42. "The CEO View: Women on Corporate Boards," Catalyst, 1995, pp. 20–21.

43. "The First-Rate Careers of the Second Generation Tisches," *Business Week,* April 13, 1987, pp. 54–58; "The Tisch Boys Have a Capable Sister," *Business Week,* May 4, 1987, p. 12.

lawyers. And women in the higher reaches function as a buffer between "capital and all labour" by serving as volunteers, fund raisers, and board members for a wide range of charitable and social service organizations.[44]

Drawing on this analysis, we conclude that the men who run America's corporations have women in higher management and on their boards not only to present a corporate image of diversity, and not only to deflect criticism from their wives, daughters, and granddaughters, but to provide a valuable buffer between the men who control the corporation and the corporation's labor force (and the general public). It is not surprising, therefore, that in its 1996 study of the top corporate officers at Fortune 500 companies, Catalyst found that only 28 percent of the women officers who held the titles of executive vice president, senior vice president or vice president had positions with operational responsibility for profit and loss. Instead, many had been channeled into positions specializing in such areas as labor relations and public relations.[45] It is in these jobs especially that women are used as effective buffers. Because these staff jobs seldom lead to positions in top management, Ghiloni concluded her study of the velvet ghetto of public affairs in a top-50 corporation by noting that "women can play an increasingly important role in the corporation and still not gain power."[46]

Long before women joined corporate boards or were employed in personnel and public relations, women of the upper class interceded in the social system in ways that smoothed out the hard-edged, profit-oriented impact of a business-driven economy. In the Progressive Era, some upper-class women argued for protective labor legislation, maximum hours, and more respectful treatment of labor. They came to call themselves volunteers as they took a hand in running health, cultural, and social welfare agencies that added a humane, socially concerned dimension to their lives of wealth and privilege. First in nonprofit institutions, and now in corporations, we see the intersection

44. Michael Mann, "A Crisis in Stratification Theory? Persons, Households/Families/ Lineages, Genders, Classes, and Nations," in Rosemary Crompton and Michael Mann, eds., *Gender and Stratification* (London: Polity, 1986), 47. See also Peta Tancred-Sheriff, "Gender, Sexuality, and the Labour Process," in Jeff Hearn, Deborah L. Sheppard, Peta Tancred-Sheriff, and Gibson Burrell, eds., *The Sexuality of Organization* (London: Sage, 1989), 45–55. Tancred-Sheriff suggests that women in corporations use "implicit sexuality" as a form of "adjunct control" that serves to "facilitate the operation of the capitalist enterprise" (53).

45. "Catalyst Census of Women Corporate Officers and Top Earners," 8.

46. Beth W. Ghiloni, "The Velvet Ghetto: Women, Power, and the Corporation," in G. William Domhoff and Thomas R. Dye, eds., *Power Elites and Organizations* (Beverly Hills, Calif.: Sage, 1987), 21–36.

of gender and class in a way that serves the power elite by providing a buffer zone between the wealthy few and the rest of society.[47]

WOMEN AS CEOS AND WOMEN ON CORPORATE BOARDS

In 1978 the futurist Herman Kahn was asked how long he thought it would take before 25 percent of the chief executives of the Fortune 500 were women. "About two thousand years," he replied, "but make it 10 percent, and I'll say within twenty years."[48] Kahn was not the only one in the late 1970s to predict that by the 1990s more than just a few women would become CEOs of *Fortune*-level companies. In 1976 *Business Week* identified the "top 100 corporate women" and claimed that it would not be long until some became chief executive officers of *Fortune*-level companies. But when the magazine interviewed these one hundred women eleven years later, it found that their progress up the corporate ladder had been quite slow. As *Business Week* summed up the situation in 1987: "Many are sticking it out, though, resigned to the idea that they may advance — but never to the highest corporate offices. Others have abandoned big companies to start their own businesses, new careers, or families."[49]

In that 1987 article *Business Week* acknowledged that "now, more than a decade later, it is clear that the optimism was overblown." Optimism, however, springs eternal in the *Business Week* breast, for the very article that acknowledged the previous "overblown" optimism was titled "Corporate Women: They're About to Break Through to the Top," and it listed "fifty women to watch." Only one of the fifty had been on the 1976 list of one hundred. The fifty corporate women on the 1987 list, *Business Week* assured its readers, were different from the hundred on the 1976 list: "These women are vastly different — better educated, more single-minded, and more confident about their prospects. They have reason to be: Their generation has achieved far greater success in the corporate world in much less time than the original 100, and many are poised at the CEO's doorway."[50]

The *Wall Street Journal* chimed in with its own prediction in 1987. In an article entitled "Five Future No. 1's" the *Journal* identified five women who

47. See G. William Domhoff, *The Higher Circles* (New York: Random House, 1970), 35; Susan Ostrander, *Women of the Upper Class* (Philadelphia: Temple University Press, 1984).

48. Robertson, "Top Women," 59.

49. "Where Are They Now? Business Week's Leading Corporate Women of 1976," *Business Week,* June 22, 1987, p. 76.

50. Ibid., 80.

were likely to become CEOs of Fortune 500 companies by 1997: Deborah Coleman (then vice president of Operations for Apple Computer), Karen Horn (then chairman and CEO-elect of Banc One Corp's Cleveland Unit), Kay Koplovitz (then president and CEO of USA Network, which was jointly owned by Time, Inc., Paramount Pictures, and MCA), Colombe Nicholas (then president of the American arm of Christian Dior), and Linda Wachner (president of Warnaco). In that article, James P. Smith, an economist at the Rand Corporation, asserted: "It's inevitable. Large numbers of women are in the middle-management pipeline now, and in 10 years you'll see far more than one in the CEO ranks."[51]

The envelopes, please. In 1977, Katharine Graham of the *Washington Post* was the only woman CEO of a Fortune 500 company. When she retired in 1991, she was one of two, for Linda Wachner had been president and CEO at Warnaco since 1986, when she engineered a hostile takeover of the company. By late 1996 there were four women CEOs of Fortune-1000 companies: Wachner (Warnaco was number 972); Marion Sandler, who was co-CEO and co-founder with her husband of Golden West (number 491 that year); Loida Lewis, who assumed control of TLC/Beatrice (number 561) after the death of her husband, the company's founder; and Jill Barad, who was named CEO of Mattel (number 342) in August 1996.[52]

What about the *Wall Street Journal*'s surefire five? Deborah Coleman took a five-month leave from Apple shortly after the article appeared and then resigned in 1992 to join Teletronic; three years later she became CEO of Merix, a

51. Quoted in Carol Hymowitz, "Five Future No. 1's: It's a Good Bet That One of These Women Will Lead a Fortune 500 Firm in the 1990s," *Wall Street Journal,* March 20, 1987. Surprisingly, only two of the five on the *Wall Street Journal* list were on the list of fifty women identified by *Business Week*. Throughout the article, Linda Wachner is referred to as Linda Wachman.

52. Loida Lewis is from an upper-class Filipino family. Her wedding to Reginald Lewis in August 1969 was "a lavish ceremony that made the society pages of Philippine newspapers [and whose guests included] many of the country's top business and social elite. The country's then Vice President, Fernando Lopez, acted as one of the godfathers of the couple." Reginald F. Lewis and Blair S. Walker, *"Why Should White Guys Have All the Fun?" How Reginald Lewis Created a Billion-Dollar Business Empire* (New York: Wiley, 1995), 106–107. See also Jonathan P. Hicks, "Reginald F. Lewis, 50, Is Dead; Financier Led Beatrice Takeover," *New York Times,* January 20, 1993. ·

Although Mattel announced in August that Barad would become CEO, she did not officially take charge until January 1997. See Lisa Bannon, "Mattel Names Jill Barad Chief Executive," *Wall Street Journal,* August 23, 1996; Dobrzynski, "Women Pass Milestone in the Board Room."

small start-up company selling $100 million worth of computer circuit boards each year.[53] Karen Horn remained president of Banc One Cleveland until October 1996, at which time she became managing director at Bankers Trust in New York. (According to *American Banker,* she was one of the few people given serious consideration as Clinton's FDIC chairman.)[54] Kay Koplovitz was named Advertising Woman of the Year in 1991 but has not become the CEO of a *Fortune*-level company — as of April 1997, she was still the chairwoman and CEO of USA Networks.[55] Colombe Nicholas resigned as president of Dior in 1988, gave an interview in 1989 in which she said, "Maybe I should have left sooner," and then dropped out of sight.[56] Only Linda Wachner, who was already in charge at Warnaco before the 1987 *Wall Street Journal* article, was a CEO in 1996. So the *Journal* in its predictions of five "future No. 1's" of *Fortune*-level companies did no better than *Business Week* in its predictions of fifty who were "about to break through to the top." Perhaps such articles keep hopes alive.[57]

There are now women heading large divisions of major corporations, and others who are chief financial officers, and there continues to be speculation that some of these women might become CEOs of their companies. Many of the women identified on the *Business Week* list of fifty do sit on the boards of *Fortune*-level companies. In fact, when we cross-checked to see how many of the fifty women on the 1987 *Business Week* list of "women to watch" were also listed by Catalyst as corporate directors in 1994, we found that eight of the fifty held thirteen directorships (Jill Barad was one of the women on that list).

53. Kerry A. Dolan, "Fairfield Bound?" *Forbes,* February 27, 1995, p. 142.

54. Jacqueline Gold, "A Bank President Who Was About to Give Birth," *American Banker,* November 28, 1994, p. 4; "She's Always a Good Soldier," same issue, 4; "Want a Hot Tip on FDIC Chairman Race? We've Got Plenty," *American Banker,* February 1, 1993, p. 7.

55. Lawrie Mifflin, "USA Networks to Sponsor Charlie Rose's PBS Programs," *New York Times,* November 14, 1995; see also Kay Koplovitz, "Manager's Journal," *Wall Street Journal,* March 6, 1995; Geraldine Fabrikant, "In Cable's World of Boutiques, a Generalist Thrives," *New York Times,* September 15, 1991.

56. Dyan Machan, " 'Maybe I Should Have Left Sooner,' " *Forbes,* May 29, 1989, pp. 320–322.

57. There was no way for us to develop a control group of males who have been identified as surefire future CEOs. Although it is true that only a small percentage of men attain one of the few CEO positions, it is also the case that for the past few decades, about 996 to 999 of the 1,000 CEOs of *Fortune*-level companies in any given year have been white men. So, however small the percentage of white men who move upward through the corporate ranks to become CEOs, the percentage for women has been smaller.

Lynda Woodworth of Catalyst is surely accurate in her claim that "there are between 25 and 50 of these women, just beneath the CEO level."[58] What is less clear is how many of them, if any, will make the jump to CEO slots. Some might, but if the fate of the *"Business Week* fifty" is an accurate predictor, many are likely to continue to hover near the top, some will leave to head smaller companies, and some will become consultants when they conclude that they have gone as far as they are going to go.

It is noteworthy that in the early 1990s relatively few male CEOs believed that their companies would select women to run their companies in the near future. In a study of 201 chief executives at the country's largest corporations, the respondents were asked, "How likely is it that your company will have a female CEO in the next ten years?" Only 2 percent said "very likely," and 14 percent said "somewhat likely." Correspondingly, women constitute only about 5 percent of the participants in the executive training seminars run by business schools, considered at many companies to be "an indispensable credential for future CEOs."[59]

Very few women have emerged as CEOs of *Fortune*-level boards, and women constitute less than 10 percent of all directors of *Fortune*-level boards.[60] There is also evidence that they have been marginalized in terms of the actual board responsibilities that they have been — or not been — given. As Diana Bilimoria and Sandy Kristin Piderit have demonstrated in their research on the makeup of various committees within corporate boards, there is empirical evidence of "sex-based bias" against female board members. Using regression analyses, the authors systematically looked at committee memberships on the boards of the 133 companies in the top 300 on *Fortune*'s list for 1984 that had at least

58. Phone interview by Richard Zweigenhaft with Lynda Woodworth, September 26, 1995. See also Judith H. Dobrzynski, "Way Beyond the Glass Ceiling: Billion-Dollar Command Now, a C.E.O. Chair Next?" *New York Times,* May 11, 1995.

59. Fisher, "When Will Women Get to the Top?" 44.

60. Women have made it into the highest circles of the legal world and on Wall Street, to about the same degree. A study by the National Law Journal found that 13.6 percent of all partners in the country's 250 largest law firms are women (but only 54 percent of these women are equity partners, which means they share in the firm's profits; 74 percent of the men who are partners share in profits). Claudia H. Deutsch, "Women Lawyers Strive for Chance to Make it Rain," *New York Times,* May 21, 1996. Similarly a study of the leading Wall Street investment and brokerage houses found that only about 8 percent of the managing directors were women. The women had tended to rise through "less coveted administrative, management and research jobs," but "the more glamorous and high paying jobs, such as investment banking and trading, are even more of a male preserve than Wall St. itself." Peter Truell, "Success and Sharp Elbows," *New York Times,* July 2, 1996.

one woman director. They examined the makeup of six committees. Even after controlling for work experience, they found that men were more likely to serve on three of the six committees studied (compensation, executive, and finance), women were more likely to serve on one of the committees (public affairs), and there were no differences on the other two (audit and nominating). These findings, they concluded, demonstrate that the underrepresentation of women on key committees is not, as is often claimed, simply a result of their having less relevant work experience; instead, they "indicate the pervasive presence of sex-based bias in the selection of committee members." Moreover, "the pattern of bias appears to follow traditional sex-typing: committees stereotypically perceived as attending to hard governance issues favored male membership, and the committee stereotypically perceived to deal with soft governance issues favored female membership."[61]

## Women in the Cabinet

Since the Eisenhower administration, 15 women and 194 men have served in the cabinets of nine presidents. The names of all of the women who have served in cabinets, and the positions they held, are listed in table 2.3.

Eisenhower appointed only one woman (as compared with twenty men). The next three presidents—Kennedy, Johnson, and Nixon—named seventy people to their various cabinets, but not one woman, so the cabinet was an exclusively male club from 1955 until 1975, when Gerald Ford appointed a woman to be secretary of housing and urban development (HUD). Of the twenty-one Carter cabinet members, three were women, one of whom held two different positions. Reagan's cabinets included thirty-three people, three of whom were women. Three of Bush's nineteen appointments were women (including Elizabeth Dole, who had also served in Reagan's cabinet), and Clinton's initial cabinet included three women. In 1997, Clinton added two more women to his cabinet. The percentage of women in presidential cabinets

61. Diana Bilimoria and Sandy Kristin Piderit, "Board Committee Membership: Effects of Sex-Based Bias," *Academy of Management Journal* 37, no. 6 (1994), 1453–1477. Quotation appears on p. 1465. These findings challenge the earlier work of Idalene F. Kesner, "Directors' Characteristics and Committee Membership: An Investigation of Type, Occupation, Tenure, and Gender," *Academy of Management Journal* 31 (1988), 69–84.

For a similar conclusion based on a study of senior executives, see Karen S. Lyness and Donna E. Thompson, "Above the Glass Ceiling? A Comparison of Matched Samples of Female and Male Executives,' *Journal of Applied Psychology* 82, no. 3 (1997), 359–375.

Table 2.3
*Women in the Cabinet*

|  | President | Years | Position |
|---|---|---|---|
| Frances Perkins | Roosevelt | 1933–45 | Labor |
| Oveta Culp Hobby | Eisenhower | 1953–55 | Health, education, and welfare |
| Carla Anderson Hills | Ford | 1975–77 | Housing and urban development |
| Juanita Kreps | Carter | 1977–80 | Commerce |
| Patricia Harris | Carter | 1977–79 | Housing and urban development |
| Harris | Carter | 1979–81 | Health, education, and welfare |
| Shirley Hufstedler | Carter | 1979–81 | Education |
| Elizabeth Dole | Reagan | 1983–87 | Transportation |
| Margaret Heckler | Reagan | 1983–85 | Health and human services |
| Ann McLaughlin | Reagan | 1987–89 | Labor |
| Dole | Bush | 1989–90 | Labor |
| Lynn Martin | Bush | 1990–92 | Labor |
| Barbara H. Franklin | Bush | 1992 | Commerce |
| Hazel O'Leary | Clinton | 1993–97 | Energy |
| Janet Reno | Clinton | 1993– | Attorney general |
| Donna Shalala | Clinton | 1993– | Health and human services |
| Madeline Albright | Clinton | 1997– | State |
| Alexis Herman | Clinton | 1997– | Labor |

*Note:* The sole female cabinet member prior to the election of Dwight David Eisenhower was Frances Perkins, who served as Roosevelt's secretary of labor from 1933 to 1945. (Mills does not refer to her in *The Power Elite*.)

has thus increased since Mills wrote his book, but it has not gone beyond a distinct minority.

The number of cabinet positions held by women is but one measure of their presence in the political elite. Another perhaps more important measure is the specific cabinet positions they have held. As the political scientist Thomas Cronin wrote in 1980: "Vast differences exist in the scope and importance of cabinet-level departments. The three million–person Defense Department and the sixteen thousand–person or so departments of Labor or Housing and Urban Development are not similar."[62] Cronin acknowledges that one can rank-order the cabinet positions in a variety of ways, including longevity, annual expenditures, and number of personnel, but his view is that the "contemporary cabinet" is best differentiated into "inner and outer cabinets." The

62. Thomas E. Cronin, *The State of the Presidency,* 2d ed. (Boston: Little, Brown, 1980), 275.

inner cabinet includes the secretaries of state, defense, and treasury and the attorney general, all of which include "broad-ranging, multiple interests" and serve in a counseling role to the president. The remaining members of the cabinet are part of the outer cabinet; their departments tend to focus on domestic policy issues, and they tend to assume an advocacy role rather than a counseling role.[63]

Thirteen of the fifteen women cabinet members have been in the outer cabinet — only Janet Reno, Clinton's attorney general, and Madeline Albright, Clinton's secretary of state beginning in 1997, have held positions in the inner cabinet. In their 1981 study of women in the power structure, Faye Huerta and Thomas Lane concluded that the women of the cabinet have held the "so called 'soft issue' areas such as housing, commerce and welfare." Until the Clinton presidency, this continued to be the case.[64]

In her study of the social backgrounds of all members of the cabinet between 1897 and 1973, Beth Mintz found that almost two-thirds (63 percent) had fathers who held professional or managerial positions; 80 percent were Protestants (48 percent were either Episcopalian or Presbyterian); and 86 percent had completed four years of college or more. Many had direct links to the business community. "Typically," she noted, "a cabinet position is one of several governmental positions held in a process of business-government interchange."[65]

The fifteen women who have served in the cabinet since 1953 have backgrounds similar to those Mintz found when she studied all cabinet members. Most of these women were born into economically secure families in which the fathers, or both parents, were well-educated professionals. The father of Oveta Culp Hobby, Eisenhower's secretary of health, education, and welfare, was a lawyer, and her husband owned the major newspaper in Houston; both parents of Hazel O'Leary, Clinton's secretary of energy, were physicians; the parents of Barbara Franklin, Bush's secretary of commerce, were both educators; the parents of Janet Reno, Clinton's attorney general, were both journalists; and the fathers of Carla Hills (Ford's secretary of HUD), Elizabeth Dole (Reagan's secretary of transportation and Bush's secretary of labor), and Ann McLaughlin (Reagan's secretary of labor) were successful businessmen. Madeline Albright, Clinton's secretary of state, was born in Czechoslovakia,

63. Ibid., 275–276.

64. Faye C. Huerta and Thomas A. Lane, "Participation of Women in Centers of Power," *Social Science Journal* 18, no. 2 (1981), 71–86.

65. Beth Mintz, "The President's Cabinet, 1897–1972: A Contribution to the Power Structure Debate," in "New Directions in Power Structure Research," a special issue of *Insurgent Sociologist* 5, no. 3 (1975), 131–148.

where her father was a diplomat. (She grew up speaking Czech, French, and some Polish.)

Of the fifteen, two seem to have come from genuine working-class origins — Heckler's father was a doorman at a New York City hotel, and Patricia Harris's father was a waiter on a railroad. (Both Heckler and Harris attended college on scholarships.) Three others were from middle-class backgrounds: Hufstedler's father was a contractor, who had to move frequently during the Depression to find work, and her mother was a teacher; Shalala's father, a real estate salesman, was a leader in the Syrian-Lebanese community in Cleveland, and her mother was a physical education teacher who put herself through law school at night while Shalala and her twin sister were young girls; and Alexis Herman's father was a mortician and political activist — after suing the state's Democratic Party to secure for blacks the right to vote, he became the first black ward leader in Alabama — and her mother was a reading teacher.[66] Juanita Kreps's class background is a bit harder to categorize: her father was a "struggling mine operator" in Kentucky; her parents were divorced when she was four, and she lived with her mother until she was twelve, at which time she attended a Presbyterian boarding school; she later said of her childhood (during the Depression), "Everyone was having economic problems, and we weren't any worse off than anyone else."[67]

All fifteen of these women graduated from college, and thirteen did post-graduate work. Eight graduated from law school (two went to Harvard, one each to Boston College, George Washington, Rutgers, Stanford, Texas, and Yale). Three did doctoral work (Kreps received a Ph.D. in economics from Duke, Shalala a Ph.D. in political science from Syracuse, and Albright a Ph.D. in international affairs from Columbia), and two attended M.B.A. programs (McLaughlin at the University of Pennsylvania, Franklin at Harvard).

Kreps and Shalala came to the cabinet after rising through the academic hierarchies of large research universities (Kreps had been a vice president at Duke, and Shalala was chancellor of the University of Wisconsin). Heckler and Martin had served a number of terms in Congress and then been defeated in reelection bids before Republican presidents named them to their cabinets.

---

66. As a teenager, Shalala was to encounter another future member of the power elite in an unlikely context. A gifted athlete, she played shortstop and left field for the West Boulevard Annie Oakleys, a team that won the Cleveland city softball championship. The coach of the team was young George Steinbrenner, son of a Cleveland shipping magnate, who was home for the summer from Williams College. See "Donna Shalala," *Current Biography* (1991), 515; Michael Wines, "Friend Helped Labor Nominee Move Up, Then Almost Brought Her Down," *New York Times,* March 12, 1997.

67. "Juanita Kreps," *Current Biography* (1977), 259.

Janet Reno had also been elected to office — she served four terms as state attorney in Dade County, Florida.

Most of the rest came to the cabinet from other government positions or from the corporate world, and some had spent time in both settings. Hills was a partner in a law firm and had been working in the Justice Department; Hufstedler was a judge of the U.S. Court of Appeals; McLaughlin was the highest-ranking woman executive at Union Carbide and had then worked at high-level positions in the Treasury and Interior departments; O'Leary was an executive vice president at Northern States Power, one of the largest gas and electric utility companies in the Midwest.

Many of these women had served on major corporate boards before being nominated for cabinet positions. Before she was nominated by Carter to be secretary of commerce, Juanita Kreps held an endowed chair in economics at Duke University, but her income from that chair was only half what she earned as a director on boards that included R. J. Reynolds, Eastman Kodak, and J. C. Penney. (In 1976 her income as a professor at Duke was $30,106, and her income from boards was $61,150.)[68] When Bush appointed Barbara Franklin to be secretary of commerce, the *New York Times* described her as "a well-connected management consultant, corporate director and Republican fund-raiser." Franklin was at the time a director on seven boards, which provided her with as much as $327,000 a year, depending on how many meetings she attended. Only one woman in history had served on more Fortune 1000 boards simultaneously — Ann McLaughlin, who was secretary of labor during Reagan's second term.[69]

Others, of course, have been asked onto boards after leaving their cabinet positions. In 1983 five of these women sat on a total of twenty boards, and by 1994 six of them sat on twenty-seven boards. All but Reno, Shalala, and Herman have been married. Most have had children. A few have been in major Washington power marriages. Hills's husband, Roderick Hills, also a lawyer, was head of the Securities and Exchange Commission (SEC) from 1975 to 1977. Elizabeth Dole met Senator Robert Dole of Kansas while she was working in the White House Office of Consumer Affairs during the Nixon administration. They were married in 1975. During the Reagan years, some considered them "the second-most powerful couple in the nation's capital."[70] Ann

68. Ibid., 261.

69. Keith Bradsher, "Bush Picks Nominee for Commerce Post," *New York Times*, December 27, 1991.

70. "Elizabeth Dole," *Current Biography* (1983), 117.

McLaughlin was married to John McLaughlin, a former Jesuit priest turned Nixon speechwriter turned television talk show host. ("Father McLaughlin," we're told in one profile of Ann McLaughlin, "defended Nixon throughout the Watergate scandal, predicting publicly that the president would eventually come to be regarded as 'the greatest moral leader of the last third of this century.' "[71])

Patricia Harris was African American, as are Hazel O'Leary and Alexis Herman. The others have been white. Three are (or were) Episcopalians (Hobby, Hills, Kreps), one a Congregationalist (Franklin), and one, Dole, a Methodist (though in an apparent effort to help her husband please the right wing of his party as he campaigned for the 1996 Republican nomination, she left the Methodist church in Washington that she had attended for years—the same church the Clintons attended—and joined a more "traditional Christian church").[72] Five have been Catholics (Heckler, Herman, O'Leary, McLaughlin, and Martin). Albright, as we have noted, was raised a Catholic but became an Episcopalian when she married (see Chapter 1, note 48).

## Women in the Military Elite

As was typically the case, Mills did not mince words when he wrote about those at the top of the military hierarchy. Mills refers in general to military men throughout history and throughout the world as "warlords," and he refers more specifically to "the men of violence: the United States warlords."[73]

In 1956, there were no women among the warlords. The only mention Mills made of women when he wrote about the military was to demonstrate the importance of rank in such an extremely hierarchical institution. Even the social lives of the women married to military men were affected by the rank of their husbands. Mills quotes the wife of General George C. Marshall, describing a social event for military wives between the two world wars: "At a tea such as this one you always ask the highest-ranking officer's wife to pour coffee, not tea, because coffee outranks tea."[74]

Indeed, it was not until 1967 that Congress passed legislation allowing women to be promoted to any general officer grade in the army and the air

71. "Ann McLaughlin," *Current Biography* (1988), 368.

72. Richard Reeves, "Church and Statesmen: Sen. Bob Dole's Church Isn't Politically Correct," *Greensboro News and Record,* May 15, 1995.

73. Mills, *Power Elite*, 186.

74. Ibid., 190.

force. (The sanction of corresponding promotions for women in the navy and the marines took another decade.) When General William Westmoreland officiated at the 1970 ceremony at which the first two women were promoted to the rank of brigadier general, he surprised everyone present. First, as he pinned the stars on Anna Hays, a twenty-eight-year army veteran who had served in three wars, he kissed her "squarely on the mouth." A few minutes later, after pinning a star on the second woman in history to become a general, he intoned "And now, in accordance with a new Army custom, . . . " and he kissed her, too.[75]

In their 1981 study of women in power, Huerta and Lane looked at those positions in the military hierarchy mentioned by Mills for the years 1958, 1965, 1972, and 1978. Of the 478 positions they examined in the Department of Defense, the army, the navy and the air force, they found only seven that had been occupied by women. Five of these were with the women's branches of the army and the marines (since eliminated by the integration of the women's corps with the formerly all-male military). The other two were in positions identified as "general counsel." These findings, they concluded, were "not unexpected," given that the military is "almost universally recognized as a 'man's world.' "[76]

In large part as a result of the shift from conscription to an all-volunteer military in 1973, the U.S. military has become less a "man's world," at least in terms of the number of men and women on active duty. In 1972 there were slightly fewer than 45,000 women on active duty (1.9 percent of the total force); by 1994 that number had increased to nearly 200,000 (about 12 percent), though most of the increase had taken place by the early 1980s, and the percentage of women in the military has remained stable for the past decade. The percentage of women officers (12.7 percent) was about the same as that of enlisted personnel (11.9 percent), but the percentage of female officers in the different branches ranges from a high of 15.0 percent in the air force to a low of 3.4 percent in the Marine Corps.[77] Starting in fall 1976 women were admitted to the service academies.[78]

75. Jeanne Holm, *Women in the Military: An Unfinished Revolution,* rev. ed. (Novato, Calif.: Presidio, 1992), 203.

76. Huerta and Lane, "Participation of Women," 75.

77. *1993 Handbook on Women Workers: Trends and Issues,* U.S. Department of Labor, 22–23; *Defense 94 Almanac,* issue 5, Department of Defense, 30. According to Holm, the end of the draft "more than any other factor during the seventies produced an expansion of women's participation in the armed forces that was of unexpected and unprecedented proportions" (*Women in the Military,* 246).

78. *World Almanac* (1995), 159.

In spite of their increased numbers in the past few decades, women have not yet been promoted to the ranks of the warlords. In May 1995, in addition to the five men who made up the Joint Chiefs of Staff, there were 38 officers in the armed services with "four-star rank" — 12 in the army, 11 in the navy, 3 in the marines, 11 in the air force, and 1 in the Coast Guard — but none was a woman. In fact, at that time, of the 929 highest ranking people in the army, navy, air force, Marine Corps, and Coast Guard (those who had achieved the rank of general officer), only 11 were women — 1.2 percent.[79]

Seventy women have become general officers, though none higher than two-star rank until March 1996, when Clinton nominated Marine Corps Maj. Gen. Carol Mutter to be the first woman three-star general.[80] The current number is the highest it has ever been, but the progress has been incremental. At the current rate of increase, it will be a long time before the percentage of women general officers moves out of the token range.

Who are these seventy women and how did they get there? All but five are white — four are African American, and one is Hispanic. Most are from middle-class backgrounds, and a disproportionate number have come from the personnel field. When we asked one of these women, Brig. Gen. Wilma Vaught — the president of the Women in Military Service Memorial Foundation — why this was so, she focused on what is clearly an important issue with regard to military promotions at the highest levels: combat experience. "The types of problems you have in personnel women can handle as well as men," she told us, "and, of course, you don't need combat experience to do well in personnel." Vaught also noted that with the exception of those who had been nurses, almost all of the seventy women had come from administrative rather than technical backgrounds.[81]

Four civilians serve under the secretary of defense as secretaries of the army, navy, air force, and Marine Corps. Because the appointments are made by the president and require the approval of the Senate, these are essentially political, not military, positions. The first woman to hold one of these positions, Sheila Widnall, was nominated by Bill Clinton in July 1993 to become secretary of

---

79. "Distribution of Active Duty Forces by Service, Rank, Sex, and Ethnic Group," May 31, 1995, DMDC-3035EO, Department of Defense.

80. John Mintz, "President Nominates 1st Woman to Rank of three-Star General," *Washington Post*, March 27, 1996. Just a few months later Clinton nominated another when he selected Rear Adm. Patricia Tracey for promotion to vice admiral. John Mintz, "Clinton Nominates First Black Admiral: Woman in Line to Become Vice Admiral," *Washington Post*, May 14, 1996.

81. Personal interview by Richard Zweigenhaft with Wilma Vaught, Arlington, Va., August 2, 1995.

the air force. Widnall, an aeronautical engineer who had served as a consultant to the air force, and a former professor and associate provost at MIT, encountered some resistance during the confirmation hearings because of her husband's membership in the Marblehead Yacht Club, which, according to the Anti-Defamation League, discriminated on the basis of both sex and religion. She was nonetheless confirmed.[82]

There are, then, very few women in the military who have even approached warlord status, and prospects are not good for more than token presence in the highest military circles for a long time. The percentage of women officers remains quite small, and the system of promotion remains riddled with biases against women. As Holm — the third woman promoted to the rank of general, and the first in the air force — concludes in the 1992 revised edition of the book she wrote in 1982, "It would be unrealistic to believe that a system still so heavily weighted toward operational experience of the kind as yet available on only a limited basis for women will be able to operate in an unbiased fashion."[83]

## Women in Congress

### THE SENATE

As can be seen in table 2.4, nineteen women have served in the Senate since 1950. They fall into two clusters: those who served in the Senate before 1978, when Nancy Kassebaum was elected, and those who have been elected since then.

Only one woman served in the U.S. Senate from the time Mills wrote *The Power Elite* until 1972: Margaret Chase Smith of Maine.[84] Smith's husband, a Maine politician "who ran for office 48 times in his lifetime without a defeat," was a member of the House from 1937 to 1940.[85] He became gravely ill and, dying, asked his constituents to elect his wife, a former teacher and newspaperwoman. They did, and she served in the House for eight years before successfully running for the Senate in 1948.

During her long tenure in the Senate, Smith had some female company, but it tended to be brief, and it was invariably the result of the death of a male

82. "Air Force Nominee Denies Club Is Biased," *Greensboro News and Record,* July 30, 1995.

83. Holm, *Women in the Military,* 278.

84. Donald E. Matthews, *U.S. Senators and Their World* (New York: Vintage, 1960), 13.

85. Martin Gruberg, *Women in American Politics* (Oshkosh, Wis.: Academia, 1968).

Table 2.4
*Women in the Senate Since 1950*

| Margaret Chase Smith | R-Maine | 1949–1973 |
|---|---|---|
| Eva Bowring | R-Neb. | April–Nov. 1954 |
| Hazel Abel | R-Neb. | Nov.–Dec. 1954 |
| Maurine Neuberger | D-Ore. | 1960–1967 |
| Elaine Edwards | D-La. | August–Nov. 1972 |
| Muriel Humphrey | D-Minn. | Jan.–Nov. 1978 |
| Maryon Pittman Allen | D-Ala. | June–Nov. 1978 |
| Nancy Kassebaum | R-Kan. | 1978–1997 |
| Paula Hawkins | R-Fla. | 1981–1987 |
| Barbara Mikulski | D-Md. | 1987– |
| Barbara Boxer | D-Calif. | 1993– |
| Dianne Feinstein | D-Calif. | 1993– |
| Patty Murray | D-Wash. | 1993– |
| Carol Moseley-Braun | D-Ill. | 1993– |
| Kay Bailey Hutchison | R-Tex. | 1993– |
| Olympia Snowe | R-Maine | 1995– |
| Sheila Frahm | R-Kan. | 1996 |
| Mary Landrieu | D-La. | 1997– |
| Susan Collins | R-Maine | 1997– |

senator during his elected term of office.[86] In 1954, when Dwight Griswold, the Republican senator from Nebraska, died, the state's governor named Eva Bowring to replace him until a special election could be held. The special election was for the final two months of Griswold's term, and it was open only to candidates who were not going to seek the subsequent six-year term. This election was won by another woman, Hazel Abel. Six years later, Richard Neuberger, the Democratic senator from Oregon, died during his term, and his wife, Maurine, won the special election that was held to complete his term. She then ran for that seat in 1960 and won; she chose not to run again in 1966.

After six more years as the sole woman in the Senate, Smith had another woman colleague for a very brief time. When Allen Ellender, the 82-year-old Democratic senator from Louisiana, died in August 1972, Governor Edwin

86. See Diane Kincaid, "Over His Dead Body: A Positive Perspective on Widows in the United States Congress," cited in Barbara Boxer, *Strangers in the Senate: Politics and the New Revolution of Women in America* (Washington, D.C.: National Press Books, 1994), 90.

Edwards was faced with the task of appointing a temporary successor. There was already a heated campaign for the seat, and Edwards wanted to avoid making a costly partisan choice. So, as he put it, in the hopes of making a "meaningful, symbolic gesture to the women of Louisiana who have for too long been underrepresented in the halls of Congress," he chose his own wife, Elaine. She was quick to assert that "I'm no U.S. Senator, but with the help of Senator Russell Long and the Louisiana congressional delegation, I will get along fine."[87] Edwards became the eleventh woman ever to serve in the Senate and at that point her service was much more typical than Margaret Chase Smith's: of these eleven women, eight had served for less than a year.[88] When Smith was defeated in her bid for reelection in November 1972, the Senate was again, for six years, an all-male club.

Two more male senators died in 1978, which led to very brief Senate terms for their widows. First Hubert Humphrey, Democrat from Minnesota, died, and his wife, Muriel, was appointed to serve until a special election could be held (she did not enter that race). Then, James Allen, Democrat from Alabama, died, and Governor George Wallace appointed his widow, Maryon Pittman Allen, to replace him; she ran in the election for the remaining two years of her husband's term but lost.

Nancy Landon Kassebaum's election to the Senate in 1978 represented a genuine breakthrough, for she was the first woman to be elected who had not replaced a deceased male. Kassebaum was not, however, without valuable political connections. Her father, Alf Landon, had been governor of Kansas and had run for president against Franklin Delano Roosevelt in 1936. The *New York Times* asserted in an editorial that if her "middle name were Jones her campaign would have been a joke."[89] In addition to a name familiar to the voters of Kansas, she had something else that helps one become a member of the Senate: a net worth of millions of dollars that enabled her to finance her campaign.

Two years later, the number of women senators doubled when Paula Hawkins was elected from Florida. Hawkins had run for the Senate in 1974 and for lieutenant governor in 1976. She lost both of those races, but she won the Republican primary in 1980 and was elected as part of the Reagan landslide that year. Six years later, she was defeated by Governor Bob Graham. Another woman senator was elected in 1986 — Barbara Mikulski, a Democrat from Maryland, who had previously served five terms in the House of Representa-

87. "Governor Names Wife Senator," *Washington Post,* August 2, 1972.
88. Gruberg, *Women in American Politics,* 123.
89. "Nancy Kassebaum," *Current Biography* (1982), 192.

tives — so there continued to be two women in the Senate (Kassebaum was the other).

In 1992, on the heels of the Clarence Thomas confirmation hearings — which captivated the nation and demonstrated quite persuasively to many that the Senate Judiciary Committee (and, by extension, the U.S. Senate) consisted of white men determined to ignore women's concerns while professing empathy — four women were elected to the Senate, tripling the number of women in that body from two to six. Carol Moseley-Braun, the first African-American woman ever to be elected to the Senate; Barbara Boxer, who had served five terms in the House; Dianne Feinstein, the former mayor of San Francisco; and Patty Murray, a former preschool teacher, state legislator and self-described "mom in tennis shoes," all joined Kassebaum and Mikulski.[90]

In June 1993 the number of women in the Senate climbed to seven when Kay Bailey Hutchison, a Republican, won a special election after Clinton selected Lloyd Bentsen, a Democratic senator from Texas, as secretary of the treasury. In November 1994, when Maine elected Olympia Snowe, who had been an aide to Senator William Cohen when he served in the House, she became the eighth woman in the Senate.[91] When Bob Dole resigned from the Senate in May 1996 to pursue his quest for the presidency full-time, the Republican governor of Kansas selected Sheila Frahm, a moderate pro-choice Republican, to replace him, increasing the number of women in the Senate to nine, but she soon lost any chance of continuing when an antiabortion ultraconservative defeated her in the Republican primary. In that 1996 election, Mary Landrieu was elected to the Senate from Louisiana. Like Nancy Kassebaum, who was elected to the Senate eighteen years earlier (and who chose not to run for reelection in 1996), Landrieu was the daughter of a successful politician whose name was well-known throughout the state: her father, Moon Landrieu, had been mayor of New Orleans and secretary of housing and urban development in the Carter administration. Susan Collins, also elected in 1996, had worked for more than a decade as adviser on business affairs to William Cohen when he served in the House of Representatives.

Clearly there have been two eras, each bringing women to the Senate via very different routes. In the pre-Kassebaum era, women had to be in the right place

90. Jamieson, *Beyond the Double Bind*, 193. Because of the number of women elected to the Senate, the House, and state legislatures in the 1992 election, the media incessantly designated 1992 as "the year of the woman."

91. Snowe and her second husband, John R. McKernan Jr., who served as governor of Maine for two terms, were referred to as "Maine's political power couple" in the *Congressional Quarterly*, November 12, 1994, p. 13.

at the right time when a male Senator died, and these requirements were best met by being his widow. The post-Kassebaum era, from 1978 to the present, includes women whose elections did not require such a morbid prerequisite.

The women who have been elected to the Senate differ from those who have been appointed to the cabinet in some obvious ways. For one, they are much less well educated and less likely to have attended prestigious colleges and universities. With the exception of Paula Hawkins, who attended Utah State but did not receive a degree, all earned undergraduate degrees. But only one attended an elite undergraduate institution (Feinstein, whose B.A. is from Stanford), and none has an undergraduate or postgraduate degree from an Ivy League school. Four have advanced degrees: Mikulski has an M.S.W., Kassebaum an M.A. in history, and both Moseley-Braun and Hutchison have law degrees.

Correspondingly, they are much less likely than the women in the cabinet to have come from privileged backgrounds, and much more likely to have come from genuinely working-class families. Only Kassebaum, Feinstein, and Landrieu, two Republicans and a Democrat, came from upper-middle-class or upper-class backgrounds. The others grew up in either middle-class or working-class families.

These women are much more heterogeneous religiously than the women of the cabinet (or the men of the Senate). Five are Catholic, two are Episcopalians, two are Jewish, one is a Mormon, and one is Greek Orthodox. All but Mikulski and Collins have been married, and all but Mikulski, Collins, Hutchison, and Snowe have had children.

THE HOUSE

The 1990s have seen a corresponding increase in the number of women in the House. In the November 1990 election, twenty-nine women were elected or reelected to the House, twenty Democrats and nine Republicans. The dramatic increase in the number of women senators in 1992 was accompanied by a sharp increase in the number of women elected in the House — forty-seven, thirty-five Democrats and twelve Republicans. Two years later, when the Republicans gained control of the House, the number of women increased by one, to forty-eight, but the number of Republicans increased by six, to eighteen. In 1996, fifty-one women were elected, thirty-five Democrats and sixteen Republicans.[92] A systematic look at the seventy-eight women who

92. *Congressional Quarterly,* November 10, 1990, p. 3836; November 7, 1992, p. 8; November 12, 1994, p. 10; January 4, 1997, p. 29. These figures are based on voting members of the House, and therefore we have not included Eleanor Holmes Norton, Democrat from the District of Columbia.

have been elected to the House in the 1990s indicates that they, like the women elected to the Senate in the post-Kassebaum era, are less well-educated and much less likely to have been educated at elite schools, less likely to have come from privileged backgrounds and more diverse religiously than the women in the power elite.

The power elite is no longer the all-male enclave it was in the 1950s. The presence of women has increased most clearly and steadily in the corporate world and cabinets, but the percentage of women on corporate boards has only recently topped 10 percent; in some presidential cabinets it has been higher, with the peak thus far being the Clinton cabinet at 21 percent in his first term and 31 percent at the beginning of his second term. Although women were almost 13 percent of the officers in the military at the end of 1993, less than 2 percent of those who achieved the rank of general officer (the equivalent of a one-star general) were women. There have been no women among the highest-ranking military officers, the Joint Chiefs of Staff. The women in the corporate, cabinet, and military elites are thus still numerical tokens, even though a few, like Katharine Graham of the *Washington Post,* Janet Reno, and Madeline Albright clearly have attained positions of real power.

The participation of women in Congress increased dramatically between 1978 and 1995, with the strongest surge coming in the 1990s. Still, women make up less than 10 percent of the Senate and only 12 percent of the House. Most have been Democrats, though it is not as pronounced a majority as is the case for Jews in Congress.

Unlike Jewish men, who, over the generations, can become virtually indistinguishable from the Christian men in the power elite, the women in the power elite and Congress remain identifiably different. Still, the more similar they are to the men who have long dominated the power elite in terms of attitudes and values, class background, and education, the more acceptable they are and the more likely to move into the higher circles. The women who have been elected to Congress have come from more varied backgrounds, as have both the women and the men who have gone the furthest in the military.

Predictions and projections concerning the increasing number of women in important positions in the corporate world do not take into consideration one important possibility: the male-centered climate of the corporate world may lead some women to leave before they reach the highest levels. This possibility, which has been broached in many anecdotal articles in the past dozen years, is confronted in a more systematic way in a *Fortune* article in September 1995, which drew on a survey of three hundred career women conducted by Yankelovich Partners. Entitled "Executive Women Confront Midlife Crisis," the article tells of the many women who have decided that the struggle is not worth it. Nor did they identify the usual suspects — the desire to have children and the glass ceiling. Instead, as one analyst put it, "There is some kind of profound something going on — a reassessment, a rethinking, a big gulp, whatever. It is not biological. It has to do with self-image and the workplace."[93]

The idea that the chief problem for women in the power elite is the often coarse and typically competitive nature of male interactions, not lack of numbers, is reinforced by the fact that men who are tokens in female-dominated work settings do not suffer the same kinds of problems as women who are tokens in male-dominated work settings, as would be expected if the cause was essentially being a part of a small minority. According to Christine Williams, a sociologist who has studied both women who do traditionally men's work and men who do traditionally women's work, "Discrimination is not a simple by-product of numbers: The social organization of work tends to benefit certain groups of workers over others, regardless of their proportional representation in an occupation. Consequently some groups (like women) suffer because of their minority status; other groups (like men) do not."[94]

If there is indeed a difficult conflict between feminine self-image and male-oriented corporate culture, then perhaps not many women will be willing to sustain a competitive persona for very long. If so, that means few women would ever make it to the top because many of the most likely candidates would no longer be available. But it does not mean that women would not continue to have a function within the power elite. Indeed, they would have the ideal role from the male point of view. They would serve as tokens and buffers until they reached their early forties and would then become the consultants and corporate directors who are the role models and instructors for the new generation of buffers.

Whether or not very many of them make it to the innermost circles, we believe that the power elite is strengthened by the presence of women. They take some of the sting out of an impersonal corporate system that can be hard on workers at the lowest levels (and those beneath them who cannot find

93. Betsy Morris, "Executive Women Confront Midlife Crisis," *Fortune*, September 18, 1995, 65.

94. Christine L. Williams, *Still A Man's World: Men Who Do "Women's Work"* (Berkeley: University of California Press, 1995), 20–21. See also Christine L. Williams, *Gender Differences at Work: Women and Men in Nontraditional Occupations* (Berkeley: University of California Press, 1990); Christine L. Williams, ed., *Doing "Women's Work:" Men in Nontraditional Occupations* (Newbury Park, Calif.: Sage, 1993); Joel Heikes, "When Men Are the Minority: The Case of Men in Nursing," *Sociological Quarterly* 32, no. 3 (1991), 389–401; Janice Yoder, "Is It All in the Numbers? A Case Study of Tokenism," *Psychology-of-Women-Quarterly* 9, no. 3 (1985), 413–418.

work). Their presence helps to legitimate the system, for it feeds into the Horatio Alger mythology that anyone who works hard can rise to the top. A close look at the class backgrounds of those women who have made it to the top, however, demonstrates that the upper classes are overrepresented by a factor of about ten or fifteen to one.

# 3

# Blacks in the Power Elite

On June 23, 1964, a headline on the business page of the *New York Times* read: "Negro Lawyer Joining U.S. Industries Board." The subject of the story was Samuel R. Pierce Jr., a graduate of Cornell University, where he had been a Phi Beta Kappa student and a star halfback on the football team. When Pierce joined the board of U.S. Industries, he became the first black to sit on the board of a Fortune 500 company.[1]

The same week Pierce joined the board of U.S. Industries, another African American, Asa T. Spaulding, became a member of the board of W. T. Grant, a nationwide chain of more than one thousand general merchandise stores. Spaulding was the president of the North Carolina Mutual Life Insurance Company of Durham, the largest black-owned business in the country.[2]

## Blacks in the Corporate Elite

Obviously, the appointment of two black men to corporate boards in 1964 was a product of the civil rights movement, but why these particular companies at this particular time? The chairman and chief executive officer of

1. "Negro Lawyer Joining U.S. Industries Board," *New York Times,* June 23, 1964. U.S. Industries was number 465 in the Fortune 500 that year.

2. Leonard Sloane, "Negroes in Business: A New Era is Signaled by Election of 2 Directors by Big Corporations," *New York Times,* June 26, 1964.

U.S. Industries, John I. Snyder Jr., was both atypical and ahead of his time. When he died less than a year later, the *New York Times* described him this way: "Soft-spoken and scholarly, Mr. Snyder presented a rather contradictory picture of a millionaire businessman. He was an industrialist who cared deeply about labor. He was a stanch Democrat among Republicans. He believed strongly in the union shop as a necessity for good labor-management relations."[3] Or, as *Business Week* rather scornfully described Snyder a few years later, comparing him unfavorably to his more profit-oriented successor, "he dabbled in liberal politics, engaged in civil rights work, and argued that private business should try to fulfill its 'social responsibilities.' "[4]

The reason for the integration of the W. T. Grant board was as obvious as it was vigorously denied. The company had been under attack because many of its southern stores operated segregated lunch counters. There had been both picketing and sit-ins at Grant lunch counters, and neither had been good for business. Although the chairman of the board claimed that Spaulding's appointment had nothing to do with the "lunch counter policy," it was clearly an effort to defuse an embarrassing and potentially costly situation.[5]

Has it been more typical for boards to integrate because of socially conscious CEOs or as a reaction to protest? According to sociologist Sharon Collins, who has conducted extensive interviews with black executives, most were hired not because of a commitment to equality and diversity on the part of senior management—though some senior managers may have had such a commitment—but because of pressures of one kind or another on their companies. In addition to the specific protests against individual companies for particular policies—like the refusal of some W. T. Grant stores to serve blacks at their lunch counters—federal laws created general pressures to integrate the higher levels of management. Not only did companies have to deal with overt protests, or the threat of overt protests, but they had to adhere to newly legislated guidelines in order to obtain government contracts. Most of Collins's interviewees attributed the opportunities that opened up for them to both overt protests and federal policies against discrimination. As she puts it in *Black Corporate Executives,* the black executives she interviewed "believe that new job opportunities emerged because of this federal affirmative action legislation and because of community-based political pressures, including urban violence."[6]

3. "John Snyder Jr., Industrialist, 56," *New York Times,* April 25, 1965.

4. "Taking USI Out of the Limelight," *Business Week,* January 21, 1967, p. 51.

5. Sloane, "Negroes in Business."

6. Sharon M. Collins, *Black Corporate Executives: The Making and Breaking of a Black Middle Class* (Philadelphia: Temple University Press, 1997), 58.

Our look at the first dozen companies to add black directors to their boards leads us to conclude that the same pattern Collins observed at the senior executive levels held for board appointments. In some cases, like U.S. Industries, boards were driven by what Collins calls a "moral commitment," but more often, as was the case with W. T. Grant, the companies were responding to external pressures.[7]

But why Samuel R. Pierce Jr. and Asa T. Spaulding? What led the boards of U.S. Industries and W. T. Grant to choose these two men among the many possible candidates for integrating the American corporate elite? As was the case for the first Jews asked to join all-Christian boards and the first women to join all-male boards, the two men selected were not likely to make those already in the boardroom uncomfortable: they were highly educated, they were assimilated into the mainstream (that is to say, white) culture, and they were not prone to rock the boat.

Samuel Pierce grew up in comfortable circumstances on Long Island. His father had parlayed a menial job at the elegant Nassau Country Club into a valet service for members of the club; subsequently he opened his own dry-cleaning store, began to buy real estate, and became a devoted Republican, an affiliation that he passed on to his son. In 1943, midway through his undergraduate work at Cornell, the younger Pierce dropped out to join the army, serving in North Africa and Italy during the Second World War. After the war, he returned to Cornell, where he completed his B.A. and a law degree.

In 1955, one of his former law professors brought him to Washington to work in the Eisenhower administration; Pierce was the first black to hold the position of assistant to the undersecretary of labor. In 1959, Nelson Rockefeller, the governor of New York, appointed him to fill a vacancy as a judge. Two years later, he became the first black partner of a major New York law firm, Battle, Fowler, Stokes & Kheel. Theodore Kheel, a well-known labor arbitrator who did work for U.S. Industries, was a close friend of CEO John Snyder's. Aware of Snyder's willingness to add a black to the U.S. Industries board, Kheel suggested Pierce. Snyder had served with Pierce on the New York State Banking Board and thought it a good suggestion.[8]

Asa Spaulding, born in 1902, was 62 when he joined the W. T. Grant board. His father owned a farm in rural North Carolina and also ran a general store,

7. "Moral commitment": Sharon M. Collins, "Blacks on the Bubble: The Vulnerability of Black Executives in White Corporations," *Sociological Quarterly* 34, no. 3 (1993), 434.

8. "Negro Lawyer Joining U.S. Industries Board"; Sloane, "Negroes in Business"; "Personality: Pierce Causes Insurance Stir," *New York Times,* December 13, 1964.

cut timber, and operated a still that produced both turpentine and rosin.[9] His great-uncle, A. M. Moore, was a physician who lived in Durham and founded a small insurance company. Dr. Moore realized that Asa was proficient in math, so he persuaded Asa's parents to let their son move to Durham, where the schools were better. Asa lived with the Moores, doing odd jobs to earn his room and board. During the summers he worked as a supply clerk for Dr. Moore's insurance company. After receiving a B.A. degree from New York University and a master's degree in mathematics and actuarial science at the University of Michigan, he returned to Durham in 1932 to be the actuary at North Carolina Mutual. (He was the first black actuary in the country.) In 1959, Spaulding became president of the company after the death of his cousin Charles C. Spaulding, who had been the president for some thirty years.[10]

A 1967 *New York Times Magazine* profile of Spaulding stressed his "cautious way of life," contrasting him to the militant Black Power types prone to demonstrations and boycotts. "No, sir, I didn't get out and picket or demonstrate anywhere during the civil-rights drive," Spaulding told the reporter. "I felt I could contribute much more toward racial advancement in other ways. . . . We mustn't get impatient. We've made progress, though not everyone is satisfied."[11]

U.S. Industries and W. T. Grant didn't exactly open the floodgates, but by mid-1971 there were a dozen blacks on Fortune 500 boards. A close look at their backgrounds reveals a few general patterns that characterize them as a group: they were highly educated, many were from families that were economically comfortable or even quite wealthy, and some had developed valuable political connections.

Clifton R. Wharton Jr., who joined the board of Equitable Life in 1969, and William T. Coleman Jr., who joined the boards of Penn Mutual in 1969 and Pan Am in 1970, are examples of those among the first wave of black corporate directors who came from highly educated and economically privileged families. Wharton's father, a lawyer, was the first African American to pass the

9. John Ingham and Lynne B. Feldman, "Asa T. Spaulding," *African-American Business Leaders: A Biographical Dictionary* (Westport, Conn.: Greenwood, 1994), 395.

10. Charles C. Spaulding, who was president of the company from 1923 until his death at age seventy-eight in 1952, is considered by some to have been the most prominent black businessman in the first half of the twentieth century. See James J. Podesta, "Charles Clinton Spaulding: Insurance Executive," in L. Mpho Mabunda, ed., *Contemporary Black Biography: Profiles from the International Black Community,* vol. 9 (New York: Gale Research, 1995), 213–217.

11. Bill Surface, "The World of the Wealthy Negro," *New York Times Magazine,* July 23, 1967, pp. 10, 35, 38, 40.

Foreign Service exam, and in the early 1960s he became the country's first black career ambassador when he was named ambassador to Norway. Indeed, Wharton's father cast such a formidable shadow that Wharton abandoned his own plans for a diplomatic career: "I began to think that if I went into the U.S. Foreign service and did well, I would never know whether it was because I'm good or because I'm my father's son."[12]

Because of his father's postings around the globe, Wharton's early education was unusually cosmopolitan. He was trilingual from his childhood, graduated from Boston Latin, a prestigious public high school, and entered Harvard at the age of sixteen. While at Harvard he was active with the radio station and helped to found the National Student Association. In 1947, at the age of twenty, he graduated with a B.A. in history.[13]

After receiving an M.A. in international affairs at Johns Hopkins, Wharton spent five years working for Nelson Rockefeller's American International Association for Economic and Social Development. He then enrolled in a Ph.D. program in economics at the University of Chicago. Five years later, Ph.D. in hand, he went to work for another Rockefeller — John D. Rockefeller III, who had established a nonprofit organization called the Agricultural Development Council.

In 1970, a year after he joined the board of Equitable Life, Wharton became the first black president of a major American university when he assumed that post at Michigan State. After eight years there, he became chancellor of the State University of New York from 1978 to 1987, then chairman and CEO at TIAA-CREF, the country's largest private pension fund. At TIAA-CREF, Wharton became the highest-paid black executive in the United States: in 1990 his total compensation was $1,283,650.[14] Along the way, Wharton joined a number of other *Fortune*-level boards (Ford Motor Company and Burroughs in 1973, Time, Inc. in 1983, Federated Department Stores in 1985, and TIAA in 1986).[15]

---

12. "Clifton R. Wharton, Jr.: The Nation's Highest-Paid Black Executive," *Ebony,* September, 1987, p. 32.

13. "Clifton R. Wharton, Jr.," *Current Biography Yearbook* (1987), 598.

14. Gerald H. Rosen, "TIAA-CREF: Declining Returns," *Academe* 78, no. 1 (January–February 1992), 8. According to Rosen, this was "an astonishing salary figure for the not-for-profit community."

15. As Wharton became part of the corporate elite, so, too, did his wife, Delores. The daughter of a Harlem undertaker, Delores, who once studied dance with Martha Graham, became a director on numerous *Fortune*-level boards, including Kellogg, Phillips Petroleum, and Gannett. In 1980 she founded the Fund for Corporate Initiatives, designed to help minorities and women become CEOs and corporate directors. Each year she organizes a weeklong retreat for twenty or so promising young executives from Fortune 500

He became deputy secretary of state in Clinton's administration, the number two position under Warren Christopher, but Christopher was said to have considered Wharton's performance "lackluster," and he was asked to resign after only ten months in office.[16]

William T. Coleman Jr., had impeccable educational, professional, and social credentials. From a solidly middle-class family that claimed six generations of teachers and Episcopal ministers on one side and numerous social workers on the other, Coleman grew up outside Philadelphia, where his father was the director of the Germantown Boys Club. Through his father and other members of the family, he met many of the most distinguished black leaders of the 1920s and 1930s, including W. E. B. DuBois and Thurgood Marshall. After graduating from the University of Pennsylvania summa cum laude in 1941 and the Harvard Law School in 1946 (interrupted by a stint in the Army Air Corps during the war), Coleman became a law clerk to Supreme Court Associate Justice Felix Frankfurter.

One of Frankfurter's other law clerks was Boston Brahmin Elliot Richardson, whom Coleman had met when they both served on the editorial board of the *Harvard Law Review*. Each morning, before turning to their legal work for Justice Frankfurter, Coleman and Richardson spent about an hour reading poetry together. Richardson became the godfather to Coleman's daughter. When his clerkship ended, Coleman joined the prestigious New York law firm of Paul, Weiss, Rifkind, Wharton & Garrison; a few years later, he returned to his hometown to join a prominent Philadelphia law firm, and he soon became a partner in Dilworth, Paxson, Kalish, Levy & Coleman. As a high-powered and socially connected Republican corporate lawyer, Coleman was an unsurprising choice when corporate boards sought to integrate in the late 1960s and early 1970s. In addition to his seats on the boards at Penn Mutual and Pan Am, over the years Coleman served on the boards of the First Pennsylvania Corporation, the First Pennsylvania Banking and Trust Company, the Philadelphia Electric Company, IBM, Chase Manhattan, PepsiCo, the American Can Company, AMAX, and INA. Coleman was such a successful corporate lawyer and on so many boards that when he agreed to become secretary of the treasury under President Ford, his income dropped dramatically — he sold his

companies. Patricia O'Toole, "Another Kind of Wharton School," *Lear's*, March 1991, pp. 26–27.

16. Elaine Sciolino, "With Foreign Policies Under Fire, Top State Dept. Deputy is Ousted," *New York Times*, November 9, 1993. See also Lee A. Daniels, "Abrupt Exit: Racism, Leaks, and Isolation Drove Clif Wharton to Resign from the State Department," *Emerge*, February 1994, pp. 28–33.

shares of Pan Am stock, gave up all his directorships, and accepted a salary that was one-fifth what he had earned in private life.[17]

Others among the first wave of black corporate directors had valuable political connections that made them even more desirable additions to corporate boards that wished to integrate. Hobart Taylor Jr., who joined the board of Standard Oil of Ohio in 1971, was from a wealthy Texas family with long-standing political connections to Lyndon B. Johnson. His grandfather was a slave who worked on a plantation as a shoemaker. Family lore has it that he saved $600 in dimes and then, during Reconstruction, invested it in real estate. Hobart Taylor Sr., a businessman, became a multimillionaire and a longtime friend and early political supporter of Johnson.[18] When Johnson first ran for the Senate in 1948, Hobart Taylor Sr. was one of his key financial backers.[19] Johnson appointed him as a delegate to the 1956 Democratic National Convention, and in 1960, Hobart Taylor Jr., by then a Detroit lawyer, was one of LBJ's key supporters in his quest for the presidency.

Hobart Taylor Jr. attended Prairie View State College and then earned an M.A. at Howard before attending the University of Michigan Law School, where he was editor of the *Law Review*. After law school he stayed in the Detroit area, spending a decade as chief legal and financial adviser for public improvements in Wayne County. In 1961, Taylor went to Washington to become special assistant to Vice President Johnson, and in 1964 he became associate counsel to President Johnson. One of Johnson's biographers described Taylor as "a mild, go-slow civil-righter and son of the Houston Negro millionaire."[20]

After leaving the Johnson administration in 1965 to become a director of the Export-Import Bank and then a partner at a Washington law firm, Taylor became a director of the Realty Equities Corporation in 1968.[21] In 1971 he joined the boards of Standard Oil of Ohio, A&P, and Westinghouse Electric. He was later to serve on the boards of Aetna, Eastern Airlines, and Burroughs. He died in 1981 of amyotrophic lateral sclerosis (Lou Gehrig's disease).

The first eleven black corporate directors had one characteristic in common:

17. "William T. Coleman, Jr.," *Current Biography* (1976), 89.

18. "Hobart Taylor, Jr.," *Annual Obituary* (1981) (New York: St. Martin's, 1981), 232–233.

19. Robert Dallek, *Lone Star Rising: Lyndon Johnson and His Times, 1908–1960* (New York: Oxford University Press, 1991), 398.

20. Alfred Steinberg, *Sam Johnson's Boy: A Close-Up of the President from Texas* (New York: Macmillan, 1968), 563. Rowland Evans and Robert Novak, in *Lyndon B. Johnson: The Exercise of Power* (New York: New American Library, 1966), say that when it came to civil rights, "like Johnson, Taylor was a gradualist" (317).

21. "Realty Equities Corp. Picks a Board Member," *New York Times,* April 30, 1968.

they were all men. By early 1971 there was much speculation about which *Fortune*-level board would be the first to name a black woman and which woman would be named. Many assumed the woman would be Patricia Roberts Harris, who had served as ambassador to Luxembourg. Indeed, in May 1971 it was announced that Harris had agreed to join the boards of Scott Paper and IBM. The following year she went on the board of Chase Manhattan.[22]

Harris was born in Mattoon, Illinois. Her father was a waiter on a Pullman railroad car. In 1977, in the hearings to confirm her nomination as secretary of HUD, she bristled when Senator William Proxmire suggested that she might not be able to defend the interests of the poor. "You do not seem to understand who I am. I am a black woman, the daughter of a dining-car worker. I am a black woman who even eight years ago could not buy a house in parts of the District of Columbia. I didn't start out as a member of a prestigious law firm, but as a woman who needed a scholarship to go to school. If you think I have forgotten that, you are wrong."[23]

After graduation from Howard University summa cum laude in 1945, and after working as program director of the YWCA in Chicago, she returned to Washington and worked first with the American Council on Human Rights and then with Delta Sigma Theta, a sorority. In 1955 she married a Howard law professor and decided to attend law school at George Washington University.

After law school, Harris worked in the Department of Justice, then left to teach law at Howard. John F. Kennedy appointed her cochairwoman of the National Women's Committee for Civil Rights, and in May 1965, Lyndon Johnson — whose nomination she had seconded at the 1964 Democratic convention — selected her to be ambassador to Luxembourg. As a law professor and former ambassador, Harris was an unsurprising choice as the first black woman to join a corporate board, though some were surprised at how long it took the corporations to ask her.

One intriguing exception exists to the general early pattern of blacks named to corporate boards. Unlike his mostly well-educated, well-off, and in some cases well-connected predecessors, this corporate director came from an impoverished background and attended a non-elite college in West Virginia. He was also a minister who had led public boycotts as a means of confronting large corporations. Yet he was named to the board of the largest company in the world. This might not have come about if not for a racist slip of the tongue.

22. Marylin Bender, "Woman Lawyer Still Awaits a Bid to Board," *New York Times,* May 3, 1971.

23. Michael E. Mueller, "Patricia Roberts Harris: Former U.S. Cabinet Secretary, Ambassador, Attorney," in Barbara C. Bigelow, ed., *Contemporary Black Biography: Profiles from the International Black Community,* vol. 2 (Detroit: Gale, 1992), 99.

By January 1971 blacks had joined the boards of seven major corporations, but none was as major as General Motors, ranked number 1 by *Fortune* since it began publishing its list of the top five hundred companies in 1955. At the annual General Motors stockholders meeting in spring 1970, an antimanagement group calling itself the Campaign to Make General Motors Responsible attacked the company for its minority-hiring policies and its lack of corporate responsibility. As part of its protest, the group emphasized that there were no blacks on GM's board of directors and that only eleven of its thirteen hundred automobile dealerships were owned by blacks.[24]

Campaign GM, as the group came to be known, managed to place some proposals on the annual shareholder ballot, including one that would have added three public representatives to GM's board and another that would have created a one-year Shareholders' Committee for Corporate Responsibility. None of the proposals garnered support on more than 3 percent of the ballots cast, but some shareholders who voted the proposals down acknowledged sympathy with Campaign GM's principles. Various colleges and foundations holding substantial shares of GM stock cautioned management that their continued support depended upon improved corporate responsibility. The Rockefeller Foundation, for example, criticized GM for its "defensive and negative attitude" toward the critics.[25]

At that stockholders meeting, James Roche, CEO and chairman at General Motors, who had been on his feet for most of the troubled six-and-a-half-hour meeting, made an embarrassing slip of the tongue. He was challenged by a young minister from Dayton, Ohio, about GM's failure to send a representative to a television station there to respond to Campaign GM's proposals. Wasn't GM, the minister asked, a "public corporation"? Roche responded by claiming, "We are a public corporation owned by free, white . . . " At this point, as some people in the audience gasped and others laughed at his use of a well-known racist phrase, Roche lamely added "umm . . . and . . . and . . . and black and yellow people all over the world." Though Roche later tried to downplay any meaningfulness to the slip and asserted that he simply had become confused by the audience's laughter, it was clearly an embarrassing episode in a long and difficult day.[26]

A few months later, with unhappy memories of the annual stockholders meeting, and well aware that the Rockefeller Foundation and other institu-

24. "A Black for GM's Board," *Time,* January 26, 1970, p. 72.

25. "After the Courtesy, a Crisis of Costs," *Fortune,* June 1970, p. 31.

26. William Serrin, "For Roche of G.M., Happiness Is a 10% Surcharge," *New York Times Magazine,* September 12, 1971, pp. 36–37, 109–125. Quotation appears on p. 116.

tional stockholders were watching closely, Roche called Leon Sullivan, an activist minister in Philadelphia, and asked him to come to New York to discuss joining the GM board. Sullivan told Roche that he was too busy, but that Roche was welcome to visit him in Philadelphia. Roche accepted this demand for respect, and Sullivan agreed to go on the board.

Who was Leon Sullivan? Born in Charleston, West Virginia, in 1922, he grew up poor. His parents divorced when he was young, and he was able to attend college because he received a football scholarship at West Virginia State University. He injured his knee during his sophomore year and lost the scholarship but was able to stay in school by working in a steel mill. During his sophomore year he also became the minister for a small Baptist congregation in Charleston. The following year, learning that the New York politician and minister Adam Clayton Powell Jr. was coming to town on a lecture tour, Sullivan invited him to speak to his congregation. Powell accepted and was so impressed with Sullivan that he offered him a job in New York after he graduated. Two years later, Sullivan became an assistant minister at Powell's church. He also worked on Powell's initial campaign for Congress and earned an M.A. in sociology from Columbia and a divinity degree from the Union Theological Seminary.[27]

In 1950, Sullivan became the pastor of the Zion Baptist Church in North Philadelphia. His congregation grew from six hundred to six thousand at Zion, and by the late 1950s he was leading four hundred other ministers in boycotts of Philadelphia businesses that refused to hire blacks. (In the 1930s, Adam Clayton Powell had led boycotts of New York–area white businesses.) In 1964, Sullivan set up a job-training program called Opportunities Industrialization Centers, designed to train high school dropouts; by 1971 it had training centers in seventy cities.

Roche's decision to pursue Sullivan for the GM board is revealing, for Sullivan certainly differed from the other early black corporate directors both in his academic background and in his professional and political experience. It is likely that Roche and the GM board assumed that naming a highly visible and politically active minister would serve as an effective response to those shareholders who were protesting various of the company's policies. In 1964, W. T. Grant could name a sixty-two-year-old African American who was willing to tell a *New York Times* writer that "we mustn't get impatient," but General Motors in 1971, facing vociferous and embarrassing shareholder protests, needed to make a stronger statement as it integrated its board.

One of Sullivan's first acts as a board member was to vote against the entire

27. Ernest Holsendolph, "A Profile of Leon Sullivan," *Black Enterprise,* May 1975, pp. 47–51.

board on a controversial resolution. In its coverage of GM's 1971 shareholders meeting, the *Wall Street Journal* reported: "The meeting's dramatic highlight was an impassioned and unprecedented speech by the Rev. Leon Sullivan, GM's recently appointed Negro director, supporting the Episcopal Church's efforts to get the company out of South Africa. It was the first time that a GM director had ever spoken against management at an annual meeting."[28] This challenge to boardroom hegemony may have been just what James Roche needed to demonstrate GM's willingness to tolerate criticism. As *Forbes* magazine explained, "such public dissent is rare in big business, and it certainly didn't harm GM's reputation."[29]

By June 1972, GM had started the General Motors Minority Dealer Development Academy, part of a program to encourage and provide support for minority members to become automobile dealers.[30] Years later, the guidelines that became known as the Sullivan Principles were used by many institutions, especially universities, when they decided whether or not to divest the holdings of companies that did business in South Africa.

BLACKS ON FORTUNE-LEVEL BOARDS, 1971–1995

In the early 1970s, with doors to some boardrooms finally opened, more and more *Fortune*-level companies added black directors to their boards, though few companies added more than one. By March 1971 the biweekly newsletter *Business and Society* identified only sixteen "major corporations"

28. Quoted in Ralph Nader and Joel Seligman, "The Myth of Shareholder Democracy," in Mark Green and Robert Massie Jr., eds., *The Big Business Reader: Essays on Corporate America* (New York: Pilgrim, 1980), 447–456.

29. "Roche of General Motors: Thus Far and No Further," *Forbes,* May 15, 1971, p. 48. In the same article *Forbes* noted that Roche, who was twelve when his father had died and who had not been able to attend college, had lived "a real Horatio Alger story." Then, in all-too familiar fashion, an atypical phenomenon is made typical and used to criticize those who advocated corporate reform: "It is a real Horatio Alger story, but these days the Alger character is a villain rather than a hero to a rising generation that treasures Ralph Nader above mere captains of industry" (48).

As Michael Kinsley points out, *Forbes* has continued its efforts at "ham-handed myth-making." Kinsley explains how an ad for *Forbes* asserts that Scott McNealy, the founder of Sun Microsystems, rose to entrepreneurial heights from having been "a foreman in an auto shop." But Kinsley, who went to prep school with McNealy, explains that McNealy's father was a vice chairman at American Motors, and that the son attended Harvard and the Stanford Business School. See Michael Kinsley, "Log Cabin Fever," *New Republic,* May 9, 1994, p. 6.

30. Herschel Johnson, "The Making of Black Car Dealers," *Black Enterprise,* May, 1974, p. 14.

(not all of these made the annual *Fortune* list) that had black directors, and eleven of the sixteen had added those black directors within the previous eight months. By the end of 1971 more than thirty companies had added black members to their boards, and by 1972, that number was up to fifty-four.[31] When *Black Enterprise* magazine ran an article in September 1973 on "Black Directors," there were sixty-seven black men and five black women on the boards of slightly more than one hundred "major U.S. companies." As the article noted, with approximately fourteen thousand directors on the boards of the one thousand companies that appeared on *Fortune*'s annual list, black directorships represented less than 1 percent of the total.[32]

As was the case with many other indicators of educational and economic advancement for blacks in the 1970s, this rate of increase did not continue.[33] *Business and Society Review* prefaced "A Listing of Black Directors" in its fall 1981 issue with the observation that "in the early 1970s there was a sudden flurry of appointments for blacks to the boards of major corporations. Today the flurry has quieted down considerably, and the current tally of black directors is not very much longer than the last one we published — four years ago." The list included seventy-three blacks who held seats on 112 companies.[34]

Nor had there been a dramatic increase in the number of blacks moving up the corporate ladder. In 1980 the *Wall Street Journal* summarized the findings of two studies that demonstrated how few blacks had moved into the higher ranks of management. In one, a survey by Korn/Ferry, only 3 of 1,700 senior executives were black. In the other, there were only 117 blacks out of 13,000 managers ranked as "department head" or higher in Chicago companies.[35] George Davis and Glegg Watson wrote in their 1982 book, *Black Life in*

31. Milt Moskowitz, "The 1982 Black Corporate Directors Lineup," *Business Society Review,* Fall 1982, p. 54.

32. Lester Carson, "Black Directors: The 72 Black Men and Women Who Sit on the Boards of Major U.S. Corporations," *Black Enterprise,* September 1973, pp. 17–28.

33. As an example of another indicator, the number of blacks at the Harvard Business School rose from less than 1 percent in 1965 to more than 10 percent in the early 1970s but fell to less than 4 percent by 1980. Similarly, the percentage of blacks at many elite prep schools rose until the mid-1970s but then leveled off or dropped. See Richard L. Zweigenhaft, *Who Gets to the Top? Executive Suite Discrimination in the Eighties* (New York: Institute of Human Relations, 1984), 25; Richard L. Zweigenhaft and G. William Domhoff, *Blacks in the White Establishment? A Study of Race and Class in America* (New Haven: Yale University Press, 1981), 8–9.

34. "A Listing of Black Directors," *Business and Society Review,* Fall 1981, pp. 63–64.

35. Jonathan Kaufman, "Black Executives Say Prejudice Still Impedes Their Path to the Top," *Wall Street Journal,* July 9, 1980.

*Corporate America,* that after three years of extensive interviewing, "We heard of only a few of the *[Fortune]* five hundred that had a Black in what could be considered senior management."[36] Also in the early 1980s, John Fernandez reported that in his study of more than four thousand managers drawn from twelve large corporations, he had found only four blacks at the five highest levels.[37] Similarly, in a study of more than one thousand business executives promoted to the positions of chairman of the board, president, or vice president of leading corporations during the fiscal year 1983–1984, Floyd Bond, Herbert Hildebrandt, and Edwin Miller found that 99.2% were white and only 0.2% were black (the other 0.6% were Hispanic, "Oriental," or "other").[38]

It is therefore important to keep in mind the distinction between inside directors, those who move up through the corporate ranks and become directors of the companies they work for, and outside directors, who are asked onto a board on the basis of visibility they have achieved outside the company. The first African Americans to sit on major corporate boards were outside directors, though a few had been successful businessmen in black-owned companies. Given the data just cited indicating that few blacks were moving through the corporate ranks in the early 1980s, we might presume that black corporate directors in the 1990s have continued to be predominantly outside directors.

In Chapter 2, we presented data on women directors of Fortune 1000 companies tabulated by Directorship. Directorship also monitors the presence of blacks on *Fortune*-level boards, and we have summarized their findings for the years 1992 through 1995 in table 3.1. The data show a steady increase in the presence of blacks on *Fortune*-level boards from the 73 found by *Business and Society Review* in 1981 to 118 in 1992, but by 1995 only 2.5 percent of the board members were black, and only 3.6 percent of the board seats were held by blacks.

As can also be seen in table 3.1, far more seats are held by blacks than there are blacks who hold those seats — that is to say, many sit on more than one board. In fact, on average, blacks who sit on Fortune 1000 boards sit on two of them. A breakdown by sex reveals that black men who are directors sit on an average of 1.9 boards, and black women who are directors sit on an average of about 2.4 boards. Though she was referring to her appointment as

36. George Davis and Glegg Watson, *Black Life in Corporate America* (Garden City, N.Y.: Anchor, 1982), 77.

37. John Fernandez, *Racism and Sexism in Corporate Life* (Lexington, Mass.: Lexington, 1981), 10.

38. Floyd A. Bond, Herbert W. Hildebrandt, and Edwin L. Miller, *The Newly Promoted Executive: A Study in Corporate Leadership, 1983–84* (Ann Arbor: University of Michigan, Division of Research, Graduate School of Business Administration, 1984), 26.

Table 3.1
*Black Directors on Fortune 1000 Boards in the 1990s*

|  | Dec. 1992 | Dec. 1993 | Dec. 1994 | Oct. 1995 |
|---|---|---|---|---|
| Number of blacks holding seats |  |  |  |  |
| Men | 92 | 115 | 116 | 137 |
| Women | 26 | 25 | 32 | 38 |
| Total | 118 | 140 | 148 | 175 |
|  | (1.6%) | (1.9%) | (2.0%) | (2.5%) |
| Number of seats held by blacks |  |  |  |  |
| Men | 164 | 203 | 219 | 265 |
| Women | 59 | 61 | 74 | 88 |
| Total | 223 | 264 | 293 | 353 |
|  | (2.3%) | (2.7%) | (3.0%) | (3.6%) |

*Source:* Directorship.

ambassador to Luxembourg and not to corporate directorships, a comment by Patricia Harris may help to explain why so many corporate boards, seeking to appear diversified, select black women: "When I'm around, you get two for the price of one — a woman and a Negro."[39]

BLACK INTERLOCKING DIRECTORS, 1994

In 1994 *Ebony* magazine, drawing on data provided by Directorship, published an article on "Top Black Corporate Directors." The article included the names and directorships held by the thirty-four black men and women who sat on three or more corporate boards. We shall compare this elite group of interlockers with the earliest black directors.

The most obvious difference between the blacks who became directors between 1964 and 1971 and those who were interlocking directors in 1994 is that far more of the recent group are women. Only one of the first twelve black *Fortune*-level directors, Patricia Roberts Harris, was female, but eleven of the 1994 interlockers were women (an increase from 8 percent to 32 percent). (Of all the blacks on Fortune 1000 boards from 1992 to 1995 — that is, those referred to in table 3.1 — women accounted for about 20 percent overall.)

About 40 percent of the 1994 black interlockers came from families that were economically comfortable, a slightly lower figure than for those who be-

39. Bender, "Woman Lawyer."

came directors between 1964 and 1971. One of the 1994 interlockers, for example, is former Congressman William H. Gray III, who sat on seven boards, including Chase Manhattan, Warner-Lambert, and Westinghouse. Gray's father and grandfather were clergymen; his father had also been a college president, and his mother taught high school. Another is Barbara Scott Preiskel, a graduate of Wellesley and Yale Law School, who sat on five boards, including General Electric and the Washington Post. Preiskel's father was a lawyer who became a real estate broker, and her mother taught high school chemistry.

About 25 percent were from solidly working-class backgrounds. One was Walter E. Massey, a physicist who became the head of the National Science Foundation and then president of Morehouse College; by 1994 he sat on the boards of Amoco, BankAmerica, and Motorola. Massey's father was a steelworker and his mother a teacher. Another interlocker with a working-class background was Delano Lewis, president and CEO of National Public Radio, who sat on the boards of Colgate-Palmolive, Chase Manhattan, and GEICO. Lewis's father worked for the Santa Fe railroad, and his mother was a domestic who became a beautician. Steven Minter, a foundation executive who sat on the boards of Goodyear Tire and Rubber, Consolidated Natural Gas Company, Keycorp, and Rubbermaid, came from a similar background. Minter's father, whose last year of formal education was the eleventh grade, was a county supervisor of highways, and his mother, who dropped out of school after the eleventh grade but subsequently earned a high school equivalency degree, became an accounts manager for a small company.

The other 35 percent came from poverty. Although their families had very little money, some of these people emphasized that their parents had "middle-class values." John Jacob, former head of the National Urban League, who sat on five corporate boards in 1994, including Anheuser-Busch and Coca-Cola, grew up as one of five sons in a three-room house with an outhouse in the front yard. His father was a Baptist minister who helped make ends meet by doing carpentry. Jacobs emphasized that his parents, though poor, had "very rigid middle-class standards" in addition to their "southern Baptist principles — no drinking, no dancing, no card playing, no movies on Sunday."[40]

The former U.N. ambassador Donald McHenry, who in 1994 sat on the boards of AT&T, Bank of Boston, Coca-Cola, and International Paper, grew up in East St. Louis, Illinois. His father, an autoworker, left the family when McHenry was a small boy, and his mother, a cook, raised him and his two siblings alone. John Slaughter, the president of Occidental College, grew up in Topeka, Kansas, where his father, whose last year of formal education was the

40. "John E. Jacob," *Current Biography Yearbook* (1986), 247.

third grade, worked as a custodian; in 1994, Slaughter sat on five *Fortune*-level boards, including Atlantic Richfield, IBM, and Monsanto.

Four of the thirty-four were the children of immigrants. (As we shall discuss in our final chapter, we consider being an immigrant, or the child of an immigrant, an important factor in overcoming the psychological impact of white prejudice in the United States.) Clifford Alexander's father came from Jamaica in 1919. After starting out as a waiter, he "worked his way up to becoming in succession, business manager of the Harlem YMCA, branch manager of a group of apartment buildings, and manager of the Harlem branch of the New York Bank for Savings." Alexander was a student at the exclusive Fieldston School, Harvard, and Yale Law School.[41] The mother of Franklin A. Thomas emigrated from Barbados. Ernesta Procope's parents were from the West Indies, and Lois Rice Dickson's parents came to the United States from Jamaica.

As was true of the first twelve black corporate directors, the 1994 black interlockers have been very well educated. All but two are college graduates, and thirty-one of the thirty-four earned postgraduate degrees. In a careful study of the pathways to the top positions in the corporate world, Michael Useem and Jerome Karabel examined the backgrounds of 2,729 senior officers and outside directors of 208 companies on *Fortune*'s 1978 lists. They found that within this group, those who had attended various top-ranked undergraduate institutions, M.B.A. programs, or law schools were significantly more likely to have become chief executive officers and to sit on multiple boards. They demonstrate that even within such a high-achieving group of corporate managers, the school that one attended was an effective predictor of who attained the highest levels of success.[42]

In table 3.2, we have used Useem and Karabel's categories to summarize the educational credentials of their sample as well as those of the first black *Fortune*-level directors and the 1994 interlocking black directors. More than half of those in Useem and Karabel's sample either did not complete college (16.4 percent) or completed only a B.A. (38.8 percent); in contrast, this was true of less than 10 percent of both groups of black directors. Useem and Karabel also demonstrate that upper-class credentials contribute to one's chances of rising to the top of the corporate hierarchy. Those with fewer academic credentials were more likely to be from upper-class backgrounds, suggesting that their class-linked personal contacts overcame their relative lack of education.

41. "Clifford L. Alexander, Jr.," *Current Biography* (1977), 10.

42. Michael Useem and Jerome Karabel, "Pathways to Top Corporate Management," *American Sociological Review* 51 (1986), 184–200. See 187–188 for the lists of the top-ranked undergraduate institutions, M.B.A. programs and law schools.

Table 3.2
*Educational Backgrounds of Corporate Directors*

|  | All Directors (1977)[a] | First Black Directors (1964–1971) | 1994 Interlockers[b] |
|---|---|---|---|
| No college or dropped out | 16.4% | 8% | 3% |
| B.A. only (from top-ranked school) | 38.8 (11.2) | 0 | 6  (3) |
| M.B.A. (from top-ranked school) | 17.1 (14.0) | 0 | 24 (24) |
| LL.B. or J.D. (from top-ranked school) | 17.4  (7.4) | 42 (25) | 33 (12) |
| Other degrees | 10.1 | 50 | 36 |

[a]Useem and Karabel, "Pathways to Top Corporate Management."
[b]*Ebony* 50th Anniversary Issue, November 1995.

Useem and Karabel conclude: "Upper-class origins confer a significant advantage on the career prospects of senior managers with the same educational credentials. Credentials also make a substantial independent difference in the careers of senior managers, though less so for the minority of managers from upper-class backgrounds than for the majority who are not."[43]

Not surprisingly, then, because virtually none of the black directors had the kind of upper-class credentials Useem and Karabel refer to (either inclusion in the *Social Register* or attendance at one of fourteen exclusive prep schools), the black directors were more likely than those in Useem and Karabel's sample to have gone on to earn higher degrees (especially law degrees and Ph.D.'s). This not only demonstrates that the black directors needed more education to get to the same place, but it alerts us to the fact that they traveled different pathways to get there — though as we shall see shortly, it is not really the same place.

PATHWAYS TO THE CORPORATE ELITE FOR BLACK DIRECTORS

As we look at the career pathways the 1994 interlockers have taken to the corporate elite, seven different routes emerge. The first and most prominent pathway is via the academic hierarchy, starting as a researcher or professor and then becoming a senior administrator (most likely a college president). Just as Clifton Wharton earned his Ph.D. and later became a college president, five of the 1994 directors were, or had been, college presidents. We have already mentioned John Slaughter, president of Occidental College. An-

43. Ibid., 193.

other is Jewell Plummer Cobb, the former president of California State University, Fullerton, who in 1994 sat on the boards of Allied-Signal, CPC International, First Interstate Bancorp, and Georgia-Pacific. In addition to the five who were or had been college presidents, three others were senior administrators at academic institutions; one headed a business school, and two headed medical schools.

Some of the 1994 directors followed a second pathway, the same one that Asa Spaulding traveled — they founded, or rose to the top of, black businesses. This category included Jesse Hill Jr., the former president, CEO, and chairman of the board of Atlanta Life, the nation's second-largest black-owned insurance company, who sat on the boards of Delta, National Service Industries, and Knight-Ridder; and Ernesta Procope, the president and founder of E. G. Bowman Company, the nation's largest black-owned insurance brokerage agency, who sat on the boards of Avon, the Chubb Corporation, and Columbia Gas Systems.

Some followed the path of Leon Sullivan — their work as civil rights activists led to their invitation to join corporate boards. Two men on the 1994 list had been the head of the National Urban League (Vernon Jordan, who was first on the list with seats on ten major companies, and John E. Jacob, sixth on the list, with five).

Some followed the path that Samuel Pierce and William Coleman had traveled — they were lawyers who had experience in high-powered corporate law firms and in government. C. Wright Mills and others have noted that it is not unusual for members of the power elite to move from one of the higher circles to another and back again. Indeed, Mills wrote that "the inner core of the power elite" included men "from the great law factories and investment firms, who are almost professional go-betweens of economic, political and military affairs, and who thus act to unify the power elite."[44] Consider, for example, the career of Aulana Peters, one of the 1994 interlockers. After finishing law school, she worked for a decade for the Los Angeles law firm Gibson, Dunn, and Crutcher. She then spent four years during the Reagan administration working for the U.S. Securities and Exchange Commission. In 1988 she returned to Gibson, Dunn, and Crutcher as a partner, and in 1994 she sat on the boards of Mobil, Merrill Lynch, Minnesota Mining and Manufacturing, and Northrop Grumman.

Clifford Alexander Jr. provides another example of a lawyer who has moved back and forth from private practice to government positions and along the way has become a director on multiple boards. Educated at Harvard and Yale,

44. C. Wright Mills, *The Power Elite* (New York: Oxford University Press, 1956), 289.

he was in private practice in New York City in the early 1960s, then served in a variety of posts in Lyndon Johnson's administration, including as deputy special counsel for the Equal Employment Opportunity Commission. After six years with the prestigious Washington law firm of Arnold and Porter, he returned to government to serve as secretary of the army under Jimmy Carter. In 1994, Alexander sat on the boards of MCI, Dun & Bradstreet, and American Home Products.

The fifth pathway—that of the person who has been asked onto boards because of his or her work as a management consultant—is one of the new routes to the corporate elite. Among those who have taken that route are Arthur Brimmer, a Harvard-trained economist who is president of Brimmer and Company, an economic and financial consulting firm; and Claudine Malone, a graduate of Wellesley and the Harvard Business School who since 1982 has been president of Financial Management Consulting, Inc. (Brimmer, who sits on eight boards, is second on the 1994 list to Vernon Jordan; Malone is seventh on the list with five.)[45]

The 1994 interlockers have taken two additional pathways that were not available to the earlier black directors but have long been standard routes to the corporate board for white men. The first is rising through the ranks of white corporations. The second is having been born to someone who founded a major corporate enterprise.

A. Barry Rand and Richard D. Parsons are both among the highest-ranking executives in Fortune 500 companies. Rand, the only child of college-educated middle-class parents in Washington, D.C., went to work for Xerox at the age of twenty-four, shortly after he graduated from American University with a degree in marketing. After two years as a sales representative and ten years as a regional sales representative (during which time he earned an M.B.A. from Stanford), Rand became corporate director of marketing in 1980, and in 1984 he became vice president of eastern operations. In 1986 he became corporate vice president and president of U.S. marketing, and in 1992 he became executive vice president, a promotion that placed him as one of the four most senior executives at the company. As early as 1987, *Black Enterprise* asserted that "he has a good chance of doing what no other black professional has ever

45. Malone is part of a sizable contingent of Wellesley women who sit on *Fortune*-level boards. In fact, more women who sit on Fortune 500 boards attended Wellesley than any other college. See Judith H. Dobrzynski, "How to Succeed? Go to Wellesley," *New York Times,* October 29, 1995. Two of the eleven black women interlockers went to Wellesley—Claudine Malone and Barbara Preiskel.

done: become president of a Fortune 500 company."[46] By 1994, Rand sat on the boards of Honeywell, Abbott Laboratories, and Ameritech.

Four years younger than Rand, Richard D. Parsons also emerged as a senior executive at a major American corporation — Time Warner — though his route to this position was quite different from Rand's steady rise at Xerox. Parsons, one of five children, was born in the Bedford-Stuyvesant area of Brooklyn. His father was an electrician and his mother a homemaker. Parsons graduated from the University of Hawaii and attended Albany Law School. After law school, he took a job as an assistant counselor to New York Governor Nelson Rockefeller. When Rockefeller became vice president in 1974, Parsons went to Washington as his deputy counsel. (Parsons, whose parents were Democrats, says, "I wasn't born a Republican, I became a Republican.")[47]

In 1977, Parsons left the White House to join what the *New York Times* called a "blue chip New York law firm," and in 1988 he became the chairman and chief executive of Dime Savings Bank. Under his guidance, the bank overcame $1 billion in bad debts, and when Dime merged with Anchor Savings Bank in 1994, Parsons became the chairman and CEO of Dime Bancorp, the fourth-largest savings bank in the nation and the largest on the East Coast. A mere six months later, Parsons became the highest-ranking black at any Fortune 500 company — he was named president of Time Warner, second in command behind chairman Gerald M. Levin. As *Black Enterprise* put it, "Parsons' appointment may signal a crack in the wall that has traditionally prevented black executives from attaining the highest level positions in corporate America."[48] By 1994, in addition to a seat on the boards of the Dime Bancorp

---

46. Alfred Edmond Jr., "Can This Man Keep Team Xerox No. 1?" *Black Enterprise,* August 1987, p. 60. The following year *Business Week* singled out Rand as one of four black executives who might become chief executive officers of major U.S. corporations in the next decade ("The Black Middle Class," *Business Week,* March 14, 1988, p. 63).

47. Fonda Marie Lloyd and Mark Lowery, "The Man Behind the Merger," *Black Enterprise,* October 1994, p. 76.

48. Mark Lowery, "Second in Command at Time Warner," *Black Enterprise,* January 1995, p. 15. The November 1995 issue of *Ebony* notes that in January 1995, Kenneth I. Chenault became vice chairman of American Express and thus "the highest-ranking Black executive of a Fortune 500 company." *Ebony* quotes an assertion in *The Wall Street Journal* that "many executives of the company predict that Mr. Chenault . . . will eventually become American Express chairman" (114). In February 1997, Harvey Golub, the chairman of American Express, wrote a letter to employees indicating that Chenault was "the primary internal candidate to succeed me when the time comes" but also indicating that he did not plan to step down for another eight years. See Saul Hansell, "American Express

and Time Warner, Parsons was a director at Philip Morris and the Federal National Mortgage Association.

Rand and Parsons are among the three youngest people on the 1994 list of directors. The youngest, born in 1958 and thus ten years younger than Parsons, is Linda Johnson Rice. Her route to multiple seats on *Fortune*-level boards is one that has been a traditional pathway for white men and has recently been traveled by women — she was born into a family that founded a successful business. Rice is the daughter of John H. and Eunice W. Johnson, who in 1942 founded the Johnson Publishing Company, the largest black-owned publisher of magazines in the United States.[49] Rice's father is one of only five blacks ever to appear on the annual list published by *Forbes* magazine of the four hundred richest Americans.[50]

When she graduated at twenty-two from the University of Southern California with a degree in journalism, Linda Rice (then Linda Johnson) became vice president of the company; when she received her M.B.A. from Northwestern University in 1987, she became, at the age of twenty-nine, the president and chief operating officer (her father, then sixty-nine, remained CEO and chairman).[51] Along the way, she has been asked to sit as an outside director on the boards of Bausch and Lomb, Continental Bank, and the Dial Corporation.

Though none of the 1994 interlocking directors was the beneficiary of the social programs that emerged in the 1960s to enhance educational opportunities for academically promising black youngsters from economically impoverished circumstances, it is likely that over the next decade some black corporate directors will be the graduates of such programs. We are thinking

---

Names Apparent Successor to Chief," *New York Times,* February 28, 1997. The Associate Press article referred to this as "the first public anointment of a black executive to run one of the country's biggest companies." Patricia Lamiell, "American Express Names Black CEO as First in Position," *Greensboro News and Record,* February 28, 1997.

49. John H. Johnson is no relation to George E. Johnson, the founder of Johnson Products Company, and one of the first twelve black corporate directors — he went on the board of Commonwealth Edison in 1971. These two Johnsons were the two richest black men in Chicago and, for a time, perhaps the two richest black men in the country. In a chapter titled "Johnson vs. Johnson," Stephen Birmingham describes the "long-standing friction between the two men." See Stephen Birmingham, *Certain People: America's Black Elite* (Boston: Little, Brown, 1977), 29–40.

50. Andrew Hacker, "Who They Are," *New York Times Magazine,* November 19, 1995, p. 71. The other four are Berry Gordy (of Motown Records), Reginald Lewis (of Beatrice Foods), Oprah Winfrey, and Bill Cosby.

51. Laurie Freeman, "Linda Johnson Rice: Publishing Company Executive," in L. Mpho Mabunda, ed., *Contemporary Black Biography: Profiles from the International Black Community,* vol. 9 (New York: Gale Research, 1995), 194–196.

especially of A Better Chance, a program about which we have written, which has placed more than ten thousand youngsters in elite prep schools.[52] The earliest graduates of the program are in their late forties, and some are likely to be named to corporate boards. Deval Patrick, for example, was the assistant attorney general in charge of the civil rights division, one of the highest-ranking blacks in the Justice Department, until he resigned in November 1996. Patrick grew up in one of Chicago's poorest South Side neighborhoods, but when he was in the eighth grade one of his teachers recommended him for the ABC program. Through ABC he was able to obtain a scholarship to Milton Academy, one of the most prestigious boarding schools in the country; after graduating from Milton he attended Harvard College and the Harvard Law School. After working for the NAACP Legal Defense and Education Fund, he joined Hill & Barlow, a prestigious Boston law firm.[53] It would not be surprising to see Patrick join a *Fortune*-level board. Similarly, former ABC students Jesse Spikes and Oliver Lee, both partners at major Atlanta law firms, or Bill Lewis, a managing director at Morgan Stanley, might become board members at *Fortune*-level companies.[54]

### ARE THE BARRIERS COMING DOWN, AND FOR HOW MANY?

As the data we have presented make clear, from 1964, when Samuel Pierce and Asa Spaulding joined *Fortune*-level boards, to 1995, when Barry Rand and Richard Parsons hovered near the top of two of the country's largest companies, much has changed. Some seats in the boardroom and some positions in senior management have opened up to blacks. There are Jews, there are women, and there are blacks in the corporate elite.

At the same time, the aggregate data collected by Directorship, summarized in table 3.1, indicate that blacks (like women, but not Jews) remain underrepresented on corporate boards. Although blacks accounted for about 11 percent of the U.S. population in 1964 and about 12 percent in 1995, the percentage of seats held by blacks on *Fortune*-level boards during that same period rose from zero to only about 3.6 percent. If that rate of increase

52. See Zweigenhaft and Domhoff, *Blacks in the White Establishment?*

53. Steven A. Holmes, "Street Survivor Via Harvard," *New York Times,* February 2, 1994; Clarence Page, "Critics Overlook Patrick's Reputation as a Consensus Builder," *Greensboro News and Record,* February 7, 1994; "Civil Rights Chief is Resigning," *New York Times,* November 15, 1996.

54. For profiles of Spikes and Lewis see Zweigenhaft and Domhoff, *Blacks in the White Establishment?* 113–117, 131. For a profile of Oliver Lee see Rochelle Sharpe, "Oliver's Twist: Affirmative Action Lifted Mr. Lee, and He Has Never Forgotten," *Wall Street Journal,* December 27, 1995.

continues, it will take another sixty years or so before blacks are proportionally represented on corporate boards.

But what about the pipeline? Are there other younger blacks, like Rand, Parsons, and Rice, coming through the ranks? There are certainly some, but the evidence is not encouraging. Studies in the early 1980s revealed that there were very few blacks at the higher levels of management in the largest companies. A 1990 study by the executive search firm Korn-Ferry International indicated that the number of blacks in "high-level management positions" had increased during the previous decade, but only from 0.2 percent to 0.6 percent.[55] In fact, in the report of the Glass Ceiling Commission, the authors use the metaphors of "concrete wall" and "brick wall" rather than "glass ceiling" in stressing that the barriers seem even more impenetrable for black men and women in the corporate world than for white women.[56]

In her interviews with senior executives at major corporations, Sharon Collins found that social protests and federal legislation opened up opportunities for black professionals in predominantly white corporations. Many of these jobs, however, were what Collins calls "racialized" rather than "mainstream." Racialized jobs are those that were created "to administer corporate policies sensitive to blacks and, hence, lessen racial pressures on white corporate environments." Mainstream jobs have "goals oriented to general (i.e., predominantly white) constituencies, not jobs produced in response to black protest and subsequent social policy." Fully two-thirds of the managers Collins interviewed were in, or had been in, racialized jobs; of these, half had been hired to perform racialized work, and the other half had started in mainstream jobs but, within a few years, had been moved into racialized jobs. The other third of Collins's interviewees had careers made up only of white corporate mainstream jobs.[57]

Collins's findings are especially relevant because, as she argues convincingly, the very forces that led to the hiring of many African Americans — a federal commitment to affirmative action and the enforcement of equal opportunity guidelines — fell by the wayside in the 1980s and 1990s. As Collins writes, "The attack on race-specific programs reduced the role of the federal government as a strong advocate of black employment. If federal policies assisted in

55. Lena Williams, "Not Just a White Man's Game," *New York Times,* November 9, 1995.

56. *Good for Business: Making Full Use of the Nation's Human Capital, a Fact-Finding Report of the Federal Glass Ceiling Commission* (Washington, D.C.: U.S. Government Printing Office, 1995), 69.

57. Collins, *Black Corporate Executives,* 12, 75, 77.

the creation of jobs for middle-class blacks, then a retreat from racial policies may undermine blacks' gains in the labor market."[58] This, indeed, was confirmed by the interviews Collins conducted. Far more black executives in racialized jobs than in mainstream jobs reported, for example, that their companies had eliminated, reduced, or redistributed their functions to managers in other areas of the company.[59]

Collins concludes that "the gains blacks have made over 25 years may be in jeopardy." Especially in the recent atmosphere of corporate downsizing, the jobs of many workers are likely to be eliminated. Those who perform central work in the company's mainstream are likely to survive, but "workers employed in affirmative action, community relations, and other support jobs dealing with the federal government will find little demand for those talents."[60] Even if blacks keep their management jobs, Collins's findings remind us that the small percentages of blacks in higher management actually inflate the number who really have a shot at getting into the corporate elite, for only through mainstream jobs does someone like Barry Rand or Richard Parsons emerge at or near the top of the corporate hierarchy.

It is likely that for the foreseeable future, the blacks in the corporate elite will have arrived there from the outside, just as was true in the late 1960s and in 1994. They will be lawyers, they will be university presidents (or the deans of medical schools or business schools), they will have been successful in businesses founded by blacks, or they will be "management consultants."

In this respect, black corporate directors, even those interlocking directors who are part of what Michael Useem calls the inner circle, constitute a distinctly different group from white corporate directors in the inner circle. In his systematic study of those who sit on multiple boards, Useem explains that, as a group, the directors who sit on more than one board — that is, the interlocking directors — form a network, an "interlocking directorate." This directorate, he argues, plays a political role in "defining and promoting" the shared needs of large corporations. "The members of the inner circle," he writes, "constitute a distinct, semi-autonomous network, one that transcends company, regional, sectoral, and other politically divisive fault lines within the corporate community."[61] But, unlike the thirty-four black interlocking directors we have looked at, most members of the inner circle are themselves the CEOs of major

58. Collins, "Blacks on the Bubble," 437.

59. Ibid., 438.

60. Ibid., 444.

61. Michael Useem, *The Inner Circle: Large Corporations and the Rise of Business Political Activity in the U.S. and U.K.* (New York: Oxford University Press, 1984), 3.

corporations. In describing them, Useem comments upon the relative marginality of some members of the inner circle:

> The interlocking directorate is, first of all, a network whose members are deeply rooted in the concrete practice of running big business. Though a few attorneys, university presidents, retired civil servants, foundation officials, titled nobility [Useem studied both the United Kingdom and the United States], and even church ministers appear on corporate boards, each represents little more than a token presence. . . . For most board positions, corporations seek individuals who can offer information and advice drawn from their own direct experience in managing a large organization. . . . Managing a large corporation is considered the quintessential prerequisite for effective contribution to a board.[62]

Useem goes on to note that two-thirds of all outside directors (not just those in the inner circle) are themselves senior officers of other corporations, and half are either presidents, chairmen, or CEOs. According to John H. Bryan, chairman and CEO of Sara Lee Corporation and chairman of the board of Catalyst, "The merit badge for a board we all prefer is someone who's head of a company bigger than our own."[63] Of the 1994 black interlocking directors, only Rand and Parsons qualify as senior officers of major corporations. (Johnson Industries, with Linda Johnson Rice as president, is not a *Fortune*-level company.) Blacks on corporate boards thus face a double whammy: they are statistically underrepresented and they have traveled different, less respected, pathways to their positions. As a result, they are likely to play marginal roles.

A diverse array of blacks seem to have some potential to join the corporate elite. Just as the first twelve black directors included both conservative Republican lawyers like Samuel Pierce and William Coleman and longtime liberal activists like Leon Sullivan, so, too, does the 1994 group of interlocking directors include conservative Republicans and liberal activists — though in both groups the traditionalists far outnumber the activists. As we indicated, Sullivan is an exception, for the general tendency is to select directors who will not rock the boat too much. Even the few activists who are asked and choose to join corporate boards are likely over time to become part of the establishment. In a 1993 profile in *Current Biography,* Vernon Jordan's willingness to join corporate boards is explained in the following way: "During his ten years at the helm, he greatly expanded the influence of the National Urban League by enlisting the cooperation of some of the largest corporations in the United States. As part of the effort, he began serving on the boards of directors of such corporate giants

62. Ibid., 38–39.
63. *Catalyst Perspective,* Fall 1995, p. 2.

as J. C. Penney, Xerox, and American Express."[64] Maybe so. But Jordan was also expanding his own influence, and by 1995, as a partner in a major Washington law firm, wearing shirts "custom-made in London," a confidant and golfing buddy of the president, and a director of ten corporations, Jordan had become an influential insider rather than an outsider activist.[65]

### Blacks in the Cabinet

Before Bill Clinton's election in 1992, five blacks had served in presidential cabinets (see table 3.3). The first was Robert Weaver, who in 1966 became the secretary of housing and urban development. Weaver grew up in a suburb of Washington, D.C., in one of the few black families among some three thousand neighbors. His white neighbors went to nearby all-white schools, but he and his brother had to commute forty-five minutes each day to attend black schools in Washington. "Their one ambition," Weaver said of his parents, "was to send us to New England schools."[66]

Weaver went to a New England school — Harvard — from which he earned a B.A., an M.A., and a Ph.D. (He was not the first in his family to attend Harvard; his grandfather had gone there.) He then went to Washington to be a part of Roosevelt's New Deal, serving in a variety of positions as adviser to agency heads on minority issues. He was the architect and leader of the "black cabinet," a group of blacks who lobbied for and assisted in the integration of the federal government.[67]

After the Second World War, Weaver held teaching positions at Northwestern, Columbia, and New York University. In 1955 he became the state rent commissioner in New York, and in 1960 he was appointed vice chairman of the New York City Housing and Development Board. When John F. Kennedy was elected president, he named Weaver to head the Housing and Home Finance Agency, at the time the highest federal administrative position ever held by an African American. Although Kennedy attempted to elevate the agency to cabinet status, Congress blocked his efforts. Five years later, Lyndon Johnson succeeded where Kennedy had failed; the agency, with its name changed to the Department of Housing and Urban Development (HUD),

64. "Vernon Jordan," *Current Biography* (1993), 297.

65. Ibid., 299. See also Jeff Gerth, "Being Intimate with Power, Vernon Jordan Can Wield It Quietly But Effectively," *New York Times,* July 14, 1996.

66. Robin Armstrong, "Robert C. Weaver: Government Administrator, Scholar," in L. Mpho Mabunda, ed., *Contemporary Black Biography: Profiles from the International Black Community,* vol. 8 (New York: Gale Research, 1995), 259.

67. Richard Bardolph, *The Negro Vanguard* (New York: Rinehart, 1959), 255.

Table 3.3
*African Americans in the Cabinet*

|  | President | Years | Position |
|---|---|---|---|
| Robert C. Weaver | Johnson | 1966–68 | Housing and Urban Development |
| William T. Coleman Jr. | Ford | 1975–77 | Transportation |
| Patricia Roberts Harris | Carter | 1977–79 | Housing and Urban Development |
|  |  | 1979–81 | Health, Education, and Welfare |
| Samuel R. Pierce Jr. | Reagan | 1981–89 | Housing and Urban Development |
| Louis W. Sullivan | Bush | 1989–93 | Health and Human Services |
| Ronald H. Brown | Clinton | 1993–96 | Commerce |
| Mike Espy | Clinton | 1993–95 | Agriculture |
| Hazel O'Leary | Clinton | 1993–97 | Energy |
| Alexis M. Herman | Clinton | 1997– | Labor |
| Rodney E. Slater | Clinton | 1997– | Transportation |

achieved cabinet status, and in 1966 Weaver became the first African American to hold a cabinet position.[68]

After Weaver left his position as secretary of HUD, there were no black cabinet members for another seven years. There were no blacks in Nixon's cabinets. In 1975, Gerald Ford selected William Coleman Jr. as his secretary of transportation. The third black in a presidential cabinet, Patricia Roberts Harris, held two cabinet positions during Carter's presidency: first she was secretary of HUD, and later she became secretary of HEW.

In 1981, twenty-seven years after he had become the first black corporate director on a *Fortune*-level board, Samuel Pierce Jr. became secretary of HUD under Ronald Reagan. In this capacity, Pierce came under investigation for corruption. Although other senior housing officials were convicted, an independent counsel ultimately decided not to prosecute Pierce because of his age (he was then seventy-two), his poor health, and the absence of "clear criminal intent." Pierce did, however, release a statement that read, in part, "I realize that my own conduct contributed to an environment in which these events could occur. I must take the blame for problems."[69]

Bush's only black cabinet appointee was Louis Sullivan, a physician whom Barbara Bush had come to know well when she joined the board of trustees of

68. "Robert C. Weaver," *Contemporary Black Biography,* 261.

69. "Former Secretary Pierce Spared Trial in HUD Corruption Case," *New York Times,* January 12, 1995.

the Morehouse School of Medicine, where Sullivan was Dean. After Sullivan gave a speech introducing her at the Republican National Convention in August 1988, Barbara Bush successfully lobbied for his appointment as secretary of health and human services.

Clinton was the first president to appoint more than one black to his cabinet. His initial cabinet included three: Ron Brown, the former chair of the Democratic National Committee; Mike Espy, a former congressman from Mississippi who was one of the first black leaders to endorse Clinton's presidential candidacy; and Hazel O'Leary, the corporate vice president discussed in the previous chapter. After his reelection in 1996, Clinton appointed Alexis Herman to replace Robert Reich as secretary of labor and Rodney Slater to replace Frederico Peña as secretary of transportation.

These ten black cabinet members are from a strikingly narrow slice of the black community. Whereas about half of the first twelve directors and 40 percent of the 1994 black interlockers had been born into economically comfortable circumstances, seven of the ten cabinet members came from relative privilege.

As we have already seen, William Coleman Jr. came from generations of educators, ministers, and social workers; Samuel Pierce's father was a successful businessman and property owner; and Robert Weaver, whose Harvard-educated grandfather was the first black in the United States to earn a doctoral degree in dentistry, grew up in a comfortable Washington suburb. Louis Sullivan's father was an undertaker and his mother a teacher. Ron Brown's parents were both graduates of Howard University; his father managed the Theresa Hotel in Harlem, which catered to many prominent entertainers and professionals. Mike Espy's maternal grandfather was one of the most prosperous blacks in the south: he founded a chain of funeral homes and, at the time of his death, was one of the largest landowners in Mississippi. Both of Hazel O'Leary's parents were physicians. Two of the ten, Patricia Roberts Harris and Rodney Slater, came from poverty. The other, Alexis Herman, grew up in Alabama, where her father was a mortician who became the first black elected to Alabama's Democratic Party organization.

Even more striking is the pattern that emerges when one looks at their collective educational experience. All ten went to college, four to prestigious "white" schools (Weaver to Harvard, Coleman to Penn, Pierce to Cornell, and Brown to Middlebury) and four to prestigious "black" schools (Harris and Espy to Howard, Sullivan to Morehouse, and O'Leary to Fiske). Seven of the ten went to law school, one (Sullivan) to medical school, and one (Weaver) received a Ph.D. in economics.

## Blacks in the Military Elite

In Chapter 1 we told of Midshipman Leonard Kaplan's being "sent to Coventry" — which meant that no one spoke to him during his entire four years at the Naval Academy. Benjamin O. Davis Jr., the first black to graduate from the U.S. Military Academy in the twentieth century, had a parallel experience during his four years at that institution. After he had been at West Point for a short time, there was a knock on his door announcing a meeting in the basement in ten minutes. Davis painfully recalls that meeting and its long-term effects in the autobiography he wrote almost sixty years later:

> As I approached the assembly where the meeting was in progress, I heard someone ask, "What are we going to do about the nigger?" I realized then that the meeting was about me, and I was not supposed to attend. I turned on my heel and double-timed back to my room.
>
> From that meeting on, the cadets who roomed across the hall, who had been friendly earlier, no longer spoke to me. In fact, no one spoke to me except in the line of duty. Apparently, certain upperclass cadets had determined that I was getting along too well at the Academy to suit them, and they were going to enforce an old West Point tradition — "silencing" — with the object of making my life so unhappy that I would resign. Silencing had been applied in the past to certain cadets who were considered to have violated the honor code and refused to resign. In my case there was no question of such a violation; I was to be silenced solely because cadets did not want blacks at West Point. Their only purpose was to freeze me out.
>
> Except for the recognition ceremony at the end of plebe year, I was silenced for the entire four years of my stay at the Academy.[70]

Davis stuck it out at West Point and graduated near the top of his class. Even after graduation in 1936, his classmates (among them William Westmoreland, from a wealthy textile family in South Carolina) continued their silent treatment of him for years. In fact, for the next fifteen years, as his assignments took him to different locations in the United States and around the world, not only did his classmates continue to give him the silent treatment, but they and their wives also shunned Davis's wife.[71]

Davis was to become the second black to hold the rank of brigadier general (and the first to hold that rank in the air force). The first was his father, whose military career spanned a fifty-year period from the Spanish-American War to World War II. The senior Davis enlisted in the cavalry in 1899, soon passed the

70. Benjamin O. Davis Jr., *Benjamin O. Davis, Jr., American: An Autobiography* (Washington: Smithsonian Institution Press, 1991), 27.
71. Ibid., 52.

Table 3.4
*Blacks with General Officer Rank in the Armed Forces, 1985–1995*

|      | Army  | Navy  | Marines | Air Force | Total |
|------|-------|-------|---------|-----------|-------|
| 1985 | 6.3%  | 1.2%  | 1.5%    | 1.8%      | 3.4%  |
| 1986 | 7.1   | 1.6   | 1.6     | 1.8       | 3.8   |
| 1987 | 7.1   | 1.9   | 1.4     | 1.2       | 3.6   |
| 1988 | 7.2   | 1.6   | 0       | 1.2       | 3.5   |
| 1989 | 6.4   | 1.2   | 0       | 1.2       | 3.1   |
| 1990 | 6.6   | 1.2   | 0       | 0.9       | 3.1   |
| 1991 | 6.4   | 1.2   | 1.5     | 1.9       | 3.4   |
| 1992 | 6.8   | 1 2   | 1.5     | 1.6       | 3.4   |
| 1993 | 6.9   | 1.3   | 1.5     | 1.7       | 3.5   |
| 1994 | 6.6   | 1.7   | 0       | 2.0       | 3.4   |
| 1995 | 7.3   | 2.2   | 0       | 2.6       | 4.0   |

*Note:* 1985 N = 36 (total 1,067); 1995 N = 36 (total 893).

tests to become an officer, and over the years rose through the military ranks, with various stints teaching military science at Wilberforce University in Ohio and Tuskegee Institute in Alabama.

Pioneers like the Davises helped prepare the way for a military that some have called a model of integration. According to Charles Moskos and John Sibley Butler in *All That We Can Be,* "By the mid-1950s, a snapshot of 100 enlisted men on a typical parade would have shown twelve black faces; integration had become a fact of Army life. At a time when Afro-Americans were still arguing for their educational rights before the Supreme Court and marching for their social and political rights in the Deep South, the Army had become desegregated with little fanfare."[72]

By 1985, of the 1,067 men with general officer rank (the equivalent of one-star general or higher), 36, or 3.4 percent, were black. As can be seen in table 3.4, this figure has since fluctuated between 3 and 4 percent, with higher figures for the army than for the other three branches of the service. By 1995 there were still only 36 blacks with general officer rank, but there were fewer generals overall, so the percentage of blacks was higher.[73] In May 1996, when

72. Charles C. Moskos and John Sibley Butler, *All That We Can Be: Black Leadership and Racial Integration the Army Way* (New York: Basic, 1996), 31.

73. Moskos and Butler report that in 1995 the 145,000 blacks in the army were about half of all blacks in military uniform and accounted for about 27 percent of all those on

Bill Clinton nominated Vice Adm. J. Paul Reason to become a four-star admiral, he became the first black four-star in that branch of the service. (The air force had promoted a black to four-star rank twenty years earlier and the army in the mid-1980s; the marines still had never done so.)[74]

Some indication of the future of African Americans in the military elite can be seen in the rising number of graduates from the three military academies, which produce a disproportionate number of generals and admirals. At West Point the number of black graduates increased from an average of two or three a year between 1955 and 1967 to an average of seventy per year from 1990 through 1994. The starting point was even lower at the Naval Academy, fewer than two a year until 1967, but the average was seventy-seven a year from 1990 through 1994. At the Air Force Academy, there were, on average, fewer than two black graduates a year until 1967, but the figure reached sixty-two between 1986 and 1989, the last years for which numbers are available.[75]

One might expect that the few dozen blacks who have achieved general officer status—almost all of them men—would become, at the time of their retirement, prime candidates for senior corporate positions. As C. Wright Mills pointed out back in the 1950s, there was "increased personnel traffic . . . between the military and the corporate realms" because of "the great cultural shift of modern American capitalism toward a permanent war economy."[76] As a result, Mills added, "Get me a general" became the slogan of corporate recruiters. But Moskos and Butler found, much to their surprise, that this has not been the case for black generals. In numerous interviews with retired generals over the years, they found that "even the most qualified black generals" have not been hired as consultants and have not been asked onto corporate boards. "This is particularly puzzling," they write, "considering that most of these retired generals once had responsibility for thousands of soldiers and oversaw logistic systems of enormous cost and complexity. . . . It is difficult not to conclude that the discrimination these people overcame in the military overtakes them again when they return to civilian life."[77]

---

active duty in the army. The percentage of blacks in the army, they note, was "approximately twice the proportion found in the navy, air force, or marine corps" (6).

74. The data in table 3.4 are courtesy of the Department of Defense. John Mintz, "Clinton Nominates First Black Admiral," *Washington Post*, May 14, 1996.

75. *Black Americans in Defense of Our Nation* (Washington, D.C.: U.S. Government Printing Office, 1991).

76. Mills, *Power Elite*, 215.

77. Moskos and Butler, *All That We Can Be*, 50.

Still, a retired black general has become one of the best-known and most admired Americans. It was a major breakthrough in 1989 when Colin Powell was named chairman of the Joint Chiefs of Staff. And, indeed, Powell's ascendance to the top of the military hierarchy has had as much impact for civilians as for soldiers. According to Moskos and Butler, "the elevation of Colin Luther Powell to the chairmanship of the Joint Chiefs of Staff in 1989 was an epic event in American race relations, whose significance has yet to be fully realized."[78]

Powell's parents were both Jamaican immigrants, a fact he makes much of, and so will we when we explore the reasons for the success and failure of minorities in the United States in the final chapter. While a student at the City College of New York, Powell joined ROTC, and when he graduated in 1958, he was commissioned as a second lieutenant. Powell has emphasized that he "found himself" in ROTC: "Suddenly everything clicked. . . . I had found something I was good at. . . . For the first time, in the military I always knew exactly what was expected of me."[79] Equally important, the military had become a place where blacks could do well. "I had an intuitive sense that this was a career which was beginning to open up for blacks," says Powell. "You could not name, in those days, another profession where black men routinely told white men what to do and how to do it."[80]

Powell rose through the ranks. He served as a junior officer in Vietnam, then held a series of command and staff jobs. In 1972 he became a White House Fellow; noting that race worked to his advantage in this appointment, he said to a friend, "I was lucky to be born black."[81] Four years later, Jimmy Carter appointed Clifford Alexander as secretary of the army, and the number of black generals tripled while Alexander held that position. "My method was simple," Alexander revealed. "I just told everyone that I would not sign the goddam promotion list unless it was fair."[82] In 1979, at the age of forty-two,

78. Ibid., 114.

79. David Halberstam, "There Is Something Noble to It," *Parade*, September 17, 1995, p. 5.

80. Ibid.

81. John F. Stacks, "The Powell Factor," *Time*, July 10, 1995, p. 25.

82. Henry Louis Gates Jr., "Powell and the Black Elite," *New Yorker*, September 25, 1995, pp. 63–80. In 1993, Clinton named Togo West Jr., a black, as secretary of the army. Noting Alexander's appointment in the late 1970s and that since that time there had been other blacks in senior positions on the civilian side of the army, Moskos and Butler write that "with the appointment of Togo West, Jr., as secretary of the Army in 1993, the presence of a black in the senior Army Secretariat had become almost the norm" (*All That We Can Be,* 35).

Colin Powell achieved the rank of general. By 1987 he had become national security adviser under Reagan, and in 1989, under Bush, he became the first black — and the youngest man ever — to be chairman of the Joint Chiefs of Staff. After the Gulf War, polls consistently indicated that Powell was among the most admired people in America.[83]

### *"Thing Is, I Ain't That Black"*

Throughout the century scholars have demonstrated that a disproportionate number of black professionals have been light skinned, and that blacks with darker skin are more likely to be discriminated against. Horace Mann Bond found, for example, that many "early Negro scholars" were "light-complexioned" individuals from families that had been part of the antebellum "free colored population" or born to "favored slaves." He explained their success in the following way: "The phenomenon was not due, as many believed, to the 'superiority' of the white blood; it was a social and economic, rather than a natural selection. Concubinage remained an openly sustained relationship between white men and Negro women in the South for fifty years after the Civil War; the children of such unions were more likely to have parents with the money, and the tradition, to send a child to school, than the former field hand slaves who were now sharecroppers and day laborers."[84]

The authors of the report of the Glass Ceiling Commission argue that "gradations in skin color" have continued to affect the career chances of men and women of color. As they put it in their report:

> *Color-based differences* are inescapable but nobody likes to talk about them. These are complicated differences because they are not exclusively racial and not exclusively ethnic. The unstated but ever-present question is, *"Do they look like us?"*
>
> Though it is mostly covert, our society has developed an extremely sophisti-

83. Moskos and Butler, *All That We Can Be*, 115.

84. Horace Mann Bond, "The Negro Scholar and Professional in America," in John P. Davis, ed., *The American Negro Reference Book* (Englewood Cliffs, N.J.: Prentice-Hall, 1966), 559. See also Franklin E. Frazier, *The Black Bourgeoisie: The Rise of the New Middle Class* (New York: Free Press, 1957); Horace Mann Bond, *Black American Scholars: A Study of Their Beginnings* (Detroit: Balamp, 1972); H. Edward Ransford, "Skin Color, Life Chances, and Anti-White Attitudes," *Social Problems* 18 (1970), 164–178; Elizabeth Mullins and Paul Sites, "The Origins of Contemporary Eminent Black Americans: A Three-Generation Analysis of Social Origins," *American Sociological Review* 49 (1984), 672–685.

cated, and often denied, acceptability index based on gradations in skin color. It is not as simple a system as the black/white/colored classifications that were used in South Africa. It is not legally permissible, but it persists just beneath the surface, and it can be and is used as a basis for decisionmaking, sometimes consciously and sometimes unconsciously. It is applied to African Americans, to American Indians, to Asian and Pacific Islander Americans, and to Hispanic Americans, who are described in a color shorthand of black, brown, yellow, and red.[85]

Although this issue is generally not commented upon directly, some accounts of African Americans in positions of power allude to it indirectly. For example, Patricia Roberts Harris is described in the following way in *Current Biography:* "Among her ancestors were Negro slaves, Delaware and Cherokee Indians, and English and Irish settlers. . . . In some of her facial features she resembles Sophia Loren."[86]

Not surprisingly, therefore, when we looked at photographs of those black Americans who had made it into the power elite, we noted that they were lighter skinned than many other black Americans. We were able to confirm this observation more systematically by asking two raters, working independently, to use the Skin Color Assessment Procedure, a skin-color rating chart developed by two psychologists, to rate the skin color of many of those we have identified as members of the power elite and various control groups of other black Americans. The differences were powerful: the blacks in the power elite were rated as lighter skinned than the blacks in the control groups, and this was especially true for the black women in the power elite, who were rated as lighter than any of the other groups.[87] In fact, when the raters scored the photographs in *Ebony* magazine's 1996 list of the "100 Most Influential Black

85. *Good for Business,* 29.

86. "Patricia Robert Harris," *Current Biography* (1965), 191.

87. The Skin Color Assessment Procedure is described in Selena Bond and Thomas F. Cash, "Black Beauty: Skin Color and Body Images Among African-American College Women," *Journal of Applied Social Psychology* 22, no. 1 (1992), 874–888.

The two raters had a high rate of interrater agreement (the interjudge reliability, as determined by a Pearson product moment correlation, was $r = .87$). The ninety magazine-quality photographs used were drawn from *Current Biography,* from various articles in *Ebony*'s fiftieth-anniversary issue in November 1995, and from the October 1994 *Ebony* article on the black interlocking directors. A regression analysis looking at the effect of both power-elite status and gender on skin-color rating was highly significant ($F = 20.23$, $p < .0001$). Gender was a stronger predictor (beta = .50, $p < .0001$) of skin color than power elite status (beta = .20, $p < .02$).

Americans and Organization Leaders," Hazel O'Leary had the lowest score (and was thus seen as the lightest) of anyone on the list.

These findings not only make sense in terms of the earlier research on skin color among eminent black Americans, they are also consistent with our findings on Jews and women in the power elite. As we have indicated in the previous two chapters, those Jews who have made it into the power elite are likely to have been highly assimilated in the first place. The longer they were in the power elite — especially the corporate and military elite — the less distinguishable they became from their Gentile counterparts. Similarly, the women who have made it into the corporate elite are those who fit in the best, and though it is certainly easy enough to distinguish them from men in terms of their appearance, they tend to be (or to become) quite similar to the men surrounding them in terms of class background, values, and behaviors. In Chapter 2 we quoted a woman executive who explained to us that although she perceived her sex to pose the most substantial obstacle to her advancement in her career, this did not mean that being Jewish was irrelevant. "It's part of the total package," she told us. "It's part of the question of whether you fit the mold. Are you like me or not? If too much doesn't fit, it impacts you negatively."

In the same way, being black makes it hard to "fit the mold," and being a dark-skinned black makes it even harder. This is not the only factor operating in terms of what can make one different, but it contributes to whether "too much doesn't fit." This may explain why light skin is more prevalent among black women in the power elite than among black men, for black women are already different from the white male power elite norm because of their sex. It is as if one can accumulate only so many points of difference from the norm, and a combination of gender points and skin-color points can exceed the acceptable limit.

Colin Powell captured the essence of skin color's role in the broader context of not being too different — and thus threatening — to whites. In a lengthy *New Yorker* profile, Henry Louis Gates Jr. asked Powell to explain polls that showed him with greater appeal among whites than among blacks. Powell, described by Gates as "light-skinned and blunt-featured," cut through sociological jargon and the need for statistical analyses:

> One, I don't shove it in their face, you know? I don't bring any stereotypes or threatening visage to their presence. Some black people do. Two, I can overcome any stereotypes or reservations they have, because I perform well. Third thing is, *I ain't that black.* . . . I speak reasonably well, like a white person. I am very comfortable in a white social situation, and I don't go off in a corner. My features are clearly black, and I've never denied what I am. It fits into their

general social setting, so they do not find me threatening. I think there's more to it than that, but I don't know what it is.[88]

## Blacks in Congress

### THE SENATE

There have been just two blacks in the U.S. Senate in the twentieth century: Edward Brooke and Carol Moseley-Braun.[89] They represent a study in contrasts. Brooke was a Republican who represented the state of Massachusetts from 1967 until 1979. His father was a lawyer, and Brooke grew up in upper-middle-class neighborhoods in the Washington area. The family lived mostly in black neighborhoods, though for a while they lived in a white neighborhood that was so rigidly segregated that blacks who did not live there could not pass through the neighborhood without a note from a white person. According to one account, "He spent his boyhood summers on his mother's family plantation in Virginia, where his grandparents told the light-skinned youth that he was a descendant of Thomas Jefferson and of a British admiral, Sir Philip Bowes Brooke, and that he was related to Rupert Brooke, the English poet."[90]

After graduating from Howard in 1941 and serving in the army during World War II, he attended Boston University Law School, where he edited the *Law Review*. After he graduated in 1948, he started a one-man law practice outside Boston, and a few years later he entered state politics. In 1948 and again in 1952 he ran for the state legislature both as a Democrat and as a Republican (it was then legal to do so); both times he lost the Democratic nomination but won the Republican one, then lost in the general election. In 1960 he ran for secretary of state as a Republican, losing by fewer than twelve thousand votes. Two years later he won the election for attorney general, the second-highest office in the state. (He gained the Republican nomination on the second ballot over Boston blueblood Elliot Richardson.) In 1966 he ran for the U.S. Senate and won, defeating the former governor Endicott "Chub" Peabody.

In running for state attorney general, Brooke downplayed his race. He was,

88. The description of Powell is in Gates, "Powell and the Black Elite," 66; the quotation appears on p. 70.

89. Two blacks from Mississippi, Hiram Revels and Blanche Cruce, served in the Senate during Reconstruction. They were both selected by the state's legislature, not by the voters. "Edward W. Brooke," *Current Biography* (1967), 42.

90. "Edward W. Brooke," *Current Biography,* 41

he asserted, an American first, a Republican second, and "a black incidentally." He declared: "I'm not running as a Negro. I never have. I'm trying to show that people can be elected on the basis of their qualifications and not their race."[91] A few years later he remarked, "I am not a civil rights leader and I don't profess to be one."[92]

Brooke lost his bid for a third term in the Senate when he was tangled in a set of allegations about financial impropriety, fueled by bitter divorce proceedings with his wife, an Italian he met during the war. Although he was never convicted of a crime, his reputation suffered, and he lost that election to Paul Tsongas. He subsequently worked as a consultant and lawyer for various Washington law firms and real estate developers. According to one account, in the early 1990s he was living in Virginia with his second wife and son and describing himself as a "retired country gentleman."[93]

Carol Moseley-Braun, the other black elected to the U.S. Senate, has never been prone to downplay race. As a teenager in Chicago in the 1960s, she staged a one-person sit-in at a restaurant that would not seat her, refused to leave an all-white beach even when whites threw stones at her, and marched with Martin Luther King Jr. in a demonstration calling for open housing in an all-white neighborhood. She describes her upbringing in the following way: "They raised us in a world that did not acknowledge or legitimize racism. Ethnic pride was part and parcel of that world—my maternal grandparents had been Garveyites and Muslims, 'race men' as they were called at the time."[94]

Born to a middle-class family on the South Side of Chicago—her father was a policeman and her mother a medical technician—Moseley-Braun received a B.A. from the University of Illinois at Chicago and a J.D. from the University of Chicago Law School.

Six years after graduating from law school she was elected to the Illinois House of Representatives, and a decade later she was elected Cook County recorder of deeds. When, four years later, she decided to run for the U.S. Senate, entering the Democratic primary against the incumbent, Alan J. Dixon, who had voted to confirm Clarence Thomas, few at first thought she had a chance. As one account puts it, Moseley-Braun's candidacy "appeared so unpromising that political organizations created to provide seed money to women's cam-

91. Isaac Rosen, "Edward Brooke: Former U.S. Senator, Lawyer, Consultant," in L. Mpho Mabunda, ed., *Contemporary Black Biography: Profiles from the International Black Community,* vol. 8 (New York: Gale Research, 1995), 28.

92. Ibid.

93. Ibid., 29.

94. Carol Moseley-Braun, "Between W. E. B. DuBois and B. T. Washington," *Ebony,* November 1995, p. 58.

paigns across the country gave her nothing or just token contributions late in the race."[95] Nonetheless, she defeated Dixon, and when she won the general election, she became one of seven women in the Senate (see Chapter 2), and the only African American.

## THE HOUSE

The number of blacks in the House has increased during the 1990s. In the November 1990 election, 25 blacks were elected or reelected to the House; in 1992 that number rose to 38, where it remained in 1994. A Supreme Court ruling that redistricting to create black districts was unconstitutional raised concerns that the number might drop substantially in the 1996 elections, but the number of blacks elected to the House in 1996 remained almost the same — 37, or 8.7 percent of the 435 who make up that body. Although blacks are not proportionally represented in the House of Representatives, their presence there is certainly higher than the figures we have cited for blacks on boards of directors, in most presidential cabinets, and in the Senate.

When we looked more systematically at the fifty-three blacks who have served in the House since 1990, some revealing patterns emerged. First, only two of the fifty-three have been Republicans (Gary Franks of Connecticut and J. C. Watts of Oklahoma), and Franks was defeated in 1996. Second, more than 75 percent have been male; only twelve have been female. Third, although more than 90 percent have been college graduates, relatively few did their undergraduate work at elite colleges or universities. Five graduated from Ivy League schools: two went to Yale (Franks and Sheila Jackson Lee [D-Tex.]), two to the University of Pennsylvania (Chaka Fattah [D-Pa.] and Harold Ford Jr. [D-Tenn.]), and one to Harvard (Robert Scott [D-Va.]). Another six attended prestigious black colleges (Elijah Cummings [D-Md.] and Mike Espy, a Democratic congressman from Mississippi before he was named to the Clinton cabinet, went to Howard; Sanford Bishop [D-Ga.] and Earl Hilliard [D-Ala.] went to Morehouse; Alcee Hastings [D-Fla.] went to Fisk; and Bennie Thompson [D-Miss.] went to Tougaloo). The roster of the schools from which the others received their undergraduate degrees reads like a sampling of four-year colleges in America. It includes Arkansas A&M, Florida A&M, Cal State Los Angeles, New York University, North Carolina A&T, St. Louis University, Seton Hall, South Carolina State, Tennessee State, Texas Christian University, the University of the Redlands, and Western Michigan.

95. Isaac Rosen, "Carol Moseley Braun: Politician, Lawyer," in Barbara C. Bigelow, ed., *Contemporary Black Biography: Profiles from the International Black Community,* vol. 4 (Detroit: Gale, 1993), 28.

These fifty-three men and women had earned thirty-eight postgraduate degrees among them. Not surprisingly, the majority of these degrees (twenty) were from law schools. Again, a few attended the country's most elite law schools, including Harvard, Yale, Georgetown, and the University of Virginia, but most went to less prestigious schools like Cleveland Marshall Law School, Southwestern, Texas Southern, the University of Maryland, the University of Santa Clara, St. John's, and Wayne State. Seventeen earned various kinds of master's degrees, and one had a Ph.D. (from International University).

The schools attended suggest that, as a group, the black men and women who have been elected to the House have come from less privileged backgrounds than those who have been appointed to *Fortune*-level boards of directors or presidential cabinets. We were able to corroborate this by looking at the family backgrounds for all those about whom we could find information.[96]

About 19 percent of them grew up in economically comfortable backgrounds (compared, for example, with a corresponding figure of 40 percent for the interlocking directors we looked at earlier in this chapter). This includes Mike Espy, who, as we have seen, came from a wealthy Mississippi family. It includes Harvard graduate Robert Scott, whose father was a doctor and whose mother was a teacher, and Sanford Bishop, whose father was a college president and whose mother was the head librarian at the college. It also includes four who are the children of men who have been successful politicians: the father of Harold E. Ford Jr. served in the House of Representatives for twenty years (Ford was elected to his father's seat); the father of Walter R. Tucker III (D-Calif.) was the mayor of Compton, Calif.; the father of Cynthia McKinney (D-Ga.) was a longtime legislator in the state house in Georgia; and the father of Jesse Jackson Jr. (D-Ill.), though not an elected official, has been a powerful political figure in the United States for decades and entered the Democratic presidential primaries in 1984 and 1988.

Half are from solid working-class families. These include men and women whose fathers were career military men (Corrinne Brown [D-Fla.] and Alan Wheat [D-Mo.]), sold insurance (Eva Clayton [D-N.C.]), were longshoremen (Ronald Dellums [D-Calif.]), steelworkers (Earl Hilliard and Edolphus Towns [D-N.Y.]), and elevator operators (Charles Rangel [D-N.Y.]). In most of these families, the mother also worked; some were hairdressers, some were clerk typists, some were maids.

96. The various published sources yielded information on only about one-third of the fifty. We therefore phoned the congressional offices of the remainder and requested the relevant information from press secretaries. We were able to obtain sufficient information about the parents of thirty-two of the fifty-three.

About one-third came from real poverty. This includes, for example, Kwame Mfume (D-Md.), who was thirteen when his stepfather, a truck driver, left home, and sixteen when his mother, who worked as a maid, died; Carrie Meek (D-Fla.), whose parents were sharecroppers in Florida; and Mel Watt (D-N.C.), who grew up in a fatherless household and lived in a tin-roofed shack without running water or electricity in rural Mecklenburg County in North Carolina.

Three patterns emerge from our examination of blacks in the power elite and in Congress. First, as was the case for Jews and women, it is apparent that social background is important. Although some have authentic stories to tell of going from rags to riches — as do some whites — most are from either working-class or middle-class families, and many are from economically privileged backgrounds. Whether one is white or black, the advantages of being born into privilege are apparent.

Second, education is important. As we have seen repeatedly in this chapter, the blacks who have made it into the power elite and Congress are quite well educated. This not only underscores the importance of education, which we also found to be the case in the chapters on Jews and women, but reinforces the oft-heard claim that blacks have to be better-educated than whites to get ahead.

Third, the same pattern holds for blacks that held for Jews and women in the cabinet and Congress. Cabinet members tend to be from families higher in the socioeconomic spectrum than elected officials, and they include Republicans as well as Democrats. In keeping with their lower social-class origins, almost all of those who have been elected to Congress have been Democrats.

# 4

# Latinos in the Power Elite

When Roberto Goizueta left his native Havana in 1949 to begin his freshman year at Yale University, he had no idea that by the 1980s he would be running one of the largest corporations in the United States. Basque and Spanish in racial and cultural heritage, and a member of the wealthy upper class in Cuba, he returned home to Havana after he had earned a degree in engineering, and from 1954 to 1960 he worked for the Coca-Cola subsidiary.

But Goizueta and other wealthy young Cubans did not count on the actions of another Cuban-born son of a successful Spanish immigrant, Fidel Castro, who turned his back on his father's large ranch and his own elite education to create the revolutionary army that overthrew Cuban dictator Fulgencio Batista in January 1959. By the early 1960s, Castro was threatening major capitalist enterprises, leading Goizueta and more than 380,000 other Cubans to emigrate to the United States by 1980.[1] In 1960 Goizueta became assistant to the senior vice president of Coca-Cola in the Bahamas, and by 1964 he was assistant to the vice president for research and development at the company's headquarters in Atlanta.

It took only a few years before Goizueta became a vice president for engineering; shortly thereafter he was a senior vice president, then an executive

1. *Statistical Abstract of the United States* (1985), 86.

vice president. He was named president and chief operating officer in 1980 and became chairman of the board and CEO in 1981. In the early 1990s he was an outside director on the boards of Ford, Eastman Kodak, Sonat, and Sun-Trust Banks. So we can be sure that there is at least one Latino at the heart of the U.S. power elite, atypical though he may be of most of the twenty-two million people identified as Hispanic Americans.[2]

Vilma S. Martínez, born to Mexican-American parents in 1943 in San Antonio, had a very different experience. As a young girl, she was bitter about the discrimination she experienced. She recalls that her junior high school counselor recommended that she go to a vocational or technical high school, her high school counselor would not advise her about applying to college, and her father, a construction worker, was skeptical about the usefulness of college for a woman, saying that she "would not complete school, that she would get married and have children." But she insisted on an academic high school, graduated from the University of Texas in two and a half years, and did not have the first of her two children until 1976, nine years after she had earned a law degree from Columbia University.[3]

Martínez practiced civil rights law as a staff attorney for the NAACP Legal Defense Fund from 1967 to 1970 and the New York State Division of Human Rights after that. After two years as a labor lawyer with the Wall Street firm of Cahill, Gordon & Reindel, she became one of the prime movers in establishing the Mexican-American Legal Defense and Education Fund (MALDEF). In 1973 she became MALDEF's general counsel and president. Three years later, the liberal Democratic governor of California, Jerry Brown, surprised everyone by appointing Martínez, only thirty-two years old, as a regent of the University of California, where she rubbed elbows with a cross-section of the California corporate rich and lobbied for greater diversity in the faculty and student body. In May 1982 she joined the Los Angeles law firm of Munger, Tolles & Olson, where her clients included Pacific Telephone, Blue Cross, and Allstate Insurance.[4] In 1983, she joined the board of directors of Anheuser-Busch; later she joined the boards of Fluor Corporation and Sanwa Bank, the sixth-largest bank in California.

2. Estimates of the size of the Latino population are not without controversy. For a discussion of the debate that ensued after *Forbes* magazine claimed that in 1996 the "Mexican-origin" population was 32 million, see Tammy Nelson, "*Forbes* Places Mexican-origin Population at 32 Million; Experts Say Magazine is Wrong," *Hispanic Business*, April 1996, p. 64.

3. Janet Morey and Wendy Dunn, *Famous Mexican Americans* (New York: Dutton, 1989), 65–67.

4. Ibid., 70.

But not all Latinas from the Southwest are liberal enough to work for the NAACP or MALDEF. Those from New Mexico, whose ancestors were sometimes landholders before the American conquest of the territory, are often quite conservative. Patricia Díaz, born in Santa Rita, New Mexico, in 1946, was the daughter of an army sergeant who was transferred frequently. She spent her teenage years in Japan, graduated from a high school in Santiago, Chile, received her B.A. in 1970 from UCLA and a law degree in 1973 from Loyola University in Los Angeles. After three years with a large corporate firm in Los Angeles, she became a management attorney specializing in labor disputes, first with Pacific Lighting and then with ABC in Hollywood. She was working for ABC in 1983 when Ronald Reagan unexpectedly named her as a "Democratic" appointee to the National Labor Relations Board, the second woman and the first Latina in its forty-seven-year history. There she joined the majority in a wide range of decisions that were extremely damaging to labor organizing.[5] In 1986 she became a member of the Federal Communications Commission. After an equally conservative three-year tenure as an FCC commissioner, she returned to the private sector as a corporate lawyer for U.S. Sprint. In 1992, George Bush tried to improve his appeal to Mexican Americans in the Southwest by appointing Díaz as assistant secretary of state for human rights and humanitarian affairs. When Bush lost his bid for reelection, Díaz joined the Washington office of the venerable Wall Street law firm of Sullivan and Cromwell and became a director of Telemundo, the second-largest Hispanic radio and television corporation in the United States. Being a conservative Democrat has served Díaz — and the Republicans — extremely well.

Goizueta, Martínez, and Díaz are graphic examples of why social scientists stress that it is very risky to generalize about the Hispanic or Latino experience in the United States. The 1.1 million Cuban Americans, many of whom were quite well off in Cuba, have one story, while the 2.4 million immigrants from Puerto Rico usually have another. (Actually, a few of the Puerto Rican immigrants are also wealthy, but most arrived poor.) Similarly, people of Mexican descent in New Mexico, many of whom have ancestors who have lived in the area for more than one hundred years and who sometimes call themselves "Spanish Americans," are different from the Mexican-American immigrants to Texas and California, the fastest-growing Spanish-speaking minority in the country. Moreover, Mexican Americans of the Southwest range from middle-class entrepreneurs to migrant farm workers, and they vary greatly in color and appearance as well because of a history of intermarriage with the indige-

---

5. James A. Gross, *Broken Promise: The Subversion of U.S. Labor Relations Policy, 1947–1994* (Philadelphia: Temple University Press, 1995), 250–263.

nous Indian populations of Mexico. The Latino population in the United States also includes some immigrants from Spain and various Latin American countries. On a 1995 list of the seventy-five richest Hispanics, which is dominated by twenty-seven Cuban-Americans and twenty-five Mexican-Americans, there are also eight people identified as Spanish and one person each from Chile, Colombia, Costa Rica, the Dominican Republic, Ecuador, Uruguay, and Venezuela. Five Puerto Rican immigrants and three residents of Puerto Rico round out the list. At the top is Roberto Goizueta of Coca-Cola, whose net worth was estimated at $574 million.[6]

There is even disagreement among scholars and political activists about what general name, if any, should be used to characterize a group whose main common heritage is the Spanish conquest and the Spanish language. The term *Hispanic* is favored by some, *Latino* by others. In a 1990 survey, however, it was found that neither term is liked by most Americans of Cuban, Mexican-American, or Puerto Rican extraction. Most prefer labels that reflect their specific backgrounds. Moreover, the three groups have "little interaction with each other, most do not recognize that they have much in common culturally, and they do not profess any strong affection for each other." The authors of the survey go on to say that "it is particularly noteworthy that more respondents prefer to be called 'American' than 'Latino,' the label that many members of the Latino intelligentsia, including ourselves, have insisted is both the 'correct' and the preferred label."[7]

Given these disagreements, we will continue to use the terms *Hispanic American, Hispanic,* and *Latino/Latina* interchangeably when a general term is needed. When possible, we will use specific ethnic identifications.

Underlying this diversity of national origins and the tendency to identify primarily with one's own subgroup, there are nonetheless two factors that powerfully shape the degree of acceptance and assimilation of all Latino immigrants. The first is their religion. The 70 percent who are Catholics can blend in easily with the largest single church in the United States (59 million strong, and 25 percent of the U.S. population). Their Catholic heritage is an important piece

6. "Emerging Wealth: The Hispanic Business Rich List," *Hispanic Business,* March 1996, p. 18. We recognize, of course, that Puerto Ricans are U.S. citizens and that those who settle in the United States thus cannot technically be termed immigrants, but we adopt that term in order to avoid the repeated syntactical gymnastics that would otherwise be necessary.

7. Rodolfo de la Garza, Louis De Sipio, F. Chris Garcia, John Garcia, and Angelo Falcon, *Latino Voices: Mexican, Puerto Rican, and Cuban Perspectives on American Politics* (Boulder, Colo.: Westview, 1992), 13–14. See also Suzanne Oboler, *Ethnic Labels, Latino Lives* (Minneapolis: University of Minnesota Press, 1995).

of cultural capital because it provides entrée into new social circles as they attain education or a higher-status occupation. True, local parishes are sometimes differentiated by status and income levels, but new social connections can be made through new parishes if a person is climbing the social ladder.

The second major factor influencing the fate of Hispanic Americans is skin color and facial features. As two sociological studies note, there is great variation in the appearance of Latinos, ranging from a pure "European" look to a Native American look.[8] In most Latin American countries, the lighter-skinned and more European-looking people tend to be in the higher social classes, the darker-skinned and more Indian-looking people in the lower classes.[9]

Several journalists and social critics have concluded that darker-skinned Hispanics are also at a disadvantage in the United States. To test this claim, E. A. Telles and Edward Murguia used information from a nationwide survey of Hispanics in 1979 to see whether those rated as light-skinned by the interviewer had higher average earnings than those who were darker. Since the lightest-skinned group was too small for sound statistical comparisons, it was merged with a group judged to be of medium skin color, and a comparison was then made with the darkest group. The researchers found that there was a strong tendency for the lighter group to earn more than the darker one, and they argue that this cannot be explained in terms of educational differences, because the two groups were very similar in education.[10] As we shall show, our own study of the skin color of Hispanics in the corporate elite leads to the same conclusion: it is advantageous to be light-skinned.

## Latinos in the Corporate Elite

We have two sources of data on the number of Latinos on *Fortune*-level boards. The first is Directorship, the publishing, research, and consulting firm

8. Carlos H. Arce, Edward Murguia, and W. Parker Frisbie, "Phenotype and Life Chances Among Chicanos," *Hispanic Journal of Behavioral Sciences* 9, no. 1 (1987), 19–32; E. A. Telles and Edward Murguia, "Phenotypic Discrimination and Income Differences Among Mexican Americans," *Social Science Quarterly* 71 (1990), 682–96; Aida Hurtado, "Does Similarity Breed Respect? Interviewer Evaluations of Mexican-Descent Respondents in a Bilingual Survey," *Public Opinion Quarterly* 58 (1994), 77–95.

9. For excellent accounts of the association of color and racial exclusion in Latin America, see Laura A. Lewis, "Spanish Ideology and the Practice of Inequality in the New World," in Benjamin Bowser, ed., *Racism and Anti-Racism in World Perspective* (Thousand Oaks, Calif.: Sage, 1995), 46–66; Vânia Penha-Lopes, "What Next? On Race and Assimilation in the United States and Brazil," *Journal of Black Studies* 26, no. 6 (1996), 809–826.

10. Telles and Murguia, "Phenotypic Discrimination and Income Differences."

Table 4.1

*Hispanic Directors on Fortune 1000 Boards in the 1990s*

|  | 1990 | 1991 | 1992 | 1993 | 1994 | 1995 |
|---|---|---|---|---|---|---|
| Number of Hispanics Holding Seats |  |  |  |  |  |  |
| men: | 35 | 29 | 29 | 38 | 37 | 41 |
| women: | 5 | 6 | 6 | 2 | 6 | 10 |
|  | 40 | 35 | 35 | 40 | 43 | 51 |
| Number of Seats Held | 53 | 46 | 45 | 50 | 57 | 74 |

*Source:* Hispanic Business.

introduced in Chapter 2. The second source is an annual list of "the board-room elite" published in the January issue of *Hispanic Business* since 1990. The list includes Hispanics who serve on "the boards of Fortune 1000 corporations, divisions, and subsidiaries." The inclusion of "divisions and subsidiaries" makes the list less exclusive than the ones we used in previous chapters. When residents of Puerto Rico and foreign nationals are eliminated from the Directorship list, however, there is a high degree of overlap with the one produced by *Hispanic Business*. We therefore have used the annual listings in *Hispanic Business* to show the slow growth in the number of Latino directors in the early 1990s, from forty in 1990 to fifty-one in 1995 (see table 4.1). Hispanics now make up about 10 percent of the U.S. population, but they provide less than 1 percent of all corporate directors.

Although we have considerable confidence in these findings, it is important to stress that they are not perfect. Deciding who is and who is not Hispanic is not an exact science. As with Jews, names can be misleading. When a reader of *Hispanic Business* wrote to complain that John Castro, the CEO of Merrill Corporation, had been omitted from a list of corporate executives published in the January 1995 issue (along with the list of the "boardroom elite"), the editors replied that "company officials tell us he is not Hispanic."[11] Similarly, the seemingly Latino CEO of Sears, Roebuck in the mid-1990s, Arthur Martinez, is mostly Irish. The name comes from a family member who married someone from Spain generations ago. There are also Hispanics whose names don't reveal that they are Hispanic: in 1994, H. B. Fuller Company selected Walter Kissling, born and raised in Costa Rica, as its CEO.[12]

Merging the Directorship and *Hispanic Business* lists for 1993 and 1994

11. Reply to Letter to the Editor, *Hispanic Business,* April 1995, p. 8.

12. "Who's News," *Wall Street Journal,* June 8, 1995.

after eliminating foreign nationals, residents of Puerto Rico, and those found not to be Latinos, we analyzed the social, educational, and career backgrounds of seventy-one Latinos and Latinas who sat on a total of 102 corporate boards. The gender difference is large: only 20 percent were women. Still, this 20 percent is considerably higher than the comparable percentage for non-Hispanic whites on boards, less than 10 percent of whom are women; the Hispanic percentage is about the same as for African Americans.[13]

Although the available biographical information is not complete in all cases, a majority of the men and women on our list seem to have been raised in at least middle-class circumstances. Many others had an elite education at the undergraduate or graduate levels that gave them the social connections and educational credentials to move quickly into responsible positions in the corporate community. Only a few people on the list of directors could be considered genuine bootstrappers, making their way to the top of corporations without the benefit of family backing or an elite education.

As might be expected from our account of Roberto Goizueta's appointment as CEO at Coca-Cola and the large number of Cuban Americans among the seventy-five wealthiest Hispanics, the majority of highly successful entrepreneurs and executives on our list come from Cuban-American backgrounds. Most had the advantage of being born to parents who were wealthy, well-educated, or both. This was true for Roberto Mendoza, who, like Roberto Goizueta, was born in Cuba and educated at Yale, and who became the head of mergers and acquisitions at Morgan Guaranty Trust in 1987, earning him a seat on the board. It was also true for Ramon Martínez IV, who was educated at Boston College and the University of Pennsylvania's Wharton School of Business and became the managing director of the Wall Street investment firm of Lehman Brothers in 1984.

And it was certainly true for Alfonso Fanjul and his brother José. They manage a fifth-generation family business, with cane fields in Florida and Puerto Rico, that provides 15 percent of the sugar sold in the United States. Forced to relocate to the United States when Castro came to power, the Fanjuls have by far the worst labor record of any sugar-producing company in the country, frequently violating minimum wage and labor laws in the late 1980s with their predominantly Latino migrant labor force. In brushing off criticism of the Fanjuls, a New York friend of theirs says, "They are completely accepted by society [in Palm Beach] — they hang out with all the best people."[14]

13. The data on non-Hispanic white women and African-American women on corporate boards can be found in tables 2.1, 2.2, and 3.1.

14. Jane Mayer, "Sweet Life: First Family of Sugar Is Tough on Workers, Generous to Politicians," *Wall Street Journal,* July 29, 1991.

The family is estimated to be worth $500 million. Some $52–90 million of its income each year is due to price supports.[15]

Although Alfonso Fanjul is listed by *Hispanic Business* as among the board-room elite, the *New York Times* reported in 1996 that he has Spanish citizenship despite his permanent residency in the United States. Some critics suggest that he preferred Spanish citizenship to avoid U.S. estate taxes, but a flap over his large campaign finance donations to the Republicans led him to claim that he was applying for American citizenship.[16]

Two directors have a recent Spanish heritage. Like the Cuban Americans, both come from well-off families. John Arrillaga, whose net worth of $400 million made him the third-richest Hispanic in the United States in 1995, is the son of a Basque-Spanish immigrant who founded a wholesale produce business in Southern California. Arrillaga graduated from Stanford, where he was a third-team basketball All-American, then went into the development business in the Silicon Valley. He amassed his fortune by constructing futuristic, campuslike worksites for the computer and education industries. He is now on the board of Morris Knudson.[17]

Pedro Cuatrecasas was born in Spain in 1936. His father, a prominent botanist, fled to the United States during the Spanish Civil War and became curator of Columbian botany at the Natural History Museum in Chicago. After earning his B.A. and M.D. from the University of Washington, Pedro Cuatrecasas was on the medical school faculties at George Washington University, Johns Hopkins, and Duke before becoming president of the Pharmaceutical Research Division of Warner-Lambert, Inc. He is on the board of Hi-Bred International.

Several directors are Spanish Americans from New Mexico. These include Katherine Ortega, the champion board sitter among Hispanic Americans for 1995. Her paternal grandparents settled in New Mexico in the late 1880s. Her father owned a café, then a furniture business. Because he was a lifelong Republican, Ortega likes to say she was "born a Republican."[18] After graduating from Eastern New Mexico State University in 1957 with a degree in business, she started an accounting firm with her sister that the family turned into the Otero Savings and Loan Association in 1974.

15. Phyllis Berman, "The Set-Aside Charade," *Forbes,* March 13, 1995, pp. 78–80, 82, 86; Phyllis Berman, "The Fanjuls of Palm Beach," *Forbes,* May 14, 1990, pp. 56–57, 60, 64, 68–69.

16. Leslie Wayne, "Foreign G.O.P. Donor Raised Dole Funds," *New York Times,* October 21, 1996.

17. Randall Lane, "The Odd Couple," *Forbes,* September 13, 1993, pp. 130–131.

18. Susan Rasky, "A 'Born' Republican: Katherine Davalos Ortega," *New York Times,* August 21, 1984.

Ortega moved to California in the late 1960s, working first as a tax supervisor for the accounting firm of Peat, Marwick, Mitchell and Company and then as a vice president for Pan American Bank, where her bilingualism was valuable in working with the local Latino community. In 1975 she gained visibility as the first woman president of a California bank, the Latino-owned Santa Ana State Bank. Four years later she returned to New Mexico as a consultant to her family's saving and loan association, and in 1982 Reagan named her to his Advisory Committee on Small and Minority Business Ownership.[19] From 1983 to 1989 she served in the Reagan administration in the largely ceremonial position of treasurer of the United States. That office gave her the public stature to give one of the keynote speeches at the 1984 Republican presidential convention. In 1989 she left her government position and marketed herself as a corporate director who could provide both Hispanic and female perspectives. By 1995 she was on no fewer than six boards: Diamond Shamrock, ITT Raynier, Kroger Company, Long Island Lighting, Paul Revere Insurance Group, and Ralston Purina.

There are some rags-to-riches stories among the Latino directors. Most of them concern Mexican Americans. Edward Zapanta, for example, was told by his high school counselor that he should become a mechanic like his father, but he went on to earn a B.A. from UCLA and an M.D. from USC. He founded a medical clinic in a predominantly Mexican-American neighborhood near where he grew up, and he sits on the boards of Southern California Edison and the Times Mirror Company. William S. Davila provides another example. Neither he nor his parents graduated from college. Davila started as a stock boy at Von's Markets in 1948 and ended up CEO of the company in 1987 at the age of fifty-six. He retired from the position in 1992 but continued as a director at Wells Fargo Bank, Pacific Gas and Electric, Hormel Foods, and Von's.

Luís Nogales provides a third example of a Mexican-American rags-to-riches story. Nogales was born in 1943 in the central valley of California where his parents were farm workers—albeit farm workers who bought books on literature and history, in both English and Spanish, and "traveled with their own small library."[20] Nogales attended San Diego State University on a scholarship and graduated from the Stanford Law School in 1969. After working for three years as Stanford's liaison to Mexican-American students, he went to Washington as a White House Fellow and then became assistant to the secretary of the interior. He returned to the West Coast in 1973 to work for Golden West Broadcasting, owner of the California Angels baseball team as well as radio and television stations. In 1983 he became executive vice presi-

19. Morey and Dunn, *Famous Mexican Americans,* 100–101.
20. Ibid., 76.

dent and in 1985 president of United Press International. When UPI was sold in 1986, he went to work in Spanish-language television for Univision. After negotiating the sale of Univision to Hallmark in 1988, he formed his own investment and consulting company, Nogales Partners. He is on the boards of Coors, Southern California Edison, and the Bank of California.

But not all the Mexican Americans in the sample started at the bottom. Ignacio Lozano, a director of Bank of America, Walt Disney Company, Pacific Mutual Life, and Pacific Enterprises, became the assistant publisher of his father's highly successful newspaper, *La Opinión,* shortly after his graduation from Notre Dame in 1947. His daughter, Monica, the managing editor of the paper since 1987, is a director at First Interstate Bank of California. She is a graduate of the University of Oregon. The family's net worth was estimated at $43 million by *Hispanic Business* in 1996.

Similarly, Enrique Hernández Jr. and Roland Hernández are Mexican Americans who had the advantage of being raised in a well-to-do family. Enrique Hernández Sr., a former police officer, created Inter-Con Security Systems, a company with offices in ten countries that employs eight thousand workers, and is estimated by *Hispanic Business* to be worth $48 million. Enrique Jr., a graduate of Harvard, sits on the board of Great Western Financial Corporation, and Roland, also a Harvard alumnus, is a director at Beneficial Finance Corporation and CEO of Telemundo Group (of which the Hernández family owns 5 percent).

THE CORPORATE PIPELINE

Only five women and only one African American held positions as CEOs in Fortune 1000 companies in the 1980s and early 1990s.[21] By the mid-1990s there had been five Latino CEOs of Fortune 1000 companies. We have already referred to Roberto Goizueta, the CEO at Coca-Cola, and Walter Kissling, the CEO at H. B. Fuller. The other three are Carlos H. Cantu, a Mexican-American graduate of Texas A & M who headed Service Master Company in Illinois; Benjamin F. Montoya, a Mexican-American retired rear admiral with a law degree from Georgetown, who was CEO of Public Service Company of New Mexico; and J. Phillip Samper, born in Salt Lake City of a Colombian father and an Anglo mother and educated at MIT, who was CEO at Cray Research.[22]

21. These five women are Katharine Graham of the *Washington Post,* Marion Sandler of Golden West, Linda Wachner of Warnaco, Loida Lewis of TLC/Beatrice, and Jill Barad of Mattel. The African American is Clifton R. Wharton Jr. of TIAA-CREF.

22. David Fuente, the CEO of Office Depot in Florida, might be considered Hispanic, but it requires expanding the meaning of the term further than is generally done. Fuente,

At the same time, the number of Latino executives in Fortune 1000 companies who were at the vice presidential level or above climbed from 167 in 1994 to 217 in early 1996, accounting for about 1.4 percent of the top positions in these companies. A survey by *Hispanic Business* found that these executives were most frequently in telecommunications, commercial banking, or food. They fared worst in industries like retailing that have very little business with the federal government and do not have to bother with the federal guidelines that have to be followed in order to bid for contracts.[23]

*Hispanic Business* also was able to use reports filed with the Equal Employment Opportunity Commission to see how well eighteen major corporations were doing in promoting Latinos to management positions at all levels. The figures ranged from 5–6 percent of all officials and managers at Citibank, Pepsi-Cola, and Sears, Roebuck to 1–2 percent at General Electric, Proctor and Gamble, General Motors, Ford, and DuPont.[24]

Latinos constitute about 10 percent of the U.S. population, so they are clearly underrepresented on boards of directors and in top management positions. They are even underrepresented in general management positions in companies that employ a large percentage of Latinos. At Citibank, for example, where 9.9 percent of the company's overall workforce is Latino, only 5.6 percent of the "officials and managers" are Latinos. At Pepsi-Cola, where 11.8 percent of the overall workforce is Latino, only 5.5 percent of all officials and managers are Latino. Nonetheless, it is clear that Latinos have made gains in recent years.[25]

To develop a more general and long-term picture of Latino involvement in the corporate community, we drew on a Distinctive Hispanic Names technique developed by the sociologist Abraham Lavender.[26] We used fifteen distinctive Hispanic names to estimate the number of Latinos listed in *Poor's Register of Executives and Directors* — the most comprehensive and readily accessible list of top managers and directors at more than fifty-thousand public companies. We first determined that these fifteen names (Álvarez, Díaz, Fernández, Flores, García, González, Hernández, López, Martínez, Pérez,

---

born and raised in Chicago, is a Sephardic Jew: in all likelihood his ancestors were expelled from Spain or Portugal in the fifteenth century.

23. Maria Zate, "Breaking Through the Glass Ceiling," *Hispanic Business,* January–February 1996, p. 34.

24. Rick Mendosa, "The Numbers Do the Talking," *Hispanic Business,* January–February 1996, pp. 17–28.

25. Ibid.

26. Abraham D. Lavender, "The Distinctive Hispanic Names (DHN) Technique: A Method for Selecting a Sample or Estimating Population size," *Names* 40, no. 1 (1992), 1–16.

Table 4.2
*Estimated Number of Hispanics in Higher Management, 1965–1995*

|  | 1965 | 1975 | 1985 | 1995 | 1995 N/1965 N |
|---|---|---|---|---|---|
| Hispanics | 78 | 131 | 235 | 374 | 5.3 |
| Est. *Poor's* total | 75,639 | 73,649 | 76,449 | 68,423 | |

Ramírez, Rivera, Rodríguez, Sánchez, and Torres) accounted for 23 percent of the names appearing on lists of corporate directors and executives in *Hispanic Business* for 1993, 1994, and 1995, which gave us a factor of 4.35 for estimating the total number of Latinos listed in *Poor's* at the midpoint in each decade since the 1960s.[27]

According to this analysis, the total number of Latinos listed in *Poor's* rose from 78 in 1965 to 374 in 1995 (table 4.2). Although these raw estimates provide a generally accurate picture of the rising rate of Hispanic participation in the business community from 1965 to 1995, they in fact slightly underestimate the overall increase in rate of participation because there were approximately 7,200 fewer names in *Poor's* in 1995 (68,423) than there were in 1965 (75,639). Correcting for the slightly smaller size of the *Poor's* list in 1995, we estimate that the number of Latinos in executive and director roles in corporations in the United States increased by a factor of 5.3 over the thirty-year period. This notable increase reflects not only that there has been greater Latino involvement in non-Hispanic companies but that there are more Latino-owned businesses. Still, Latinos represented only 0.5 percent of executives and directors at publicly owned companies large enough to be listed in *Poor's* in 1995.

It is clear that Latinos have come a long way in thirty years: some are in the corporate elite, and the number is increasing; some are or have been CEOs of non-Hispanic *Fortune*-level companies; and there are more and more Hispanics moving through the pipeline. Given the many Hispanics in America, though, a percentage of the population that is increasing substantially, they remain very much underrepresented in the higher levels of the corporate world.

SKIN COLOR AMONG HISPANICS

Taking our cue from the findings on skin color and income presented earlier in the chapter, we examined the skin color of 188 magazine quality

27. That is, because 4.35 × 23% = 100%, multiplying the number of times these fifteen names are found in *Poor's* for a given year by 4.35 provides an estimate of the total number of Hispanic Americans listed in *Poor's* for that year.

photographs of people who were selected as "top influentials" by *Hispanic Business* for 1993 and 1994. First, we wanted to see whether those identified as influential Hispanics in general were light skinned, and second, we wanted to see whether those who were *Fortune*-level directors were even more light-skinned than the other "influentials." We used the same nine color cards and the same two raters that we used to assess the photographs of African Americans in the previous chapter.[28]

We used the average score based on the two raters' responses to each photograph. As was true for the African-American sample, the two had a high level of agreement (89 percent of their ratings were within one point of one another on the nine-point color scale). As expected, the influentials as a group were light skinned. The overall mean score was 3.5 (on a ten-point scale), and less than 5 percent had ratings higher than 5; in contrast, the overall mean score for the African Americans rated in Chapter 3 was 5.9. In order to compare the scores of these Hispanic influentials with a group of whites, the photographs that accompanied the biographical sketches of those on the 1994 and 1995 *Forbes* lists of the "400 Richest Americans" were rated. Not every sketch included a photograph, and we omitted the one African American on the list for whom there was a photograph (Oprah Winfrey), but we were still left with 170 photographs to rate (96 in 1994, and 74 in 1995). The range of scores was from one to six, and the mean score was 2.9. Thus the skin-color ratings of Hispanic influentials were much closer to those of non-Hispanic rich whites than to those of prominent African Americans.

We also looked to see whether there were differences based on sex and whether those Hispanic influentials who sat on *Fortune*-level boards were rated as lighter skinned than the other influentials. Both variables were significant: the Latinas were rated as lighter (with a mean score of 2.82) than the Latinos (3.58), and the nine men and three women who sat on *Fortune*-level boards were rated as lighter (2.92) than the other Hispanic influentials (3.42).[29]

We were struck not only by the light skin color of the Hispanic corporate directors but by how overwhelmingly "Anglo" they appeared. We were sure we would have a hard time identifying some of them as Hispanics if we did not

28. The use of color cards to assess skin color is described in Selena Bond and Thomas F. Cash, "Black Beauty: Skin Color and Body Images Among African-American College Women," *Journal of Applied Social Psychology* 22, no. 11 (1992), 874–888.

29. These differences were statistically significant. When we ran a regression analysis in which skin color was the dependent variable and both gender and presence or absence on *Fortune* boards were predictive variables, the resulting $F$ was 9.83 ($p < .0001$). As was the case with African Americans, sex was a stronger predictor (beta = .29, $p < .0001$) than presence on *Fortune* boards (beta = .11, $p < .12$).

have other clues, like Hispanic-sounding names or inclusion of their photos in a magazine called *Hispanic Business*. In order to test this more systematically, we constructed a booklet with twenty-eight photographs of CEOs, chairpersons, or directors of large corporations, all of which we cut out of issues of *Fortune, Ebony,* or *Hispanic Business*. Seventeen of the photos were of white men and women, three were of black men, three of black women, three of Hispanic men, and two of Hispanic women. One of the Latinos was Cuban and the other two were Mexican American; both Latinas were from New Mexico. We showed these to ten current or recent students at Guilford College in Greensboro, North Carolina, and asked them to tell us which of the 28 people were white, which were black, and which were Hispanic. As expected, the accuracy rate was quite high for whites (87 percent); the relatively few errors were made because some students thought certain of the darker-skinned men or women were Hispanic. The accuracy rate was also quite high for black men (90 percent) and fairly high for black women (60 percent); the blacks who were misidentified were thought to be Hispanic, especially one of the three black women. In sharp contrast, and confirming our own less systematic observations, the accuracy rate for identifying Hispanics was only 40 percent for the men and 30 percent for the women; in every case but one, when errors were made the Hispanics were thought to be white. (In the one exception, a Hispanic male was perceived by one of the raters as black.) We replicated this little study on the campus of the University of California, Santa Cruz, and found that the students were a bit more accurate in identifying Hispanics but still thought they were white about half the time.[30]

---

30. The accuracy scores of the UCSC students were quite similar to those of the Guilford College students for whites (89 and 90 percent, respectively), black men (97 and 90 percent), and black women (54 and 60 percent). The UCSC students were more accurate than the Guilford College students in identifying both Hispanic men (57 and 40 percent) and Hispanic women (40 and 30 percent).

Unable to contain our curiosity, we showed the photographs to six Latino students at UCSC. They were somewhat less accurate than the other UCSC students in identifying the Hispanic men (44 percent) but more accurate in identifying the Hispanic women (67 percent). Their combined accuracy rate for the Hispanics was 53 percent — virtually the same as the non-Hispanic UCSC students.

When a Latino reader in Texas chastised *Hispanic Business* in November 1996 because the 1995 and 1996 stories on the top influentials, top executives, and multimillionaires "failed to include a single dark face," the magazine replied that each of the three lists contained Hispanics with "African ancestry" and claimed that "basing your conclusions on visual evidence alone makes for a faulty argument." But as the reader is saying, and as our evidence shows, there are few "dark faces" at the top whatever their ancestry. See

## Latinos in the Cabinet

It was not until 1988 that there was a Hispanic member of the cabinet, and he was an unexpected and unlikely one at that. On the eve of the Republican convention that year, as his eight years as president were about to end, Ronald Reagan's sudden announcement of Lauro Cavazos, a Democrat and college president, as the new secretary of education may have seemed a bit unusual to the casual eye. But his friend and vice president, George Bush, was struggling in his campaign for president at the time, especially in Texas. Because the Democratic nominee for vice president, Lloyd Bentson, was a popular senator from Texas, the Republicans feared that Bush would lose the state and its many electoral votes. Since Bush had already proclaimed that he would become "the education president" and that he would appoint a Latino to his cabinet, Reagan decided to help matters along with a person who just happened to be a registered Democrat from Texas. In the words of Alicia Sandoval, a spokeswoman for the National Education Association, the appointment of Cavazos was "just a ploy to help get Bush elected and carry Texas . . . a classic case of tokenism."[31] Bush did carry Texas on his way to victory, and he reappointed Cavazos, who served until December of 1990, when he was forced to resign because Bush's advisers considered him ineffectual.[32]

Cavazos grew up on an 800,000-acre ranch, where his father worked for forty-three years as a foreman in the cattle division. He was educated in a one-room schoolhouse for the children of the ranch's Mexican laborers until, when he was eight years old, his father persuaded reluctant officials in a nearby town to let his children attend what had been up to that time an all-Anglo school. After graduating from high school in 1945, Cavazos served for a year in the army, then began what was to become a lengthy and conventional climb through the ranks of academe. First, he received a B.A. and an M.A. in zoology from Texas Technological College (now Texas Tech University) and a Ph.D. from Iowa State. After teaching at the Medical College of Virginia for ten years, he left to become professor and chairman of the anatomy department at the Tufts University School of Medicine. He rose through the administrative ranks over the next sixteen years, becoming the dean in 1975. He left in 1980 to return to Texas Tech as president, the position he held when Ronald Reagan came calling.

---

Gustavo E. Gonzales, "Are Black Hispanics Being Ignored?" *Hispanic Business,* November 1996, p. 6.

31. "Lauro F. Cavazos, Jr.," *Current Biography* (1989), 97.

32. Maureen Dowd, "Cavazos Quits as Education Chief Amid Pressure from White House," *New York Times,* September 13, 1990.

Not content with one Latino cabinet member, Bush appointed Republican Congressman Manuel Lujan of New Mexico as his secretary of the interior. Born in 1928, Lujan first won election in 1968. He is another example of a conservative Spanish American from New Mexico. In spite of twenty years as a member of the House Committee on Interior and Insular Affairs, where he usually sided with developers in their battles with environmentalists, Lujan showed little understanding of any important land, water, or environmental issues when he assumed his cabinet post. *Time* declared that his record was "dismal" and that he was "clueless on environmental issues and often embarrassed himself making policy statements on matters of which he was ignorant." The conservative British magazine the *Economist* said he had a "blank interior." An article in the *Audubon* spoke of his "incompetence," and the *New Republic* called him "the dregs of the Bush cabinet."³³

Lujan was raised near Santa Fe in privileged circumstances. His father ran a successful insurance agency and served three terms as mayor of Santa Fe, although he did fail in his bids for Congress and the governorship. Lujan joined his father's business in 1948 after graduating from the College of Santa Fe and worked there for twenty years, eventually moving the business to Albuquerque. He won a seat in Congress in the 1968 elections by making an ethnic appeal to the traditionally Democratic Mexican-American voters in his district. By 1995 he was a Fortune 1000 director for the Public Service Company of New Mexico, a gas and electric utility.³⁴

In January 1993 two Latino men — Henry Cisneros and Frederico Peña — became members of Bill Clinton's cabinet. There are some striking similarities between the two. Both were born in Texas in the spring of 1947 into stable middle-class families (Cisneros's father was a civilian administrator for the army, and Peña's father was a broker for a cotton manufacturer). Both attended Catholic schools, received B.A. degrees from universities in Texas, went on to earn postgraduate degrees (a Ph.D. for Cisneros, a law degree for Peña), became the first Latino mayors of the cities in which they lived in the early 1980s (Cisneros of San Antonio in 1981, Peña of Denver in 1983), were reelected throughout the 1980s, and, by the early 1990s, were partners in private investment companies (Cisneros, Asset Management, and Peña, Investment Advisors, Inc.). By spring 1995, both were out of the investment

33. Ted Gup, "The Stealth Secretary," *Time,* May 25, 1992, p. 57; "The Blank Interior of Manuel Lujan," *Economist,* September 22, 1990, p. 34; "Talk of the Trail," *Audubon,* July 1989, p. 20; Bruce Reed, "Half Watt: The Dregs of the Bush Cabinet," *New Republic,* October 16, 1989, p. 20.

34. "Manuel Lujan," *Current Biography* (1989), 354–358.

business and were being investigated by the Justice Department, Cisneros for allegations that he misled federal investigators during his prenomination interviews about payments he made to a former mistress, and Peña in connection with a contract awarded in 1993 to an investment firm he had just left.[35] Though both had their troubles, both got through them. Peña remained in Clinton's cabinet, and Cisneros became president of Univision.

## Latinos in the Military Elite

There have been few Latinos of general officer rank in the armed forces of the United States. Of the 1,067 people who held that rank in 1985, only two were Latinos (one in the navy, the other in the air force). Over the next decade, the number of Latinos with general officer rank increased steadily, but only to ten; the corresponding percentage increase was from 0.2 percent to 1.1 percent. None of the Latino general officers during that decade was a marine, and none of the ten in 1995 was a woman. (From 1986 through 1988, there was one Latina in the air force with general officer rank.)

An examination of the next few levels of the officer ranks for the same years suggests that Latino generals and admirals will remain rare. The percentage of Latinos at those levels increased from a meager 1.6 percent to only 2.5 percent. Because there are high attrition rates for all ethnic groups between colonel and general, there is very little chance of a substantial increase in Latinos at the elite level of the military over the next few years.

As with African Americans in the previous chapter, we considered the longer-term prospects for an increasing Latino presence in the top levels of the military by looking at graduation figures for the three major service academies. For all three services the numbers on Latinos are available only from 1975 to 1989. They show a rise from five or fewer graduates a year in 1975 to forty-seven at West Point, fifty-two at the Naval Academy, and forty at the Air Force Academy in 1989. In each of the three academies there were more blacks than Latinos in 1989, so the military is likely to remain a more important avenue of upward mobility for blacks than for Latinos.[36]

35. "Henry G. Cisneros," *Current Biography* (1987), 87–96; "Frederico F. Peña," *Current Biography* (1993), 460–464; David Johnston, "Concluding That Cisneros Lied, Reno Urges a Special Prosecutor," *New York Times,* March 15, 1995. Shortly after the 1996 election, Cisneros resigned. See Steven A. Holmes, "Housing Secretary Resigns, Citing Financial Pressures," *New York Times,* November 22, 1996.

36. "Hispanic-American Graduates of the Military Academies, 1966–1989," in *Hispanics in America's Defense* (Washington, D.C.: Department of Defense, U.S. Govern-

## Latinos in Congress

Due to a concentrated population base in the state of New Mexico and in some congressional districts, Latinos have gradually developed a small amount of political representation in Congress. The story could begin with those few who were elected from the territories of Florida and New Mexico in the nineteenth century, or with those elected to the House from Louisiana or New Mexico after 1912, but we will restrict ourselves to the two senators elected since 1935 and the twenty-two members of the House first elected after 1960.

### THE SENATE

There have been two Latino senators, Dennis Chávez and Joseph Montoya, both Democrats from New Mexico whose families had lived in the area for several generations. Chávez, first appointed to the Senate in 1935, was born in 1888 on a family-owned ranch in New Mexico that traced back to a land grant from the king of Spain in 1769. Still, his parents were poor, he was one of eight children, and he was forced to drop out of school in the eighth grade to go to work. He drove a grocery wagon and then was hired to work in the Albuquerque Engineering Department. In the 1916 election, he worked as a Spanish interpreter for Democratic Senator A. A. Jones. When Jones won the election, he took Chávez to Washington, where he became a Senate clerk. He studied law at Georgetown University (which required that he pass a special examination, because he held no high school diploma), and received his LL.B. in 1920.

Chávez then returned to Albuquerque, set up a law practice, and was elected to the New Mexico House of Representatives and then the U.S. House of Representatives as a Democrat. In 1934 he ran for the U.S. Senate and lost a bitterly contested election to Bronson F. Cutting. While he was in the process of challenging the election, Cutting was killed in a plane crash, and Chávez was appointed to replace him. He went on to win a special election and was reelected to serve four more terms in the Senate. Although he had been ill with cancer for more than a year, he ran again for the Senate in 1962, was reelected, returned to the hospital the day after the election, and died a few weeks later.[37]

Montoya's parents were descended from Spanish immigrants who settled in New Mexico in the eighteenth century. His father was a sheriff. Montoya won

---

ment Printing Office, 1990), 181. See also *Black Americans in Defense of Our Nation* (Washington, D.C.: Department of Defense, U.S. Government Printing Office, 1991), 241–276.

37. "Dennis Chávez," *Current Biography* (1946), 109–112; "Senator Chávez, 74, Is Dead in Capital," *New York Times,* November 11, 1962.

election to the Senate in 1964. Like Chávez, he studied law at Georgetown Law School. While still a student there, he was elected to the New Mexico House of Representatives on the Democratic ticket. He moved from the state house to the state senate, became lieutenant governor, and in 1957 was elected to the U.S. House of Representatives. After serving four terms in the House, he was elected to the Senate in 1964. Montoya was defeated in 1976 after a series of newspaper articles detailed alleged improprieties involving a shopping center he owned in Santa Fe, claiming that he had received "special treatment" from the IRS, whose budget was reviewed by a committee he headed. In addition, Montoya's name was one of those mentioned when South Korean businessman Tongsun Park was accused of attempting to buy influence in the United States by making contributions to the election campaigns of politicians. When Montoya died in 1978, he was "said to be a millionaire" according to the *New York Times*.[38]

### THE HOUSE

Of the twenty-six Latinos first elected to the House after 1960, twenty-two have been Democrats and only four Republicans. Typically, the Democrats are Mexican Americans from Texas or California and Puerto Ricans from New York, although a Mexican American from Arizona was elected to the House in 1990 and a Puerto Rican from Illinois was elected in 1992. Until 1996 none of the Mexican Americans had been from a well-to-do background. Three of the four Republican Latinos, on the other hand, came from solidly middle-class or higher backgrounds. Secretary of Interior Lujan is one of those well-to-do Republicans. The other two are Cuban Americans, an unsurprising finding, given the prominence of Cuban Americans in the corporate elite.

There are some exceptions to these generalizations, but they turn out to be very atypical. Robert Menéndez, elected in 1992 as the first Hispanic American from New Jersey to serve in the House, is an unusual Cuban-American Democrat. But Menéndez was born in New York City in 1954, before Castro came to power, and he did not have to leave his parents' native land under pressure. He grew up in New Jersey and was elected to the school board in Union City in 1974 while he was working on his B.A. at St. Peter's College. He received his law degree from Rutgers in 1976 and became mayor of Union City in 1986 and a member of the state legislature in 1987, moving from the assembly to the senate in 1991. He is married to a non-Hispanic

38. "Joseph M. Montoya Is Dead at 62; Was Senator in Watergate Inquiry," *New York Times,* June 6, 1978.

white, the former Jane Jacobsen. About 22 percent of the voters in his district are Latinos.[39]

Another Democrat, William Richardson, is even more atypical. Richardson's father, an Anglo, was a well-to-do banker, and his mother was a Mexican citizen. Richardson, born in Pasadena, California, grew up in Mexico City, where his father was an executive for Citibank, the only foreign-based bank in the city at the time. He went to Middlesex, an exclusive New England prep school, then to Tufts for a B.A. in 1970 and an M.A. in international relations in 1971. After graduation he spent three years in the State Department as a liaison to Congress, followed by three more years as a staff member for the Senate Foreign Relations Committee. Obviously looking for a place to settle where he could win a seat in Congress, Richardson moved to Santa Fe in 1979 to become executive director of the Democratic State Committee. In 1980, despite charges that he was a classic carpetbagger, he almost unseated the Republican incumbent, Manuel Lujan, outspending the affluent Lujan by more than $200,000. In 1982 he won a seat in a newly created district, carefully crafted by his Democratic friends in Congress to give him a strong Latino base, and in 1985 he was elected to a term as chair of the Congressional Hispanic Caucus. In December 1996, Bill Clinton appointed Bill Richardson chief delegate to the United Nations, replacing Madeline Albright.[40]

The second Republican Hispanic elected to the House since 1960, Illena Ros-Lehtinen, a Cuban American from Miami who had served in the state legislature since 1982, was seated in 1989 just as Lujan was leaving to become secretary of the interior. A 1975 graduate of Florida International University, she owned a private school in Miami. She was joined on the Republican side of the aisle in 1992 by a second Cuban American from southern Florida, Lincoln Díaz-Balart, whose wealthy family had once been active in Cuban politics.

Lujan, Ros-Lehtinen, and Díaz-Balart are prototypical Republicans, but the fourth Republican Hispanic, Henry Bonilla of Texas, most decidedly is not. His victory over an incumbent Latino Democrat, however, was an unlikely one based on very unusual circumstances. Born in 1954 in San Antonio into a low-income Mexican-American family, Bonilla graduated from the University of Texas in 1976, started as a radio announcer in Austin, and worked his way up in the television industry, including jobs in New York and Philadelphia, before returning to San Antonio in 1986 as an executive producer of the news and

39. *Congressional Quarterly,* January 16, 1993, p. 108.

40. See "Bill Richardson," *Current Biography* (April 1996), 37–40; James Brooke, "Traveling Troubleshooter Is Ready to Settle Down at the U.N.," *New York Times,* December 14, 1996.

later a public relations officer for a network affiliate. His wife, Deborah Knapp, a non-Hispanic white, was well known as the station's nightly newscaster.

Bonilla jumped into the 1992 election as a rare Mexican-American Republican because the four-term Democrat, Mexican-American Albert Bustamante, had been caught in the House banking scandal. He also was exposed for building a $600,000 home just outside his district in a wealthy neighborhood, and he was convicted of taking $340,000 in bribes. Under these circumstances, Bonilla attracted the votes of angry Mexican-American Democrats (who overwhelmingly supported the Clinton-Gore ticket) even though he was an extremely conservative candidate. Sensing Bustamante's vulnerability, leading Republicans from around the country came to the area to boost Bonilla's candidacy.[41]

The three Mexican Americans first elected to Congress in 1996 follow the patterns described so far in some ways, but they were distinctive in others. Like most Mexican Americans, all three were elected as Democrats. Silvestre Reyes started as a farm worker as a youngster but was regional chief of the Border Patrol in El Paso when he retired to run for office. He won his spurs with Mexican Americans and Anglos alike in 1993 when he stationed his staff one hundred yards apart for twenty-four hours a day along the border to halt illegal immigration. Laura Sánchez, like Reyes, was the child of immigrant parents (she was one of seven children). But Sánchez had married Stephen Brixey III, a bond salesman, earned an M.B.A., and become a Republican. In 1996 she switched her registration to Democratic, dropped her Anglo married name, and defeated an extreme right-wing incumbent in the Republican stronghold of Orange County, California, with the help of donations from women's groups, environmentalists, and gays and lesbians, all of whom found her opponent, "B-1 Bob" Dornan, to be one of their worst enemies in Congress.

Though the third Mexican American elected in 1996, Ruben Hinojosa, is also a Democrat, he came from more fortunate economic circumstances than any of the Mexican Americans previously elected to Congress. Hinojosa's family had owned and operated a successful family meatpacking company, H & H Meats of Mercedes, Texas. In the mid-1990s, with Hinojosa as its president, it was the thirty-ninth-largest Hispanic business, with $52 million in sales and 320 employees. Hinojosa is the first Hispanic business leader of major stature to be elected to Congress.

Hispanic Americans are part of the corporate community and will continue to be included, especially those with light skin and/or high-status social backgrounds in their ancestral countries. Such people are racially and culturally similar to the Europeans who came directly to the United States. In the case of Cuban Americans, they build on a strong immigrant business community in southern Florida that will continue to generate a disproportionate number of new members in the corporate elite. This point is underscored by the fact that only eleven of the seventy-five wealthiest Latinos for 1995 sat on a Fortune 1000 board, so there is a large pool of likely directors ready to be tapped.

The acceptance of light-skinned Hispanic Americans into American society in general and the corporate elite in particular can be seen most clearly in the marriage partners of the three women corporate directors we have highlighted in this chapter. Vilma Martínez married Stuart Singer, a fellow lawyer, in 1968. Patricia Díaz married Michael Dennis, also a lawyer, also in 1968, and she goes by the surname of Díaz Dennis. Katherine Ortega also married a lawyer, Lloyd Derrickson, in 1989.

The military has not been as important an avenue of upward mobility for Latinos and Latinas as for African Americans, but it has not been notable for discrimination against Latinos in the past, either. As for participation in the political arena, our conclusions are more tentative because there are too few cabinet appointees and elected officials to study. As with the other groups, though, appointed officials tend to come from higher socioeconomic backgrounds and to be present in both Republican and Democratic administrations. Elected officials, on the other hand, with the important exception of Cuban Americans, tend to come from the middle and lower levels of the society, and to be Democrats.

5

# Asian Americans in the Power Elite

If we were told that Shirley Young was a graduate of Wellesley College who became a vice president of General Motors in 1988 and serves on the boards of Bell Atlantic and the Promus Companies, most of us would be likely to see her as an example of the kind of success story that belongs in our earlier chapter on women. So, too, with Phyllis Campbell, the president and CEO of the U.S. Bank of Washington in Seattle, where she is also a director of Puget Power and Light Company, chairwoman of the Association of Washington Business, and vice chairwoman of the Greater Seattle Chamber of Commerce. In fact, although both might have been included in the chapter on women in the power elite, both are also Asian Americans.

Shirley Young was born in Shanghai in 1935, the daughter of a career diplomat in Chiang Kai-shek's Nationalist Chinese government who was killed by the Japanese in 1942. Arriving in the United States after the war, Young earned a B.A. in economics from Wellesley in 1955 and became one of the first members of the Wellesley corporate network as a market researcher, first with the Alfred Politz Research Organization, then with Hudson Paper Corporation, and then in 1959 with Grey Advertising, where she helped such companies as Proctor and Gamble, General Foods, and General Motors "understand how consumers go from thinking about a product to actually buying it."[1] In 1988 she left Grey to become a vice president at General Motors. In 1995 she was lauded in a headline in the *Wall Street Journal* for acting as a bridge to her native country after helping General Motors to "clinch a deal in China."[2] Along with her GM position and corporate directorships, she is chairwoman of the Committee of 100, a Chinese-American leadership group, and a member of the Committee of 200, an international organization of successful businesswomen.

Phyllis Campbell, born Phyllis Takisaki in Spokane in 1951, is a third-generation Japanese American whose grandfather lost his grocery store when he and his family were taken to a detention camp during World War II. The oldest of five children, she worked for her father after school in his small dry-cleaning business, where she developed a strong interest in accounting and finance. Her mother was a medical technologist. Campbell received B.A. and M.A. degrees in business administration from Washington State University and graduated from the University of Washington's Pacific Coast Banking School. She worked her way from branch manager to vice president in the banking corporation that she now heads. Her husband is a civil engineer.[3]

As members of minority groups, Shirley Young and Phyllis Campbell are not typical of most women in the power elite. Except for gender, however, they are typical of the Chinese Americans and Japanese Americans over the age of forty-five who have made it big in the United States. Unlike most Chinese immigrants before 1965, who came from low-income backgrounds, the great majority of the Chinese Americans at the top levels of the U.S. economy are from well-to-do or at least well-educated families in China, Taiwan, or Hong Kong. William Mow, for example, founder of Bugle Boy Industries in 1977, is the son of the man who was chief of Chiang Kai-shek's United Nations military committee when the Communists took over. Mow grew up in Great Neck, New York, studied engineering at Rensselaer Polytechnic Institute, and earned a Ph.D. in that field from Purdue.

Successful Chinese Americans often downplay the advantages they had on

1. Jim Henry, "Shirley Young," *Notable Asian Americans* (New York: Gale Research, 1995), 437–438.

2. Gabriella Stern, "GM Executive's Ties to Native Country Help Auto Maker Clinch Deal in China," *Wall Street Journal,* November 2, 1995.

3. Nancy Moore, "Phyllis Jean Takisaki Campbell," *Notable Asian Americans,* 24. For a detailed study of the Japanese-American experience that demonstrates just how typical Campbell's childhood was, see Edna Bonacich and John Modell, *The Economic Basis of Ethnic Solidarity: Small Business in the Japanese American Community* (Berkeley: University of California Press, 1980).

the way to the top in America. For example, Chang-Lin Tien, a former chancellor of the University of California and a director of Wells Fargo Bank, reports that he arrived in the United States at the age of twenty-one as a penniless immigrant, unable to speak English. True, but he also was born into a wealthy banking family in Wanchu, and his wife's father was a high-ranking officer in Chiang's army.[4]

Perhaps the best-known Chinese American is the television personality Connie Chung, daughter of a former intelligence officer in the Nationalist army who came to the United States in 1944 after losing five of his children in World War II. Chung received her B.A. from the University of Maryland in 1969.

As the very different social backgrounds of highly successful Chinese Americans like Shirley Young and Japanese Americans like Phyllis Takisaki Campbell suggest, the label *Asian American* is no more useful than *Hispanic* or *Latino*. The immigrant groups from a wide range of Asian countries included under that label do not share a common language, national heritage, or immigration pattern. Although they have formed some pan-Asian organizations to resist discrimination and ensure a fair share of social services at the local level, they often remain wary of one another because of historic enmities between their native countries.[5]

In this chapter we concentrate on the immigrant groups that come from China, Japan, and Korea, with the greatest emphasis on Chinese Americans and Japanese Americans, because we could not find more than a few members of other Asian-American immigrant groups in top positions. Their populations are too small, too recent, or too low on the income ladder to have had much national-level impact yet. The few exceptions usually came from the higher social levels of their native country.

In spite of the many differences among the various Asian-American immigrant groups, there are four generalizations that hold at least for the three groups on which we shall concentrate. First, they are very highly educated, either in their country of origin, in the case of immigrants since 1965, or else in the United States.[6] Second, and not fully appreciated in understanding

---

4. Chang-Lin Tien, "A View from Berkeley," *New York Times* Education Life Section, March 31, 1996, p. 30.

5. For an excellent account of efforts to create pan-Asian institutions, see Yen Le Espiritu, *Asian American Panethnicity* (Philadelphia: Temple University Press, 1992). Espiritu begins her account by noting that she is "a Vietnamese American who is married to a Filipino American" (xi).

6. For detailed information on the educational backgrounds of Asian Americans, see Deborah Woo, "The Glass Ceiling and Asian Americans," Glass Ceiling Commission, U.S. Department of Labor, Washington, D.C., 1994; Bill Ong Hing and Ronald Lee, eds., *Re-*

the acceptance of Asian Americans by white Americans, 63 percent of Asian Americans identify themselves as Christians according to a telephone survey of 113,000 people across the country. Christianity is strongest among Korean Americans, whose families in Korea began to adopt the religion at the turn of the twentieth century as a reaction to pressures from China and Japan. Christian churches founded by Korean Americans are also attended by Japanese Americans and Chinese Americans. Exact figures on the religious identification of Japanese Americans and Chinese Americans are not readily available, but it is known that only 4.1 percent of Asian Americans identify themselves as Buddhists.[7]

Third, many Asian Americans have ended up as "middlemen" in the United States in more ways than one, owing partly to their educational backgrounds, partly to their concentration in small businesses. Asian Americans in California, for example, say that in both large corporations and government agencies they often end up as middle managers, taking orders from white bosses and giving orders — and termination notices — to Hispanic and African-American workers; some of them cynically call themselves a "racial bourgeoisie."[8] But Asian Americans also often end up as middlemen in a second and more traditional sense, as small-business owners providing services and retailing in or near ghettoes and barrios, marketing the products of big corporations in areas where companies like Safeway, Sears, and Revco do not wish or dare to tread. This role has been especially common among Korean Americans in major cities like New York and Los Angeles in the past few decades, and this has led to some highly visible confrontations with African Americans and Mexican Americans.[9]

Fourth, there is evidence that most Asian Americans face difficulties in advancing to the highest levels of large organizations. They are stereotyped as

---

*framing the Immigration Debate: A Public Policy Report* (Los Angeles: LEAP Asian Pacific American Public Policy Institute and UCLA Asian American Studies Center, 1996).

7. Barry A. Kosmin and Seymour P. Lachman, *One Nation Under God: Religion in Contemporary Society* (New York: Harmony, 1993), 148. The overall figure is inflated somewhat by the fact that virtually all Filipino Americans are Christians, but it is the low figure for Buddhism that makes our general point. Most Asian Americans do not maintain a religious tradition that conflicts with the overwhelming predominance of Christianity in the United States. In the United States 86 percent of all people are Christian, 2 percent are Jewish, 8 percent secular, 2 percent "decline to state," and 1.5 percent "other."

8. Benjamin Pimentel, "Asian Americans' Awkward Status," *San Francisco Chronicle*, August 22, 1995.

9. See, for example, Ivan Light and Edna Bonacich, *Immigrant Entrepreneurs: Koreans in Los Angeles, 1965–1982* (Berkeley: University of California Press, 1988).

lacking in "interpersonal" and "leadership" skills and in their written or spoken English. Thus, despite high levels of educational attainment and considerable evidence of their general acceptance by white Americans, there may be limits to just how far Asian Americans can go in the power structure for at least another decade.[10]

## Asian Americans in the Corporate Elite

We have two sources of information on Asian Americans on corporate boards: a list from Directorship and a list compiled by the management consultant William Marumoto of Washington, D.C., whose company specializes in executive recruitment and selection. For information on the founders and managers of corporations we drew on three sources: a report on immigrant entrepreneurs by an Asian-American leadership group, a list compiled by Marumoto, and a sample of distinctive Chinese, Japanese, and Korean names drawn from *Poor's*.

According to Directorship's figures, the number of Asian Americans on the boards of the 750 publicly held companies in the Fortune 1000 rose from fifteen in 1992 to twenty-six in 1995 (see table 5.1). In order to obtain a large enough sample, we used past directors on Marumoto's list as well as the names provided by Directorship for a study of the social backgrounds of fifty-seven Asian-American directors.

The majority of these directors are Chinese Americans (61 percent), most of them born in China or Taiwan. With one exception, the other directors are all Japanese Americans. The exception is Korean American Wendy Lee Gramm, an economist, who is married to the ultraconservative Republican senator from Texas, Phil Gramm. Mrs. Gramm, born in Hawaii in 1945, comes to her Republican and conservative leanings naturally. Her father was a vice president of a sugar company, her mother a librarian. She received her B.A. from Wellesley in 1966 and her Ph.D. from Northwestern in 1971. She met and married Gramm in the 1970s, when they both taught economics at Texas A&M. She is a director of the Enron Corporation in Houston and was appointed by

10. For comprehensive reviews and analyses of the evidence concerning discrimination against Asian Americans in corporate, governmental, and academic settings, see Woo, "Glass Ceiling and Asian Americans," and Hing and Lee, *Reframing the Immigration Debate*. For an earlier summary of the situation facing Asian Americans and other minorities in the corporate world, and essays by minority executives on their experience, see Donna Thompson and Nancy DiTomaso, eds., *Ensuring Minority Success in Corporate Management* (New York: Plenum, 1988).

Table 5.1
*Asian-American Directors on Fortune 1000 Boards*

|  | Dec. 1992 | Dec. 1993 | Dec. 1994 | Oct. 1995 |
|---|---|---|---|---|
| Number of Asian Americans holding seats |  |  |  |  |
| Men | 14 | 30 | 27 | 23 |
| Women | 1 | 4 | 3 | 3 |
| Total | 15 | 34 | 30 | 26 |
|  | (0.2%) | (0.5%) | (0.4%) | (0.4%) |
| Number of seats held by Asian Americans |  |  |  |  |
| Men | 15 | 50 | 31 | 31 |
| Women | 1 | 5 | 4 | 7 |
| Total | 16 | 55 | 35 | 38 |

*Source:* Directorship.

George Bush in 1988 to the Commodity Futures Trading Commission. In the 1990s she was also on the board of the Chicago Mercantile Exchange.

There is less to table 5.1 than meets the eye when two factors are taken into consideration. First, five of the people on the list were directors at Wang Laboratories, founded in 1951 by Chinese-American immigrant An Wang, who died in 1990 at the age of seventy. Wang was a 1947 Ph.D. in applied physics from Harvard whose invention of magnetic core memory was the basis for major advances in the computer industry. Wang's innovative work helped make him one of the five richest people in the United States in the early 1980s, but his company failed to follow the market's turn to smaller personal computers and had to be transformed into a software and services provider in 1993 to escape bankruptcy. Second, the list is less impressive when we realize that fourteen of the directors are based in Hawaii, where they serve on the boards of relatively small companies like Hawaiian Electric Industries, Hawaiian Airlines, Bancorp of Hawaii, and First Hawaii Bank. Even at these companies, moreover, the Asian-American directors are a small presence on the boards — four of thirteen at Hawaiian Electric, three of fourteen at Hawaiian Airlines, three of nine at Bancorp Hawaii, and three of thirteen at First Hawaii Bank. Only three of these fourteen Hawaii-based directors have directorships on the mainland.

Pei-yuan Chia, former vice chairman of Citibank, was the highest ranking Asian-American executive and corporate director at a world-class U.S.

corporation until his unexpected retirement in 1996 at age fifty-six. He also was a prototypical Chinese-American member of the power elite. Born in Hong Kong in 1939, he grew up in a banking family. After receiving his B.A. from a university in Taiwan in 1961, he came to the United States in 1962 and earned an M.B.A. from the Wharton School of Business at the University of Pennsylvania in 1965. He became a U.S. citizen in 1970, and from 1965 to 1973 he was a products group manager for General Foods. In 1973 he moved to Citibank, where he worked in consumer banking, which was then secondary to corporate accounts. He caught the tidal wave of growth in credit cards and helped Citibank develop consumer banks for upscale customers in three dozen countries, making large profits in the process. In 1992 he was elevated to the six-person management group that runs Citibank, and in 1994 he became one of four vice chairmen.[11]

Although Chia was the highest-ranking Asian American in an established U.S. corporation, he was by no means the richest. In 1995 that honor went to developer Ronnie Chan, age forty-five, a naturalized U.S. citizen with an M.B.A. from the University of Southern California. Chan runs the Hong Kong–based Hang Long Development Corporation, a company that he inherited from his father. Right behind Chan is Charles B. Wang of New York (no relation to An Wang), estimated by *Forbes* to be worth $410 million in 1995. Wang was born in 1944 in Shanghai, where his father was a Supreme Court justice, and he came to New York at the age of eight. After graduating from Queens College in 1967 with a degree in mathematics, he worked for Columbia University's Riverside Research Institute and for Standard Data Corporation. In 1977 he founded Computer Associates International, which develops software for businesses and is today a Fortune 1000 company, second only to Microsoft in size and importance in the industry.

Although there are some wealthy investors and company founders on top-level boards, most Asian-American corporate directors worked their way up the corporate ladder. Robert Nakasone, for example, served as president of Toys R Us in the early 1990s. He obtained a B.A. from Claremont College in 1969 and an M.B.A. from the University of Chicago in 1971, then worked for Jewel Foods before joining the toy company in 1986. George Hayashi worked his way up to the presidency of American Presidents Lines, a shipping company. Lee Liu, president of IES, an electric utility in Iowa, worked for the firm for most of his adult life. Ross Harano, after earning a B.A. in finance from the

---

11. Michael Quint, "Moving Up at Citicorp," *New York Times,* January 19, 1992; "Chia, Citicorp's Head of Consumer Banking, Made a Vice Chairman," *Wall Street Journal,* January 20, 1994.

University of Illinois in 1965, had a variety of business jobs before becoming president of the Chicago World Trade Center in 1993.

Still other directors come from foundations, law firms, and academic institutions, common routes to the top for directors of all social backgrounds. K. Tim Yee, a director of Bancorp Hawaii, is president of the Queen Emma Foundation in Honolulu. Michael Chun, the lone Asian-American director on the nine-member board of Alexander & Alexander, a Hawaiian conglomerate, is president of Kamehameda Schools in Honolulu, which serve descendants of the native people of Hawaii. Robert Hamada, a professor of finance and onetime dean of the School of Business at the University of Chicago, is a director of Northern Trust Corporation, a Chicago bank.

### IMMIGRANT ENTREPRENEURS

There are dozens of immigrant entrepreneurs in the computer and electronic industries. It is estimated that three hundred of the nine hundred high-technology firms in Santa Clara County, California — Silicon Valley — are headed by Asian-American immigrants. Most emigrated with a strong educational background, acquired further education in the United States, and then worked for established firms before venturing out on their own. Some have received financial backing for their start-up companies from wealthy Chinese venture capitalists outside the United States.[12]

Winston Chen, for example, came from Taiwan in 1965 and received M.S. and Ph.D. degrees in applied mathematics from Harvard. After eight years at IBM, he cofounded Solectron, a company that makes circuit boards for computers. In 1993 he sat on the board of directors of Intel, one of his main customers, and in 1995 he joined the board of Southern California Edison. Daniel Kwoh, Wilson Cho, and Henry Yuen are amassing their fortunes as the owners of the Gemstar Corporation, which markets a device for programming VCRs. Kwoh earned a Ph.D. in physics at California Institute of Technology, then worked as a research scientist at TRW. Yuen also graduated from Caltech and worked for TRW. Cho was a professor of physics at Hong Kong University.[13] None of the three is on a major board.

Not all immigrant entrepreneurs are in computers and electronics, and not all are men. Eleanor Yu founded Adlands in 1984, when she was only twenty-

12. Edward Jang-Woo Park, "Asians Matter: Asian American Entrepreneurs in the Silicon Valley High Technology Industry," in Hing and Lee, *Reframing the Immigration Debate,* 165–167.

13. See Melanie Erasmus, "Immigrant Entrepreneurs in the High-Tech Industry," in Hing and Lee, *Reframing the Immigration Debate,* 179–194, for these and other examples of immigrant entrepreneurs in high-tech industries.

five. It provides marketing advice and advertising skills to corporations that want to sell their products in Asia or in Asian-American communities in the United States. Revenues in 1993 were more than $16 million, making Adlands the largest advertising agency in the country targeted to Asian Americans.

Yu's father is a British businessman and lawyer who sits on several multinational boards; her mother is from a wealthy Hong Kong family. Born in Hong Kong, at age eleven Yu was sent to Oxford to attend the Headington Aristocratic Ladies College, a school for the children of diplomats and legislators. She then went to Oxford University. Following graduation she wanted to go to the United States, but her parents objected, so she went to Canada instead for a second B.A. at the University of Ottawa. Then, two degrees in hand though only twenty years old, she headed for New York to work for the advertising agency Ogilvy and Mather. Three months later she moved to Philadelphia when her husband, Kenneth Yu, was transferred there by Bell Labs. After five years with J. Walter Thompson in Philadelphia, she moved to San Francisco when her husband became a professor at the University of California. There she opened Adlands, later establishing offices in Hong Kong, Sydney, and Toronto and a print shop in Hong Kong. In 1991 an Asian-American voluntary organization named her Outstanding Asian-American Woman of the Year, but perhaps she is more accurately described as a member of the international business community who decided to set up shop in the United States.[14]

There are, however, authentic bootstrappers among Chinese-American immigrants, and one of them, Sue Ling Gin, sat on the boards of Commonwealth Edison, a public utility in Chicago, and the Michigan National Corporation, a banking company, in 1995. Gin started working in her family's small restaurant outside Chicago at the age of ten and took on major responsibilities as a teenager after her father died. She also worked in a sewing factory and a laundromat to help make ends meet. She went to DePaul University in fall 1959 but dropped out to work at a variety of jobs before opening her own real estate firm. She hired an all-female staff — not, she explained to one interviewer, out of feminist principles, but "because women would work for lower wages."[15] She made her first million speculating in run-down Chicago real estate and acquired two restaurants. In 1983 she started Flying Fare Foods to provide food services for airlines flying in and out of Chicago's Midway Airport. In 1984, at age forty-three, she married for the first time. Her husband, William McGowan, thirteen years older than she, was born into a working-class Irish-American family, but by then he was CEO of MCI.

14. Jim Henry, "Eleanor Yu," *Notable Asian Americans,* 442–444.
15. Leslie Wayne, "Together Apart," *New York Times Magazine,* March 27, 1988, 38.

When we compare the careers of Chinese-American and Japanese-American directors, we see that they tended to follow different pathways to the top. The Chinese Americans were more likely to be investors or founders of their own companies who were later invited to serve on the boards of other companies. The Japanese Americans were more likely to have climbed the corporate ladder in established companies or to come from legal or academic backgrounds.

We found relatively few multimillionaires in the Japanese-American community, whether on Fortune 1000 boards or not. The only Japanese American on the Forbes Richest 400 list for 1995 was a farmer and developer, Katsumasa "Roy" Sakioka, with a net worth estimated at $350 million. Sakioka, who kept out of the limelight and did not sit on any major boards, was born in a farm village in Japan in 1899 and came to the United States at the age of eighteen. He had been a tenant farmer for more than two decades when he was interned at Manzanar during World War II, but after the war he and his children were able to buy farmland in Orange County, California, in anticipation of urban growth spilling over from Los Angeles. When Sakioka died in late 1995 his businesses were taken over by his surviving family of five children and seventeen grandchildren. Except for the founder's death the only mention of any Sakioka in the *Los Angeles Times* since 1980 concerned a violation of state labor laws in 1983 by Sakioka Farms for asking migrant farm workers to use short-handled hoes to weed crops, putting its workers at risk for painful back injuries.[16]

The most prominent Japanese American of great wealth in the post–World War II era, George Aritani, age seventy-eight in 1995, would have inherited the thriving import-export business that his father founded in 1936, but he had to start all over again, albeit with cash in hand, because the business was sold when the family was put into an internment camp. Fortunately for Aritani, his parents had sent him to college in Japan in the 1930s, so after the war he was able to use his contacts there and his knowledge of Japanese business to create the Mikasa Corporation, which specialized in importing Japanese china. In 1995, when Aritani was still a director, the company had sales of $331 million and 1,800 employees, but in 1985 he had been bought out by his predominantly European-American executives for $32 million, so there is no family presence in the company.[17]

16. Bill Billiter, "Workers on Farm in Orange County Issued Illegal Hoes," *Los Angeles Times,* April 9, 1983; J. R. Moehringer, "Katsumasa Sakioka: Made Fortune in O.C. Real Estate," *Los Angeles Times,* November 1, 1995.

17. Damon Darlin, "Accessorizing the Dinner Table," *Forbes,* December 19, 1994, pp. 288–290.

Unlike Sakioka and Aritani, developer Bill Naito of Portland, Oregon, is one of the best-known business figures in the city because of his visible role in restoring the historic downtown area.[18] We could name a few other multimillionaires in the Japanese-American community, especially in Los Angeles and Seattle, but they are neither as numerous nor as visible as their Chinese-American counterparts, and they rarely serve on major corporate boards.

### THE CORPORATE PIPELINE

There is little systematic information available on Asian-American executives below the top echelon of the corporate community. At a very general level, however, it is likely that Asian Americans are underrepresented in management positions even though they have excellent educational backgrounds and are well represented in the professional ranks of corporations. This is true even in Silicon Valley, where only 22 percent of the Asian-American professionals become officers and managers, as compared to 35 percent of the white professionals.[19]

The most specific information on executives was developed by William Marumoto for the late 1980s and early 1990s. He found that Asian Americans had served as senior vice presidents at Lockheed, U.S. West Communications, Microsoft, Burlington Northern, Pitney Bowes, Pacific Bell, Hughes Aircraft, Bank of America, Sony, Tristar Pictures, Turner Broadcasting System, and First Interstate Bank of Washington.

To explore possible increases in Asian-American representation in higher management, we studied distinctive Chinese, Japanese, and Korean names listed in *Poor's* for 1965, 1975, 1985, and 1995, paralleling our use of distinctive Jewish and Hispanic names in earlier chapters. In the case of Chinese Americans, we used the names Wang, Wong, Woo, and Wu, which account for 13 percent of the 2,801 Chinese-American entries from China, Taiwan, and Hong Kong in *Who's Who Among Asian Americans*, giving us a multiplier of 7.7 to obtain estimates of the total number of Chinese Americans in *Poor's* for those years.[20] For Japanese Americans, we used any name beginning with

18. Gary Eisler, "Only in Portland," *Forbes,* April 4, 1988, p. 132.

19. Park, "Asians Matter," 166–167. See Woo, "Glass Ceiling and Asian Americans," for further details. For a quantitative study using logit regression analysis to show that Asian-American scientists and engineers are less likely than their white counterparts to be advanced to management positions, see Joyce Tang, "Glass Ceiling in Science and Engineering," *Journal of Socio-Economics* 26, no. 4 (1997), in press. Tang's work shows that being native born or, in the case of immigrants, being a longtime resident of the United States, does not improve one's odds of moving into a management role.

20. See Chapter 4, note 27, for details on the generation and use of this multiplier.

Table 5.2
*Estimated Asian-American and Hispanic Increases in Higher Management,*
*1965–1995*

|  | 1965 | 1975 | 1985 | 1995 | 1995 N/1965 N |
|---|---|---|---|---|---|
| Hispanics | 78 | 131 | 235 | 374 | 5.3 |
| Japanese Americans | 24 | 65 | 88 | 112 | 5.2 |
| Chinese Americans | 15 | 69 | 92 | 177 | 13.0 |
| Korean Americans | 0 | 0 | 20 | 20 | |
| Est. *Poor's* total | 75,639 | 73,649 | 76,449 | 68,423 | |

seven distinctive prefixes — Haya, Kawa, Koba, Miya, Naka, Taku, and Yama. These names account for 17 percent of the 882 Japanese Americans in *Who's Who Among Asian Americans,* giving us a multiplier of 5.9. Finally, we sampled Korean Americans with the distinctive surname Kim, which accounts for an amazing 25 percent of all Koreans and Korean Americans at all levels of the social ladder.[21]

In table 5.2 we present our estimated total number of Chinese Americans, Japanese Americans, and Korean Americans in *Poor's* for 1965, 1975, 1985, and 1995. To provide a further comparison, we include our earlier estimates for Hispanic Americans for the same years. As we noted in the previous chapter, the raw figures underestimate the rise in the rate of participation because there were 7,200 fewer names in *Poor's* in 1995 than in 1965. We therefore include for the first three groups in the table a percentage increase between those two years, adjusted for the decline in total entries. Because there were no Kims in *Poor's* until 1985, no such adjustment was possible for Korean Americans.

As might be expected on the basis of group size, there were more than twice as many Hispanic Americans in *Poor's* than the largest Asian-American group, Chinese Americans. But the Chinese-American group grew the most, by a factor of 13. Taken together, the three Asian-American groups and Latinos have increased their participation to the point where they collectively account

21. Eui-Hang Shin and Eui-Young Yu, "Use of Surnames in Ethnic Research: The Case of Kims in the Korean-American Population," *Demography* 21, no. 3 (1984), 347–359. The most prominent Korean-American Kims are Andrew B. Kim, who founded his own investment company, Sit/Kim International Investments, after working for many years on Wall Street, and James Kim of Gladyne, Pennsylvania, whose computer stores, the Electronic Boutique, do several hundred million dollars' worth of business each year in shopping malls nationwide.

for 1 percent of the total number of executives, officers, and directors listed in *Poor's* in 1995.

The positions held by those Asian Americans listed in *Poor's* who were below the level of director, president, or CEO were primarily confined to finance, accounting, and research. They tended to be in financial or technical firms, especially electronics. This finding is consistent with the fact that 20–40 percent of the engineers and technical staff in some major companies in the electronics industry are Asian American.[22]

Given the relatively small numbers of Asian Americans who have been in the United States long enough to arrive at the top, and the negative stereotypes they face, their record of corporate involvement is impressive. As we noted at the outset of the chapter, subtle forms of discrimination have kept all but a few Asian immigrants from making it to the very top. But a considerable number — particularly those who entered American society at its middle or higher levels thanks to wealth or educational credentials, or who have acquired a good education since coming to the United States — are poised for advancement from the middle levels should that discrimination ever cease.

## The Political Directorate

No Asian American has ever been appointed to a president's cabinet, so we will lower our political threshhold to include lower-level appointees in the executive branch. Patsy Takemoto Mink, named assistant secretary of state for ocean and international, environmental, and scientific affairs by Jimmy Carter in 1977, was the first Asian American whose executive-branch appointment required Senate confirmation. Mink was born in 1927 into modest circumstances in Hawaii, where her father was a civil engineer. After graduating from high school as class valedictorian, she earned a B.A. at the University of Hawaii and a law degree at the University of Chicago, where she met and married John Mink, a graduate student in geophysics of Eastern European extraction. In spite of her excellent educational credentials, it was difficult for her to obtain a legal position in either Chicago or Honolulu, so she finally started her own practice in Honolulu.

Mink was elected president of the Young Democrats in Honolulu in 1954. In 1957 she was elected to the state legislature, where she sponsored a law mandating equal pay for equal work. In 1965 she became the first woman from a minority background to be elected to Congress. After serving six terms in the House, she failed in a bid for the Senate, and at that point received her State Department appointment. Mink left the State Department in 1978 to serve

22. Erasmus, "Immigrant Entrepreneurs," 180.

three consecutive terms as national president of Americans for Democratic Action. In 1983 she was elected to the Honolulu City Council, and in 1990 she returned to the House of Representatives, where she continues to serve.[23]

Julia Chang Bloch, born in China in 1942, came to the United States in 1951 and obtained a B.A. at the University of California in 1964 and an M.A. in Far Eastern Studies at Harvard in 1967. Bloch had two firsts to her credit during the Republican administrations of the 1980s. When she was appointed by Reagan to be an administrator in the Agency for International Development in 1981, she became the first Asian American to head a major agency. In 1989 she became the first Asian American to serve as an ambassador, when George Bush appointed her to head the embassy in Nepal. Married to Stuart Marshall Bloch in 1968, she worked in both the legislative and executive branches of the federal government before her appointment in 1981. In 1993 she left government to become a vice president for corporate relations at the Bank of America in San Francisco.

Elaine Chao, appointed by Bush to head the Peace Corps in 1991, came to New York from Taiwan with her family in 1961 when she was eight years old. Her father soon developed a shipping and trading business, Foremost Maritime Corporation. After graduating from Mount Holyoke College and Harvard Business School, Chao worked in international finance at Citicorp from 1979 to 1983. She spent 1983 and 1984 in Washington as a White House Fellow, then became a vice president for syndications at the Bank of America. While working for the bank in California, she became more involved in Republican politics, chairing a national committee of Asian Americans for Bush and Quayle in 1988. This earned her appointments as deputy administrator of the Maritime Administration and later as deputy secretary of the Department of Transportation before her Peace Corps appointment. In 1993, Chao married Mitch McConnell, a Republican senator from Kentucky. After leaving government, she became president of United Way and a director of Dole Foods.

The highest-ranking Asian-American official in the Clinton administration has been Lon Hatamiya, a Japanese American born in 1959 in California to parents who owned a large orchard company. Hatamiya received his B.A. from Harvard in 1981, then worked as a purchasing manager for Proctor and Gamble for a few years before returning to school to earn both an M.B.A. and an LL.B. from UCLA in 1987. He worked in a corporate law firm for two years, then returned home to run the family business. Clinton appointed him administrator of agricultural marketing services in the Department of Agriculture in 1993.

Clinton's other top-level appointee from the Asian-American community is

23. Samuel R. Cacas, "Patsy Takemoto Mink," *Notable Asian Americans,* 261–262.

Dennis Hayashi, director of the Office for Civil Rights. Hayashi, a third-generation Japanese American from Los Angeles, received his B.A. from Occidental College in 1974 and his law degree from Hastings College, a part of the University of California, in 1978. He immediately went to work for the Asian Law Caucus in San Francisco, litigating civil rights cases and challenging the legality of the World War II internment. In 1991 he became national director of the Japanese American Citizens League, founded in 1929, the oldest Asian-American civil rights organization.

### Asian Americans in the Military Elite

In spite of the aspersions cast upon their patriotism and the bitter internment experience, Japanese Americans volunteered for service in World War II and fought courageously throughout Europe. Two future Democratic senators from Hawaii, Daniel Inouye and Spark Matsunaga, both decorated for bravery on the field of battle, used veterans organizations in Hawaii as their political base in winning election. Japanese Americans also served in important roles as intelligence officers and interrogators of prisoners in the war with Japan. Nonetheless, the military has never been an avenue of mobility for Japanese Americans, and there are virtually none in the military elite.

Nor have many members of the other Asian-American groups reached the higher military circles. The few who approached the top in the 1980s, like Gen. William Chen, Rear Adm. Ming Chang, and Maj. Gen. John Fugh, came from high-ranking families in China and acquired advanced degrees in engineering, law, or medicine. Fugh, for example, was judge advocate general of the army before he retired in 1993 to join a corporate law firm in Washington, D.C. Another prominent Chinese American in the military, Maj. Gen. Vernon Chong, was a physician who became head of military hospitals in Texas.

Further, there is little likelihood that more Asian Americans will emerge at the top of the military hierarchy in the foreseeable future, for the pipeline is nearly empty. Only three Asian Americans were among the 893 men and women in the top five ranks in 1995 (0.3 percent), a slight decline from 1985, when there were six out of 1,067 (0.6 percent). We must conclude that in the future the corporate elite and the political directorate will be far more important than the military for Asian Americans who aspire to the power elite.

### Asian Americans in Congress

Five Asian Americans have been elected to the Senate, four from Hawaii and one from California. Eight have been elected to the House, five from

Hawaii and three from California. But three of the five House members from Hawaii went on to be senators, so the total of Asian Americans elected to Congress is ten.

Asian-American elected officials tend to be from more modest social and educational backgrounds than members of the corporate world or appointed government officials. Although the first Asian American elected to the U.S. Senate, Hiram Fong of Hawaii, a Chinese American, became a millionaire, his father had been an indentured servant on a sugar plantation and his mother a maid. Fong earned a B.A. at the University of Hawaii in 1930 and an LL.B. at Harvard Law School in 1935, then returned to Hawaii to begin his political career, amassing his fortune along the way. Daniel Inouye, a Japanese American born in Honolulu in 1924, served in the House for four years and in 1963 became the first Asian-American Democrat elected to the Senate. His father was a file clerk. Following his service in World War II, where he lost his arm in the fighting in Italy, Inouye earned a B.A. at the University of Hawaii and a law degree from George Washington University, then entered the political arena, where he has been ever since.

Spark Matsunaga, from a poor immigrant Japanese family, worked many different jobs as a teenager, then graduated from the University of Hawaii in 1941 and served in World War II. After the war he used the G.I. bill to earn a law degree at Harvard and returned to Hawaii to serve as a Honolulu prosecutor and involve himself in Democratic Party politics. He won a seat in the House in 1962 and defeated Hiram Fong in 1976 to join Inouye in the Senate. When Matsunaga died in 1990, his seat was won by Daniel Akaka, of Hawaiian and Chinese heritage; his father had a third-grade education and worked in a machine shop. Akaka went to the University of Hawaii on the G.I. bill, earning his B.A. in education, and worked as a teacher, principal, and program specialist for the state's Department of Education before winning a seat in the House in 1976 with 80 percent of the vote.

The fifth Asian-American senator, and the only one from a mainland state, would have to be classified as atypical whatever his social or ethnic background, and he was not born in the United States. S. I. Hayakawa, a one-term Republican senator from California from 1975 to 1981, was born in 1906 in Canada, where his well-to-do Japanese parents had an import-export business. Hayakawa completed his B.A. and M.A. in Canada, then came to the United States to earn a Ph.D. in English and American literature at the University of Wisconsin in 1953. Along the way he developed a fascination with pseudoscientific claims about "general semantics," and in 1949 he wrote a best-selling popular book, *Language in Thought and Action*. Hayakawa taught at San Francisco State University from 1955 and became a vice president there in 1968. His confrontational stance toward antiwar and civil rights protesters made him a conservative celebrity. His theatrics led to his elevation to the presidency of the campus. He switched his registration from Democratic to Republican and won his Senate seat in 1974 while receiving little support from Japanese-American voters. He was an abysmal failure as a legislator, falling asleep at inopportune moments, making inappropriate remarks, and generally ignoring the details of his position. Voters rejected him for a Democrat in 1980, despite the general Republican sweep that year.

Although generalizations are premature at this point, it is noteworthy that the only Chinese-American senator, Hiram Fong, was a well-to-do and conservative Republican, whereas the senator of mixed heritage, Daniel Akaka, and the two Japanese-American senators from Hawaii were moderate-to-liberal Democrats. Hayakawa blurs the picture somewhat because he became a Republican in the 1970s, but he was also a Japanese Canadian with a very atypical personality and career.

When we turn to the House, we find that the pattern of party differences seen in the Senate is reinforced. If we set aside Inouye, Matsunaga, and Akaka, each of whom became a senator after serving in the House, then five additional Asian Americans have served there, two from Hawaii and three from California. Of the four Japanese Americans, three have been Democrats, and all either came from low-income circumstances or had parents who did. The fifth, Jay Kim, who founded his own engineering firm in Southern California, is of Korean ancestry and is a Republican.[24]

The patterns among the subgroups encompassed by the term *Asian Americans* show cleavages similar to those found among Latinos. The wealthier and better-educated immigrants — in this case Chinese Americans — tend to be the corporate directors and appointees in Republican administrations. Immigrants who came to the United States from less privileged socioeconomic backgrounds — in this case Japanese Americans — are more likely to be elected officials. Japanese Americans, with their history of communal sharing to establish small farms and small businesses, and with their common experience of arbitrary incarceration during World War II, are defenders of civil liberties who tend to be Democrats.

From the point of view of the power elite, successful Asian Americans have three main functions. First, they serve as "middlemen" in corporate management and in selling corporate products in low-income communities through

24. The four Japanese Americans are Patsy Mink (D-Hawaii), Patricia Saiki (R-Hawaii), Norman Mineta (D-Calif.), and Robert Matsui (D-Calif.).

small retail businesses. Second, they are "ambassadors" for their corporations to Asian countries and to Asian-American consumers in the United States. Third, they provide much-needed scientific and technical expertise in corporations, research institutes, engineering schools, and science departments.

We predict that Chinese Americans will become increasingly important members of the power elite. Not only are they growing in numbers, but they often arrive with strong educational credentials, considerable wealth, and conservative outlooks. They also have the ability to obtain loans from Chinese financiers in Hong Kong, Taiwan, and Singapore.[25] Japanese Americans, on the other hand, are likely to stay about where they are now as fourth- and even fifth-generation Americans. The Japanese-American community is not being infused with large numbers of new immigrants. Nor does it have strong ties to banks or corporations in Japan that might be a source of loans. Although Japanese Americans have been very successful, especially in obtaining excellent educational credentials, few have amassed large amounts of capital, so they are likely to turn to the professions even more in the future. They are also outmarrying at a very high rate, as we shall show in the final chapter, and they have a very low birthrate.[26]

Whatever the future may bring, the economic and political achievements of Chinese and Japanese Americans are such that old-line members of the power elite can claim that their circles are now diversified in terms of Asian Americans as well as women, African Americans, and Hispanic Americans.

But does the multiculturalism of the power elite extend to differences in sexual orientation on the part of either men or women? We shall address that question next.

25. Park, "Asians Matter," 167.
26. Norimitsu Onishi, "Japanese in America Looking Beyond Past to Shape Future," *New York Times,* December 25, 1995.

# 6

# Gay Men and Lesbians in the Power Elite

In June 1995, forty gay and lesbian leaders from around the country, many of them state legislators, city council members, or judges, came to Washington to meet with members of the Clinton administration. The lowlight of the event took place even before the meeting started: the security guards at the Executive Office Building, apparently afraid that they might contract AIDS if they happened to touch one of these visitors, were wearing bright blue rubber gloves when the delegates arrived. When one of the visitors, a state representative from Oregon, asked about the gloves, he was told that they were "for protection."[1]

It is dumbfounding that such an insensitive display could have taken place in an administration that had received major financial backing from gay and lesbian organizations and proclaimed a new openness to homosexuality. The glove incident symbolized both the changes that have taken place—no previous president had ever invited a group of gay and lesbian activists to Washington—and the continuing fears and prejudices that the topic of homosexu-

1. David W. Dunlap, "Clinton Names First Liaison to Gay and Lesbian Groups," *New York Times,* June 14, 1995. For a behind-the-scenes account of the glove incident, see David Mixner, *Stranger Among Friends* (New York: Bantam, 1996), 351–352.

ality inspires. It is apparent that doors have opened for gays and lesbians since Mills wrote *The Power Elite,* but fears and prejudices remain. Presumably there have always been homosexuals in the power elite, but there is no way to know who or how many. What we do know is that over the past few decades many gays and lesbians have chosen to be public about their sexual orientation, and this openness, and the political activism that has accompanied it, has contributed to changes in the lives of institutions as well as individuals. There are now openly gay men and women in almost all walks of life in America — but are there openly gay men and women in the power elite or Congress?

For the most part the answer is no, but this depends on what one means by "open." People tend to assume that homosexuals are either "in the closet" or "out" (and thus "open"), but in reality there are many shades in between. One study of hundreds of gay men and women in the corporate world found that most of those who remained closeted had revealed their sexual orientation to some of their coworkers. Many told the researchers that although they were out at work, they still did not want their real names published.[2] So there are gay men and women in the corporate world who are open about their homosexuality to certain colleagues, or even to most of their colleagues, but this information is not public in the sense that it is accessible to researchers trying to understand the extent to which the power elite has diversified.

Although the existence of a well-to-do and highly educated community of gay doctors, lawyers, entertainers, and business executives makes it possible in theory to determine who is and who is not gay in the power elite, our interest was not to "find" those who are homosexual but to explore whether or not people who happen to be homosexual and who have made it into the power elite are willing to be public about their homosexuality. So by "openly homosexual" we really mean "publicly homosexual." And, of course, we were interested in determining the extent to which continuing prejudices and barriers prevent gay men and lesbians from rising to the top.

## Gay Men and Lesbians in the Corporate Elite

There can be no doubt that the experiences of a gay man or woman working for a Fortune 500 company in the 1990s are likely to be different from those of his or her counterpart in the 1950s. The larger culture has

2. Annette Friskopp and Sharon Silverstein, *Straight Jobs, Gay Lives: Gay and Lesbian Professionals, the Harvard Business School, and the American Workplace* (New York: Scribners, 1995), 21, 24.

undergone dramatic changes in attitudes about sexuality in general, and so have some corporations.[3] Support groups for gay and lesbian employees have formed in many corporations, sometimes sanctioned by the company. According to an executive active in the gay employees' organization at Xerox, speaking in 1991, "Official or unofficial, there's a group in every large company in the U.S. Most are closeted, like the groups at Hughes and TRW. The president of the company may not know, but they're there."[4]

More significantly (and not unrelated to the growing influence of gay employees' organizations), by the mid-1990s some companies had extended health benefits to the live-in partners of homosexual employees, a development that for many was unthinkable in the late 1980s.[5] Annette Friskopp and Sharon Silverstein conducted interviews between 1990 and 1994 for their study of gay and lesbian graduates of the Harvard Business School. They found that none of those interviewed in 1990 even mentioned the lack of domestic partner benefits. When asked, they said that they did not think it was likely that such benefits would be provided in very many companies in the foreseeable future. But many of those interviewed in 1993 and 1994 raised this as an issue, and they were well aware that the number of companies providing such benefits had increased.[6] By 1995 not only had various West Coast companies already known for progressive corporate policies — Lotus, Apple Computer, and Levi Strauss, for example — added domestic-partner benefits, but even the Walt Disney Company, known throughout the years for its conservatism, had done so.[7]

3. See, for example, John D'Emilio and Estelle B. Freedman, *Intimate Matters: A History of Sexuality in America* (New York: Harper and Row, 1988); Bruce Bawer, *A Place at the Table* (New York: Poseidon, 1993), 52–54.

4. Thomas A. Stewart, "Gay in Corporate America," *Fortune,* December 16, 1991, pp. 42–56. The quotation appears on p. 43

5. Late in 1991, Lotus became the first publicly held major corporation to extend benefits to domestic partners of gay and lesbian employees. In February 1992, Levi Strauss became the second. Over the next few years, other companies also extended such benefits. James D. Woods, *The Corporate Closet: The Professional Lives of Gay Men in America* (New York: Free Press, 1993), 236–237. When IBM announced in October 1996 that it would extend benefits to the partners of gay and lesbian employees in its 110,000-person domestic workforce, it became the largest employer to extend health-care coverage to same-sex couples. See David Dunlap, "Gay Partners of I.B.M. Workers to Get Benefits," *New York Times,* September 20, 1996.

6. Friskopp and Silverstein, *Straight Jobs, Gay Lives,* 71.

7. Stewart, "Gay in Corporate America," 50; Woods, *Corporate Closet,* 236–237; Mireya A. Navarro, "Disney's Health Policy for Gay Employees Angers Religious Right in Florida," *New York Times,* November 29, 1995.

In spite of these changes, considerable evidence demonstrates that gays and lesbians continue to encounter prejudiced attitudes and discrimination in the corporate world, and there is reason to believe that the higher one moves in the executive ranks, the less likely is homosexuality to be acceptable. A survey of CEOs by the *Wall Street Journal* in the late 1980s revealed that two-thirds of the respondents said they would be reluctant to place a homosexual on their company's management committee. The author of a 1991 article noted that "though several CEOs of major companies are reputedly gay, none approached by *Fortune* was willing to be interviewed on or off the record."[8]

The literature on the experiences of homosexuals in the corporate world has been growing. Two studies are especially relevant to our focus on gays in the corporate elite. The first, by James Woods, grew out of a doctoral dissertation at the Annenberg School of Communications at the University of Pennsylvania. In 1990, Woods traveled around the country interviewing seventy gay men who worked as professionals, many (but not all) in law firms and corporations. (His was a snowball sample, in which an initial group of friends and contacts put him in touch with others.) Woods concluded: "They learn to control and monitor outward appearances, to distort them when necessary. They learn to dodge. For many the result is a calculating, deliberate way of approaching social encounters. One can say . . . that they *manage* their sexual identities at work."[9]

Woods identified three groups of gay men in the corporate world, each employing a different coping strategy. The first group he calls counterfeiters. They fabricate heterosexual identities, at times even marrying to mask their homosexuality. The second group, called integrators, are known to be gay. And the third group, which he considers the largest, he calls avoiders. They don't lie or fabricate false identities, nor are they open about their sexual orientation—instead, they remain somewhat aloof and hope the issue won't come up. In Woods's view, conditions had improved even since his own one-year stint in the corporate world (where he was a counterfeiter, and miserable) in 1985, before he enrolled in graduate school. Still, at the time Woods wrote a book based on his dissertation, relatively few companies had made major changes. He expressed the hope that "because heterosexism is expensive for both employers and employees, market forces may ultimately achieve what appeals to fairness and civil rights will not."[10]

The second valuable study of particular interest to us is Friskopp and Sil-

8. Stewart, "Gay in Corporate America," 45–46.
9. Woods, *Corporate Closet*, 28.
10. Ibid., 241.

verstein's research on the experiences of gay and lesbian graduates of the Harvard Business School. These two graduates of the business school (where they were members of the Gay and Lesbian Student Association) mailed a survey to more than one hundred people who were on the mailing list of the Harvard Gay and Lesbian Alumni Association; sixty-seven were returned. They also interviewed more than one hundred people, including some who had indicated on their returned surveys that they were willing to be interviewed. The authors spoke with gay and lesbian professionals from every graduating class since the late 1960s and with "a number" (they don't say how many) from the 1940s, 1950s, and early 1960s. All had gone to Harvard, and most had worked in the corporate world.[11]

Of their many findings and suggestions for homosexual employees and employers, most relevant for our purposes was their conclusion that "discrimination in the form of a hostile atmosphere, corporate cowardice, and unequal benefits is rampant." As a result, they write, "the fear of the lavender ceiling looms large for many," especially at "conservative" Fortune 500 companies.[12] Citing the fear of discrimination as one reason gay and lesbian employees remain closeted, Friskopp and Silverstein write:

> Those employed by America's most prominent conservative companies almost universally believed they would be discriminated against in some fashion if they were completely open about their gay identity in their current work environment. These professionals include those working for Fortune 500 manufacturers (both industrial and consumer products companies) and in construction, energy, real estate, transportation, investment banks, and utilities. To a lesser degree this fear is shared by those employed by large banks, insurance companies, pension funds, and major consulting firms.[13]

Woods's study, Friskopp and Silverstein's study, and other smaller-scale studies indicate that the higher one rises in the corporate hierarchy, the more being open about one's homosexuality serves as an impediment to one's career. As Marny Hall concluded in her study of lesbians in the corporate world: "They could advance to a certain level but not beyond because they could not project the necessary corporate image."[14]

11. Friskopp and Silverstein, *Straight Jobs, Gay Lives*, 18–23.

12. Ibid., 110–111.

13. Ibid., 157.

14. Marny Hall, "Private Experiences in the Public Domain: Lesbians in Organizations," in Jeff Hearn, Deborah L. Sheppard, Peta Tancred-Sheriff, and Gibson Burrell, eds., *The Sexuality of Organization* (Newbury Park, Calif.: Sage, 1989), 125–138. The quotation appears on p. 134

When we attempted to find openly homosexual men or women who hold senior executive positions in *Fortune*-level boards, we were not successful. There are, however, some very wealthy and influential men who have been public about their homosexuality. One such person is the media executive David Geffen.

David Geffen grew up in a three-bedroom apartment in a Jewish-Italian section of Brooklyn. His mother, Batyam, ran a brassiere and corset shop (and called her son King David). "She made the money," Geffen recalls, while his father "read a lot. He wasn't successful or ambitious. He spoke lots of languages. There were times that kids said to me, 'What does your father do?' and I had to make something up because I actually didn't know what he did."[15]

After an undistinguished record in high school, Geffen enrolled at the University of Texas but dropped out after one semester. He headed out to California, where his older brother lived, and held a number of jobs before landing a lowly but coveted position in the mailroom of the William Morris talent agency. (He told his employer he was a graduate of UCLA.)[16] Desperately wanting to be an agent, he followed the astute advice of a more experienced William Morris agent, who told him that rather than trying to persuade established stars to work with a mailroom boy in his early twenties he should seek to represent some of the undiscovered musical talent of his own generation.

He became the agent for Laura Nyro, a singer and songwriter who wrote a series of hits for herself and various other artists. When her publishing company—half-owned by Geffen—was sold to CBS in 1969, he received $2 million in CBS stock at the age of twenty-five. Within a year he had started his own record company, Asylum, which put out records by Joni Mitchell, Jackson Browne, Linda Ronstadt, and the Eagles, among others. Five years later, he sold the company to Warner Communications for $7 million.

In 1980 he started Geffen Records. With a stable that included Don Henley, Guns 'N Roses, Rickie Lee Jones, and Aerosmith, this venture, too, was extremely successful, and Geffen branched out to invest in theater (including *Cats* and *Little Shop of Horrors*) and films (including *Beetlejuice* and *Lost in America*). In 1990, Geffen concluded the time had come to join the massive

15. Bernard Weinraub, "David Geffen: Still Hungry," *New York Times Magazine,* May 2, 1993, 28–31, 38–43, 68, 78. The quotation appears on p. 43.

16. Both *Forbes* and the *New York Times* report that Geffen not only lied to get the job but, knowing that the company would request confirmation, watched for an incoming letter from UCLA. When he spotted it, he steamed open the envelope and replaced it with a bogus letter that he had prepared on UCLA stationary stating that he had graduated. Lisa Gubernick and Peter Newcomb, "The Richest Man in Hollywood," *Forbes,* December 24, 1990, p. 94–98; Weinraub, "David Geffen," 68.

move toward conglomeration, and he sold the company, the last of the major independent labels. Rather than accepting various lucrative cash offers, he decided on MCA's offer of $550 million worth of stock, foreseeing that MCA would itself be sold in the near future. When the Japanese company Matsushita bought MCA, Geffen, as MCA's largest shareholder, received a check for an estimated $670 million.[17] A 1990 article in *Forbes* described him and his wealth in the following way: "This 47-year-old chap given to blue jeans, T shirts and a fashionable day-old stubble, will be worth nearly $900 million. David Geffen is well on his way to achieving his well-known ambition of becoming Hollywood's first billionaire. And he's a bachelor to boot."[18]

He was indeed a bachelor, but not an eligible one in the conventional sense. Geffen had not yet gone public about his homosexuality, but over the next few years he became increasingly involved in fund raising for the battle against AIDS, and he told a reporter for *Vanity Fair* that he was bisexual. Then, both frightened and energized by the venomous language at the 1992 Republican national convention — especially a speech in which Patrick Buchanan claimed that there was "a religious war going on in this country for the soul of America" — Geffen became involved in Clinton's presidential campaign. Even before the Republican convention ended, he had called Clinton's campaign director, Mickey Kantor, an old friend from Kantor's days as a Los Angeles lawyer. Geffen became a major contributor and fund raiser.[19]

In late November 1992, just a few weeks after Clinton's election, in a speech to six thousand people at the Commitment to Life VI, a benefit for AIDS Project Los Angeles, Geffen went public about being gay. "As a gay man," he told the crowd, "I have come a long way to be here tonight."[20] This declaration generated considerable publicity. The *Advocate,* a magazine that addresses issues of relevance to the gay and lesbian communities, named Geffen Man of the Year. Friskopp and Silverstein write that many of the Harvard Business School graduates they interviewed cited Geffen as a public role model "for his business success and his candor about being gay."[21]

In Chapter 1 we noted that several decades ago Laurence Tisch advised young Jewish men interested in business careers to avoid the large "Gentile" companies because they would only get "bogged down." Better, said Tisch, to

17. Geraldine Fabrikant, "The Record Man with Flawless Timing," *New York Times,* December 9, 1990.

18. Gubernick and Newcomb, "Richest Man in Hollywood," 94.

19. Weinraub, "David Geffen," 40. The Buchanan quotation appears in Mixner, *Stranger Among Friends,* 249.

20. Brendan Lemon, "Man of the Year: David Geffen," *Advocate,* December 29, 1992, p. 35.

21. Friskopp and Silverstein, *Straight Jobs, Gay Lives,* 196.

work for Jews, or to be successful enough to buy your own company so that you can call the shots. Similarly, Geffen might advise young homosexual men and women interested in business careers to be selective about whom they decide to work for. A week after the AIDS fund raiser, when asked whether being gay had influenced his decision to pursue a career in show business rather than another business, Geffen acknowledged that it had been a key consideration: "When I realized as a teenager that it was possible that I might be gay — I wasn't sure until my twenties — I thought, *What kind of career can I have where being gay won't make a difference?* I thought about it a lot, and I decided that the entertainment business was a profession in which being gay was not going to be unusual or stand in my way."[22]

If the richest man in Hollywood is publicly gay, then it sends a message to those who run the many companies that do business with him. But the entertainment business is only one segment of the corporate world, and given its reputation for liberal politics and lifestyles, the public presence of one homosexual executive, even an extremely wealthy one, does not exactly indicate that the mostly conservative corporate elite is ready to accept openness about homosexuality. Still, given the real changes that have taken place at the lower tier of corporate management and the increasing tendency for younger gay men and lesbians in the corporate world to be open about their sexual orientation, it is likely that there will be a few who rise above the lavender ceiling in certain companies in certain industries.

In December 1996 many in and out of the corporate world were stunned by the decision of Allan Gilmour, the former vice chairman of the board at the Ford Motor Company, to reveal his homosexuality in an interview in a gay magazine. Gilmour, a graduate of Harvard and the University of Michigan and a lifelong conservative Republican, had retired from Ford two years earlier, though he remained on the boards of Prudential Insurance, Dow Chemical, Detroit Edison, U.S. West, and Whirlpool. Obviously, Gilmour chose to wait until he was no longer working at Ford to reveal his homosexuality. In fact, he did not even take phone calls at work from his thirty-four-year-old partner until a few months before he retired.

It is noteworthy that none of the chairmen of the boards on which Gilmour sat at the time he went public with his homosexuality asked him to leave those boards. When he contacted them after the story broke, he said, "I was told uniformly that it makes no difference." It is possible that Gilmour will serve as an important role model for younger gay men and lesbians in the corporate world. But we believe it is unlikely that in the near future they will be able to come out, remain in the corporate world, and rise as high as the corporate

22. Lemon, "Man of the Year," 38.

boardroom. Gilmour's own assessment of the impact of coming out in the corporate world is, no doubt, quite accurate: "I perceived the risk of coming out in the business world as fairly substantial."[23] Our best guess is that, like Jews in the early part of the century, most gay men and women in large corporations will either hide this aspect of their identity, top out at a lower level than they otherwise would, or leave in the hope of creating working environments that permit openness.

## Gay Men and Lesbians in the Political Elite

Contrary to the images of gays and lesbians as outrageous drag queens and butches on the one hand and as left-wing political activists on the other, the great majority of gays and lesbians tend to be straight-looking mainstream Democrats and Republicans. Like everyone else, gays and lesbians mostly reflect and express their social and educational backgrounds, as well as their occupational training and experience. They can be from high social levels as well as lower ones. Thus a wealthy ultraconservative like Phyllis Schlafley can have a gay son, an army brat like Newt Gingrich can have a lesbian half-sister, and a psychoanalyst like Charles Socarides, who claims that he can "cure" one-third of the homosexuals he treats, can have a gay son, Richard, who served in the Clinton administration as the White House liaison to the Labor Department.[24] In fact, many prominent gays and lesbians are from comfortable socioeconomic backgrounds, have had excellent educations, and have experienced considerable success in the professions, academia, and business.

There are gay Democratic clubs and gay Republican clubs across the country, but only the Republicans are organized by a national centralized office. The umbrella group is called the Log Cabin Republicans — the name derives from Abraham Lincoln, who is alleged to have grown up in a log cabin, and who supported individual rights.[25] In 1992 the group had five thousand members in fourteen states. By 1995 that figure had climbed to ten thousand mem-

23. Steve Friess, "Executive Decision," *Advocate*, April 29, 1997, pp. 24–26, 31. The quotations appear on pp. 26 and 25, respectively.

24. Laura Blumenfeld, "Schlafley's Son Out of the Closet," *Washington Post*, September 19, 1992; "Gingrich's Half-Sister Now Gay Activist," *Greensboro News and Record*, March 6, 1995; David W. Dunlap, "An Analyst, a Father, Battles Homosexuality," *New York Times*, December 24, 1995.

25. The log cabin myth is to presidents what the Horatio Alger myth is to captains of industry. At the time Abraham Lincoln was born, his father, a skilled carpenter and farmer, owned two farms of six hundred acres each, several town lots, horses, and livestock. See Edward Pessen, *The Log Cabin Myth: The Social Backgrounds of the Presidents* (New Haven: Yale University Press, 1984), 25.

bers in thirty-five states. Membership skyrocketed after Buchanan's speech at the 1992 convention, when many formerly closeted gay Republicans decided they had to become more involved in order to combat the antigay views of the religious right. The president of the Texas Log Cabin Republicans, Paul von Wupperfeld, stated that the state organization's membership had more than tripled in the twelve months ending in December 1992, an increase that he attributed in no small part to the Republican convention.[26] That year, the Log Cabin Republicans decided they could not endorse the Bush-Quayle ticket.[27]

Most gays and lesbians, however, vote Democratic, and they, too, have organized politically. In 1977 the Municipal Elections Committee of Los Angeles was formed. Its bland generic name disguised the fact that it was a gay and lesbian political action committee — the first one in the country — and made it easier for politicians to accept money from the group without having to acknowledge support from homosexuals. The adviser to this early gay PAC was David Mixner, who fifteen years later emerged as Bill Clinton's liaison to gays and lesbians during the 1992 campaign.[28]

Mixner was born in 1946 in southern New Jersey (three days after Bill Clinton was born in Arkansas). His father was the manager of the workers on an absentee-owner farm. After graduating from the local public high school in 1964, Mixner attended three different colleges before finally dropping out of Arizona State to work in Eugene McCarthy's 1968 presidential campaign. He became a key McCarthy organizer, was thrown through a window by police at the 1968 Democratic convention in Chicago, and became one of the four organizers of the Vietnam moratorium in October of 1969.

Later that year, at a reunion of those who had worked on McCarthy's presidential campaign, Mixner met Bill Clinton. Clinton had not worked on the campaign, but came to the reunion on Martha's Vineyard with a friend who had. The two twenty-five-year-olds — one a Yale Law School student, the other a college-dropout political activist — hit it off, and because both had political aspirations, they kept in touch over the years as their respective political careers unfolded. In October 1991, Mixner arranged a meeting in Los Angeles

26. Von Wupperfeld explained his preference for the Republican Party by noting that he was the son of a Goldwater conservative and therefore that "it would be unnatural for me to vote as a Democrat." As has been the case with other gay Republicans, he has encountered antagonism from liberals in the gay community. Francis X. Clines, "For Gay G.O.P. Members, a 2d Closet," *New York Times,* September 4, 1992.

27. Kathy Sawyer, "Dole Campaign Returns Gays' Donation," *Washington Post,* August 27, 1995.

28. The information in this and the next two paragraphs is drawn from Daniel Golden's profile of Mixner, "Mixner's Moment," *Boston Globe,* June 6, 1993, and from Mixner, *Stranger Among Friends.*

between Clinton, by then governor of Arkansas, and a small group of wealthy southern Californians known as Access Now for Gay and Lesbian Equality (ANGLE). The group was impressed by Clinton, in part because he agreed to their demands, including an end to the ban on homosexuals in the military.

Mixner was able to rally considerable support from the homosexual community for Clinton. Patrick Buchanan's speech at the Republican convention made this task much easier. As Mixner said to one interviewer, "Support crystallized overnight with Pat Buchanan's speech. It created a voting bloc and tripled the money."[29] According to Mixner, gays and lesbians contributed $3 million of the $25 million Clinton raised.[30]

Mixner, like Geffen, has rallied homosexual support for various Democratic politicians, just as the Log Cabin Republicans have raised money and gotten out the more conservative gay vote. But no openly gay men or women have been appointed to presidential cabinets or been elected to the Senate. There have been openly gay men in the House of Representatives, though each was first elected before it was publicly revealed that he was gay.

There is a long and lurid history of sexual scandals involving senators and congressmen, but for many years the press chose to ignore the sexual escapades of elected officials. Through the years, congressmen have been caught having sex with men and with women, with girls and with boys. Only when the media began to publicize sex scandals involving homosexual encounters did most Americans realize that some of those whom they had elected were gay. In 1978, Fred Richmond, a Democratic representative from Brooklyn, was charged with paying for sex with a sixteen-year-old boy and for soliciting an undercover male policeman. He wrote a confessional letter to his constituents, and they reelected him twice. Two years later, Jon Hinson, a conservative Republican from Mississippi, was arrested in Washington for "committing an obscene act" at a popular pickup spot for gays. He, too, was reelected but

---

29. Bruce Bawer, *A Place at the Table*, 52.

30. Golden, "Mixner's Moment," p. 4 of downloaded version; Mixner, *Stranger Among Friends*, 250. In spite of the money Mixner raised and assurances by Clinton of access to decision makers with regard to gay and lesbian issues, Mixner and other homosexual activists were frozen out and treated badly by most members of Clinton's inner circle, a sordid story that is told in Mixner's *Stranger Among Friends*, chapters 16–18. The youthful and arrogant Rahm Emanuel and George Stephanopoulos, both from white ethnic groups that had been discriminated against in the past, were the worst offenders. In May 1996, when Clinton said he would support a Republican bill denying recognition of same-sex marriages, Mixner called the decision "nauseating and appalling" and an "act of political cowardice." Todd Purdom, "Clinton Would Sign Bill Barring Recognition to Gay Marriages," *New York Times*, May 23, 1996.

resigned during his next term after being arrested in a men's restroom in a federal office building on a charge of sodomy. At about the same time, another right-wing Republican, Robert Bauman of Maryland, was caught soliciting sex from a sixteen-year-old boy. He confessed, claiming alcoholism as his excuse, ran for reelection, and lost by a narrow margin.

In 1983, Gerry Studds, a Democrat from Massachusetts, was censured by the House for having had sex with a seventeen-year-old male congressional page a decade earlier. He was subsequently reelected six times before retiring. In spring 1987, Barney Frank, a Democrat from Boston who had been in Congress since 1980, announced that he was gay. As *Newsweek* put it, "the voters shrugged and returned him to Congress by a landslide majority."[31]

In 1980, as part of the Reagan victory, twenty-nine-year-old Steve Gunderson, a Republican who had previously served in the Wisconsin state legislature, was elected to the U.S. House of Representatives. His homosexuality was, as the *New York Times* put it, "quietly known in his Wisconsin district and in Washington for years," but it was neither a public nor a political issue in six reelection campaigns, until the spring of 1994. In March of that year, Gunderson gave a speech to the Human Rights Campaign Fund, a gay political group in Baltimore, in which he mentioned that his partner of eleven years was in the audience. That same month he spoke on the House floor against a Republican-sponsored amendment to deny funds to schools "encouraging or supporting" homosexuality. When he sat down, a fellow Republican, Robert Dornan of California, leveled a highly personal attack on Gunderson. "He has a revolving door on his closet," Dornan said. "He's in, he's out, he's in, he's out, he's in. I guess you're out because you went up and spoke to a huge homosexual dinner, Mr. Gunderson." Though Dornan later withdrew his remarks from the official record, he refused to apologize. Nor was he able to withdraw comments he made later that day to a reporter: "We have a representative on our side who is a homo. I have just had it with him saying he takes second place to no one in this House upholding Christian principles."[32]

31. This quotation, and the material in the previous two paragraphs, are drawn from "Barney Frank's Story," *Newsweek,* September 25, 1989, pp. 14–18; Jonathan Alter, "Gays in Washington: Voters Aren't as Alarmed as Politicians Think," *Newsweek,* September 25, 1989, p. 19. Gerry Studds comes from an elite educational background: after graduating from Groton and Harvard, he taught in the late 1960s at St. Paul's. See August Heckscher, *St. Paul's: The Life of a New England School* (New York: Scribners, 1980), 325.

32. Chandler Burr, "Congressman (R), Wisconsin. Fiscal Conservative. Social Moderate. Gay." *New York Times Magazine,* October 16, 1994, pp. 43–45; John McCormick, " 'Poster Boy,' " *Newsweek,* July 11, 1994, p. 19.

In spite of hostility from the right wing of his own party, Gunderson won the 1994 election, but he chose not to run for reelection in 1996.[33] In August 1996 another Republican congressman acknowledged that he is gay. After voting to deny federal recognition to same-sex marriages, Jim Kolbe, a six-term representative from Arizona, was electronically "outed" by gay activists who distributed the information in e-mail messages. As a result of this campaign, Kolbe publicly acknowledged his sexual orientation. A gay activist described as an architect of the outing campaign happily noted that after Kolbe's announcement there were as many openly gay Republicans — two — as openly gay Democrats in Congress: "I think it's a terrific development that we now have an equal number of openly gay G.O.P. members of Congress."[34]

There were other signs of an increasing political presence for gays and lesbians in the political world in the 1994 elections. The first openly homosexual candidate was elected to the California legislature, four of the sixty men and women elected to the Oregon House of Representatives were openly homosexual or bisexual, and voters in Phoenix sent an openly gay man to the Arizona House of Representatives for the first time. In addition to Gunderson, Barney Frank and Gerry Studds were reelected to the House.[35]

But the only two openly gay candidates for statewide office lost in 1994 (one in New York, the other in California), and no openly gay candidate has won or even made a serious run for a Senate seat. Sheila James Kuehl, the openly gay woman elected to the California legislature, told a conference sponsored by the National Gay and Lesbian Task Force, "We've grown to the point where we can be elected locally, but not yet to the point where we can be elected statewide."[36]

In 1992, whether as a political payback for the support he received from gay voters or out of a genuine commitment to diversity in his administration, or both, Clinton appointed an openly gay man and an openly gay woman to positions senior enough to require confirmation by the Senate. Both were confirmed, making them the highest-ranking openly gay people to serve in the executive branch. Roberta Achtenberg, a former law professor and a member

33. Frank Rich, "On the Bright Side," *New York Times,* November 10, 1994.

34. See David W. Dunlap, "A Republican Congressman Discloses He Is a Homosexual," *New York Times,* August 3, 1996.

35. David W. Dunlap, "Gay Politicians Say Losses Are Partly Offset by Gains," *New York Times,* November 14, 1994.

36. David W. Dunlap, "Zelda's Unwavering Love Is No Longer Unrequited," *New York Times,* November 20, 1994. See also Michelangelo Signorile, *Queer in America: Sex, the Media, and the Closets of Power* (New York: Random House, 1993), 223–229, 321–325.

of the San Francisco Board of Supervisors, became an assistant secretary at HUD. She was confirmed by the Senate in a 58–31 vote, although Jesse Helms called her a "militantly activist lesbian" who "tried to bully the Boy Scouts of America" into permitting homosexual Scout leaders.[37] And Bruce Lehman, also a lawyer, became assistant commerce secretary and commissioner of patents and trademarks. Lehman, who had worked in Washington as a congressional aide and as a copyright lawyer and lobbyist for a major law firm, had many friends on Capitol Hill, including Republicans. His confirmation hearings produced none of the conservative wrath that marked those held for Achtenberg's appointment. Lehman noted that a conservative paper in Washington had tried to stir up some outrage from conservative Republicans, but "the problem is, they all know me, and they kind of like me, and they didn't want to make a martyr of me."[38]

It may be that Bruce Lehman received kinder treatment from the Senate than did Roberta Achtenberg simply because she is, in fact, more radical politically than he is. But it also reminds us that when homosexuals are considered for positions in or near the power elite, gender is also part of the equation. As both a homosexual *and* a woman, Achtenberg had two barriers to surmount. As we pointed out in Chapter 2, the more characteristics that differentiate a woman from the dominant WASP male majority in the power elite, the more difficult it is for her to gain acceptance. This phenomenon becomes more apparent the closer one gets to the power elite. At a level requiring Senate confirmation, an openly gay woman may pose a greater threat than an openly gay man.

Antagonism toward homosexuality persists, especially from the religious right, even though exit polls in 1994 indicated that one-third of the voters who identified themselves as gay, lesbian, or bisexual voted for Republicans in the 1994 congressional election.[39] As Kathleen Jamieson points out, it has become the pattern that powerful women are accused of being closet lesbians. In her efforts to unseat Barbara Mikulski, the incumbent Democratic senator from Maryland, the conservative Republican syndicated columnist Linda Chavez claimed that Mikulski was "a San Francisco–style Democrat," that she was "anti-male," and that she should "come out of the closet."[40] In a radio inter-

37. "Lesbian Confirmed in Housing Position with Votes to Spare," *New York Times,* May 25, 1993.

38. Teresa Riordan, "Even in a 'Big Tent,' Little Insults, Little Compromises," *New York Times,* May 29, 1994.

39. David W. Dunlap, "For Gay Republicans, the Ideological Sniping Comes From Both Camps," *New York Times,* October 4, 1995.

40. Jamieson, *Beyond the Double Bind,* 72.

view, House Majority Leader Richard Armey referred to Barney Frank as "Barney Fag," then gave a lukewarm apology, saying that he had mispronounced Frank's last name.[41] Rather than face the outspoken opposition of Jesse Helms, the Clinton White House backed away from naming James Hormel, an openly gay San Francisco businessman who had contributed heavily to Clinton's election, as ambassador to Fiji.[42]

Although they have clearly not yet become a part of the political elite, homosexuals represent an increasingly sizable, well-organized, and well-funded group of voters in some states. They have become a civil rights group with some political clout. But for politicians on the right, given the continuing hostility toward homosexuals and homosexuality among many of their constituents, even deciding whether or not to accept campaign contributions can be problematic. This was demonstrated quite clearly in late 1995, when Robert Dole's presidential campaign at first accepted a $1,000 campaign contribution from the Log Cabin Republicans, then months later returned it on the grounds that the group's agenda was "in opposition to Senator Dole's on the issues."[43] Republican congressman Gunderson, who had previously stepped down as chief deputy whip because of the intolerance exhibited by Republicans at the 1992 convention, wrote a pained letter to Dole, noting that he had first heard about this at a dinner party and, as he put it, "I assumed my friends had mistaken yours for the campaigns of other, decidedly bigoted candidates. I was embarrassed to learn I was wrong."[44]

It is not only the right that finds homosexuality a volatile issue. When delegates to the 1994 annual meeting of the highly respected Japanese American Citizens League voted to make the League the first civil rights organization to endorse same-sex marriage, a major conflict followed. Disaffected members elected a new president and several new directors. There was a wholesale firing of national staff members, who were blamed for the resolution even though it was introduced by delegates from Hawaii. Membership dropped by 11 per-

41. "The Republican Week That Was," *New York Times,* January 29, 1995.

42. David W. Dunlap, "Nomination of Gay Man Is Dropped," *New York Times,* January 1, 1995. Helms's opposition was not the only problem. Fiji has harsh laws against homosexuality that might have complicated Hormel's ambassadorship.

43. Sawyer, "Dole Campaign Returns Gays' Donation." Dole later said that an aide had made this decision, but that he did not want to object publicly because he did not want to embarrass the aide. See "Dole Changes His Tune on Donation," *Greensboro News and Record,* October 18, 1995.

44. Richard L. Berke, "Gay Congressman of His Own Party Brings Fire on Dole," *New York Times,* September 7, 1995.

cent in the next year, and the organization's attorney resigned because the endorsement conflicted with his Christian beliefs. Then the directors opposed to the new regime resigned in protest. In 1996 the organization was rebuilding, its future somewhat uncertain.[45]

## Gay Men and Lesbians in the Military

Almost immediately after he entered office, Clinton blundered into a firestorm over gays in the military. After initially taking a clear and principled stand, he crumbled in the face of opposition led by a traditional southern Democrat, Senator Sam Nunn of Georgia. The result was his endorsement of an ambiguous policy of "don't ask, don't tell." By spring 1995, as one writer put it after interviewing service members, officials at the Pentagon, and gay-rights advocates, "the results have been as ambiguous as the rules themselves."[46] According to Mixner, the new Clinton policy has made conditions in the military much worse for gays.[47]

The Joint Chiefs of Staff, Nunn (who was chairman of the Senate Armed Forces Committee), various congressmen, and the entire religious right opposed Clinton's initial plan on gays in the military. Colin Powell was also against it, although he later tried to sugarcoat his vigorous opposition by telling Henry Louis Gates Jr. that "I never presented the case in terms of there

45. Dennis Akizuki, "Turning Point for Asian Civil Rights Group," *San Jose Mercury News,* August 6, 1996; Dennis Akizuki, "Japanese Group Heals Internal Divisions," *San Jose Mercury News,* August 11, 1996.

46. Eric Schmitt, "The New Rules on Gay Soldiers: A Year Later, No Clear Results," *New York Times,* March 13, 1995.

47. In Mixner's view, by mid-1995, "It was clear to everyone, except perhaps the President and his staff, that the 'Don't Ask, Don't Tell' policy was a disaster. The facts speak for themselves. Dismissals of homosexuals from the military increased at an even greater rate than before the new policy. The Service Members Legal Defense Network, an organization dedicated to assisting gay and lesbian service members and protecting their legal rights, has monitored the policy. In its most recent report, released on February 27, 1995, their researchers found a 17 percent increase in discharges over the previous year. The report documents continuing witch-hunts on military bases, destroyed careers, heightened fear, and the absence of any efforts by the Pentagon to stop such tactics. Compounding this was the Department of Justice's insistence on fighting on the side of the military in appeals of cases we had won in the lower courts" (*Stranger Among Friends,* 350). For a more recent report by the Servicemembers Legal Defense Network that drew the same conclusions, see Philip Shenon, "New Study Faults Pentagon's Gay Policy," *New York Times,* February 26, 1997.

being something wrong, morally or any other way, with gays. I just couldn't figure out a way to handle the privacy aspect."[48] Some in the military have been more open in their views and in their condemnation of homosexuality. Admiral Thomas Moore, former chairman of the Joint Chiefs of Staff, once referred to homosexuality as "a filthy, disease-ridden practice."[49] Needless to say, there have been no openly homosexual men or women who have risen very far in the military hierarchy, and certainly none who have made it into the military elite.[50]

Gay rights activism, like the women's movement of the late 1960s, was emboldened by the civil rights and antiwar movements, and in fact some gay and lesbian leaders were part of those other movements to begin with. As the movements of the 1960s took on various forms, they affected one another and, to varying degrees, contributed to cracking the monolithic nature of the power elite.

The problem facing openly gay men and lesbians as they move closer to the power elite, while unique in some ways, is, at a deeper level, similar to the problems facing others who were previously excluded. They, too, will have to find ways to enter the comfort zone of the upper- and upper-middle-class, Ivy League–educated, white heterosexual males at the center of the power elite. They will have to do so by asserting as many similarities as possible and by managing differences that might rekindle discomfort. Most of all, they must behave in traditionally masculine or feminine ways. Woods makes this point about identity management when he asserts that many in the corporate world "don't care if someone's gay or not," but that they do care "how effeminate you are."[51] It is likely that a similar problem faces lesbians in making sure they don't appear too "masculine." But, as we concluded in Chapter 2, this is a key issue for heterosexual women as well.

Our assumption is that there are and have always been homosexuals in the

48. Henry Louis Gates Jr., "Powell and the Black Elite," *New Yorker,* September 25, 1995, 63–80. The quotation appears on p. 74.

49. Quoted in Bawer, *A Place at the Table,* 149.

50. For a detailed account of the outing of Pete Williams, the Pentagon spokesman during the Gulf War, see chapter 6, "Operation Out-the-Pentagon," in Signorile, *Queer in America,* 97–122. Signorile argues that Williams "had much more influence than the label 'spokesperson' suggested," and he quotes both *People* magazine and an unnamed congressional staffer to the effect that Williams was "a policymaker" (114), but Williams was not at a sufficiently senior level to qualify for what Mills called "the military elite." Indeed, he was a civilian, not technically even in the military.

51. Woods, *Corporate Closet,* 14.

power elite, but to remain there they have had to "manage" their image by remaining closeted. Whether openly gay men and women will be allowed into the power elite remains to be seen. It seems unlikely that this will happen soon. Rather, some homosexuals, like Geffen, will emerge as wealthy and powerful individuals, perhaps even being asked to join some progressive *Fortune*-level boards as outside directors. Gay men and lesbians will continue to function in the political arena as a civil rights group, with a handful of openly homosexual members in the House of Representatives (and maybe even the Senate), and with subcabinet appointments (and maybe even a cabinet member). A tendency may emerge for the elected officials to be Democrats, but the small number of gay elected officials up to this point does not allow for a confident prediction, despite the homophobic emphasis of the Republicans in the first six years of the 1990s. Gay men and lesbians might achieve more tolerant treatment in the military, but it is hard to picture either gay men or lesbians emerging at the top of the military hierarchy for a very long time without the creation of a liberal majority in the U.S. Congress that is strongly committed to civil rights and civil liberties for every American.

# 7

## The Ironies of Diversity

As the preceding chapters have shown in detail, the power elite and Congress are more diverse than they were before the social movements that emerged in the 1960s brought pressure to bear on corporations, politicians, and government. Although the power elite is still composed primarily of Christian white men, there are now Jews, women, blacks, Latinos, and Asian Americans on the boards of the country's largest corporations; presidential cabinets are far more diverse than was the case forty years ago; and the highest ranks of the military are no longer filled solely by white men. In the case of elected officials in Congress, the trend toward diversity is even greater for women and all of the minority groups that we have studied. At the same time, we have shown that the assimilation of the different groups has been uneven. In this final chapter, we explain the successful assimilation by women and minorities into the power elite and Congress in terms of four factors: identity management; the importance of class; the importance of education; and the importance of light skin. We conclude that class origin is the most important factor for all groups except blacks and "Indian-appearing" Latinos, and we offer a general explanation for the continuing exclusion of people with darker skins.

Ultimately we suggest that the increase in diversity at the top contains several ironies, the most important of which is related to what is perhaps the major unresolved tension in American life, between liberal individualism and the class structure. The diversification of the power elite has been celebrated, but this celebration ignores the continuing importance of the class structure. The movements that led to diversity in the power elite have succeeded to some extent, especially for women and minorities from privileged social backgrounds, but there has been no effect on the way the power elite functions or on the class structure itself.

### Identity Management

We have seen that newcomers who seek to join the power elite have to find ways to demonstrate their loyalty to those who dominate American institutions — straight white Christian males. We can recall, for example, Cecily Cannan Selby's decision to reduce tension at a dinner meeting with the previously all-male Avon Products board by lighting up a cigar, or Hazel O'Leary's realization that she had to learn to play golf if she expected to advance in her corporate career. We can envision William T. Coleman demonstrating his elite educational background by reciting great poetry with his fellow law clerk Elliot Richardson. Reading between the lines of traditional stereotypes, we can imagine Jewish and black executives being properly reserved, Asian-American executives acting properly assertive, gay executives behaving in traditionally masculine ways and lesbian executives in traditionally feminine ways. Thus we have seen the importance of identity management. As Terry Miyamoto of U.S. West put it, the challenge is to move into a "comfort zone" with those who decide who is and is not acceptable for inclusion.

At the same time, in Chapter 2 we drew on the work of sociologist Rosabeth Kanter to stress that the demand for demonstrations of outward conformity by established leaders is not primarily a matter of personal prejudice or cultural heritage. It is, instead, the need for trust and smooth working relationships within complex organizations that leads to the marked preference for women and minorities who think and act like the straight Christian males running those organizations. The social movements that arose in the 1960s were able to rock the boat enough to open up some space for nontraditional leaders, but not enough to change the way in which institutions are managed. Unless and until such changes are made in institutional governance, women and minorities will be at a disadvantage in climbing the managerial hierarchy even though they are now allowed to enter the competition.

Identity management, however, is only the final step, the icing on the cake, so to speak. Before atypical candidates for acceptance into the higher circles can even think about making adjustments in their personas, they have to meet prerequisites that are attainable by only a small percentage of the population whatever their race, ethnicity, gender, or sexual orientation. It is to these prerequisites that we now turn.

## The Importance of Class

Those who brought diversity to the power elite tended to come from business and professional backgrounds, like the white Christian males whom Mills studied more than forty years ago. Fully one-third of the women who have become corporate directors are from the upper class, and many others are from the middle and upper middle classes. Most of the Cuban Americans and Chinese Americans who have risen to the top have come from displaced ruling classes, a far cry from the conventional image of the immigrant. The Jews and Japanese Americans in high positions have mostly been the products of two- and three-generational climbs up the social ladder. The first black members of the corporate elite and the cabinet tended to come from the small black middle class that predated the civil rights movement. Although there is no systematic information on the social backgrounds of gay and lesbian leaders, who are treated in most studies as if they had no class origins, our anecdotal information suggests that many visible activists and professionals come from business and professional families as well.

A high-level social background, of course, makes it easier to acquire the values, attitudes, and styles that are necessary to hire, fire, and manage the work lives of employees with blue, white, and pink collars. This point can be extended to include even those from more modest circumstances, like Lauro Cavazos, whose father was a ranch foreman, or Katherine Ortega, Sue Ginn, and David Geffen, whose families owned small businesses, or David Mixner, whose father was in charge of minority farmhands on a farm he did not own. Most of those we studied, in other words, learned firsthand that a few people boss the majority or have independent professions based on academic credentials, and that they were expected to be part of this managerial and professional stratum.

When we compare women and minority members of the power elite with their counterparts in Congress, however, two further generalizations emerge. First, members of the power elite tend to come from more privileged social backgrounds than the elected officials. Second, the elected women and minorities are more likely to be Democrats than Republicans. These two findings suggest that there are class and political dimensions to our findings on the differences between the power elite and Congress that cut across gender and ethnic lines. If the power elite comes to be housed almost exclusively in the Republican Party as well-to-do southerners leave the Democrats and as the liberal-labor coalition becomes more important within the Democratic Party, then the country's traditional regional, racial, and ethnic politics may be replaced by a more clear-cut class-and-values politics, with both the Republicans and Democrats being able to say that they are multicultural in terms of gender and minority representation.[1]

## The Importance of Education

Class by no means explains all of our findings, however. Education also matters a great deal. The women and minorities who make it to the power elite are typically better educated than the white males who are already a part of it. This was seen with the European-American women and African Americans on corporate boards and in presidential cabinets, as well as the successful Asian-American immigrants. Education seems to have given them the edge needed to be accepted into the power elite.

Moreover, it is not merely academic degrees that matter but also where those degrees are from. Again and again, we saw that a significant minority were from the same few schools that educate Christian white male leaders — Harvard, Yale, Princeton, and MIT on the East Coast, the University of Chicago in the Midwest, Stanford and the University of California on the West Coast. Three of the five Asian-American appointees to the executive branch, for example, have at least one degree from Harvard (Julia Chang Bloch, Elaine Chao, and Lon Hatamiya). The other two attended the University of Chicago (Patsy Mink) and the University of California (Dennis Hayashi).

These elite schools not only confer status on their graduates but also provide contacts with white male elites that are renewed throughout life at alumni

---

1. On the continuing importance of class voting in the United States, contrary to recent claims based on weak methods, see Michael Hout, Clem Brooks, and Jeff Manza, "The Democratic Class Struggle in the United States, 1948–1992," *American Sociological Review* 60, no. 6 (1995), 805–828; Jeff Manza and Clem Brooks, "Continuity and Change in the Social Bases of U.S. Political Alignments, 1960–1992," paper presented at the American Sociological Association Meetings, New York, August 1996.

On class voting by Latinos, see Barry Kosmin and Ariela Keysar, "Party Political Preferences of U.S. Hispanics: The Varying Impact of Religion, Social Class and Demographic Factors," *Ethnic and Racial Studies* 18, no. 2 (1995), 236–347. In surveys of the CEOs of the largest Hispanic-owned businesses in 1989 and 1996, *Hispanic Business* found that 78 percent of them voted Republican in 1988 and that 67 percent said they were Republicans in 1996. See "CEOs and the Entrepreneurial 80s," *Hispanic Business,* April 1989, p. 30; "HB 500 CEOs Opt for Dole," *Hispanic Business,* June 1996, p. 34. On class voting by Chinese Americans, see Wendy Tam, "Asians — a Monolithic Voting Bloc?" *Political Behavior* 17, no. 2 (1995), 223–249.

gatherings and other special occasions. School connections in turn lead to invitations to attend exclusive social events and join expensive social clubs, which extend the newcomers' social networks even further. With success in business or a profession comes invitations to serve on boards of trustees of elite foundations and universities, and the circle is completed. The newcomers become part of the ongoing institutional framework that defines and shapes the power elite in the United States, even though they are unlikely to reach the very top. The individuals in the power elite may come and go, and they may diversify in gender, ethnicity, and sexual orientation, but there is stability and continuity within the overall power structure.

As was true of social class origins, there is a difference in educational attainment between those in the power elite and those in Congress: the men and women elected to Congress are not as likely as those in the power elite to have attended elite colleges and universities or to have earned postgraduate degrees.

## The Importance of Color

Just as class alone cannot explain all of our findings, neither can the combination of class and education: color also matters. African Americans and darker-skinned Latinos find it more difficult than others to use their educational credentials as a passport to occupational success. This can be seen poignantly in our skin-color comparisons of successful blacks and Latinos. Even among those who had achieved some level of prominence (measured by inclusion in *Ebony*'s fiftieth anniversary issue or the *Hispanic Business* listing of "Hispanic influentials"), those who had made it into the power elite were lighter skinned than those who had not. On this score, our data simply reinforce earlier work by others. As the Glass Ceiling Commission reported, "Our society has developed an extremely sophisticated, and often denied, acceptability index based on gradations in skin color."[2]

There is another side of the coin: darker-skinned blacks may have a harder time finding jobs and may, if convicted of crimes, receive stiffer jail sentences.[3] Furthermore, both blacks and Latinos in the United States understand (and sometimes indulge in) the discrimination against those who are darkest. Blacks speak openly of the advantage lighter-skinned blacks have, and surveys of Latinos reveal that those who are described as "Indian" in appearance report

2. *Good for Business: Making Full Use of the Nation's Human Capital, a Fact-Finding Report of the Federal Glass Ceiling Commission* (Washington, D.C.: U.S. Government Printing Office, 1995), 95.

3. James H. Johnson Jr. and Walter C. Farrell Jr., "Race Still Matters," *The Chronicle of Higher Education*, July 7, 1995, p. A48.

greater discrimination than do Latinos who are described as more Caucasian in appearance.[4]

These findings on color discrimination may be useful in explaining why the assimilation of blacks into the power elite may be slowing down. The failure of American society to accept darker-skinned citizens — especially blacks — is the single most important issue that needs to be understood by social scientists.

## Explaining Discrimination

How is the greater discrimination against blacks and against Latinos who are "Indian" in appearance to be explained? We think it hinges on a distinction between immigrant minorities, whose migration to a country was voluntary, and subjugated minorities, who have been defeated by groups with superior military technology or brought to a country against their will as slaves.

A distinction between immigrant and subjugated minorities, as opposed to a focus on race, is compatible with the general patterns of assimilation and integration in the United States. This can be seen most clearly through what social psychologist Thomas F. Pettigrew, perhaps the leading authority on race and ethnic relations of the past thirty-five years, sees as the two most important and revealing indicators of integration: residential patterns and intermarriage.[5] Asian Americans, Latinos, and African Americans are designated as "people of color," but when we look at the extent to which those in each group live among and marry people from other groups, the importance of immigration rather than race becomes apparent.

4. Carlos H. Arce, Edward Murguia, and W. Parker Frisbie, "Phenotype and Life Chances Among Chicanos," *Hispanic Journal of Behavioral Sciences* 9, no. 1 (1987), 19–32; E. A. Telles and Edward Murguia, "Phenotypic Discrimination and Income Differences Among Mexican Americans," *Social Science Quarterly* 71 (1990), 682–696; Aida Hurtado, "Does Similarity Breed Respect? Interviewer Evaluations of Mexican-Descent Respondents in a Bilingual Survey," *Public Opinion Quarterly* 58 (1994), 77–95.

5. Thomas F. Pettigrew, "Integration and Pluralism," in Phyllis A. Katz and Dalmas A. Taylor, eds., *Modern Racism: Profiles in Controversy* (New York: Plenum, 1988), 19–30. As noted in Chapter 2, intermarriage as an indicator of "assimilation" is stressed by Milton Gordon (*Assimilation in American Life* [New York: Oxford University Press, 1964]) and by Seymour Martin Lipset and Earl Raab (*Jews and the New American Scene* [Cambridge: Harvard University Press, 1995]), but here the emphasis is on "integration," which highlights the fact that African Americans have faced distinct barriers to acceptance. "*Assimilation*," concludes Pettigrew, is a concept "used in North America largely in reference to *national* groups that have arrived over the past 150 years with distinctive non-anglo cultures. *Integration* is a concept shaped by black-white relations in the United States to refer to inclusion processes for a *racial* group that has a unique history of rigorous exclusion" (20).

Table 7.1

*Intermarriage by U.S.-Born Members of Ethnic and Racial Minorities*

| | % Married to Non-Hispanic Whites | | | |
|---|---|---|---|---|
| | Male (*N*) | | Female (*N*) | |
| Filipino Americans | 61% | (106) | 66% | (103) |
| Native Americans | 57 | (1,212) | 58 | (1,234) |
| Cuban Americans | 61 | (92) | 47 | (137) |
| Chinese Americans | 47 | (140) | 52 | (152) |
| Japanese Americans | 44 | (216) | 54 | (266) |
| Puerto Rican Americans | 42 | (528) | 35 | (602) |
| Mexican Americans | 31 | (4,793) | 28 | (5,261) |
| African Americans | 5 | (9,804) | 2 | (9,581) |

*Source:* Adapted from Jacobs and Labov, "Asian Brides, Anglo Grooms," p. 23, table 4.
*Note:* The table includes only individuals under age forty and excludes war brides and grooms.

The best data on residential patterns demonstrate that blacks continue to live in predominantly black neighborhoods, but this is not the case for Latinos or Asian Americans. In *American Apartheid: Segregation and the Making of the Underclass,* the sociologists Douglas Massey and Nancy Denton demonstrate just how persistent residential segregation has been in the United States. Using computerized data from the U.S. censuses of 1970 and 1980, they looked at the thirty metropolitan areas with the largest black populations. Based on two different measures ("black-white segregation" and "spatial isolation"), they conclude that the 1970s showed virtually no increase in integration, "despite what whites said on opinion polls and despite the provisions of the Fair Housing Act."[6] Moreover, they found that degree of segregation was not the case for Hispanics and Asians. "In fact," Massey and Denton conclude, "within most metropolitan areas, Hispanics and Asians are more likely to share a neighborhood with whites than with another member of their own group." In the final chapter of their book, Massey and Denton update their work to include 1990 census data. They conclude that "there is little in recent data to suggest that processes of racial segregation have moderated much since 1980. . . . Racial segregation still constitutes a fundamental cleavage in American society."[7]

6. Douglas S. Massey and Nancy A. Denton, *American Apartheid: Segregation and the Making of the Underclass* (Cambridge: Harvard University Press, 1993), 61.
7. Ibid., 67, 223.

There have been dozens of studies focusing on the recent marriage patterns of minority groups. All of them point to increasing intermarriage occurring between the large white population and each minority group except blacks. The exact percentage of "outmarriage" varies with a number of factors, including country of birth, years of residency in the United States, region of residence, educational level, and income. For our emphasis on intermarriage as a sensitive indicator of integration and acceptance, two papers by sociologists Jerry Jacobs and Teresa Labov using a 1 percent sample from the 1990 census (539,279 marriages) provide an ideal test case. The findings of their analysis of marriages to non-Hispanic white partners by American-born minorities under the age of forty are summarized in table 7.1.[8]

There are many dramatic findings in this table, including the very high percentage of native-born Asian Americans marrying non-Hispanic whites, but none is more important to our point than the continuing low levels of intermarriage by African Americans to non-Hispanic whites. In a sample that focuses only on married couples, thereby excluding any distortion by the high percentage of unmarried males and females in the African-American community, only 5 percent of married African-American males and 2 percent of married African-American females under age forty were married to non-Hispanic whites. This is less than one-sixth the percentage for the next-lowest group, Mexican Americans, and far below the 44–66 percent figures for Asian Americans. Even among African-American college graduates, only 11 percent of the males and 3 percent of the females had married whites, whereas the percent-

8. Jerry A. Jacobs and Teresa Labov, "Asian Brides, Anglo Grooms: Asian Exceptionalism in Intermarriage," Department of Sociology, University of Pennsylvania, October 1995; Jerry A. Jacobs and Teresa Labov, "Sex Differences in Intermarriage: Exchange Theory Reconsidered," Department of Sociology, University of Pennsylvania, September 1995.

For similar findings based on 1990 survey data with native-born Latinos that are slightly lower due to a wider age range, see Rodolfo de la Garza, Louis DeSipio, F. Chris Garcia, John Garcia, and Angelo Falcon, *Latino Voices: Mexican, Puerto Rican, and Cuban Perspectives on American Politics* (Boulder, Colo.: Westview, 1992), 25, table 2.6. Jacobs and Labov find low rates of intermarriage among subgroups of Latinos, and de la Garza et al. report similarly low rates among Latino groups in the table cited. There is, however, evidence for a growing number of intermarriages among Asian Americans in California, with the rate being higher than intermarriage with whites when the size of the population is taken into account. See Larry Hajima Shinagawa and Gin Yong Pang, "Intraethnic, Interethnic, and Interracial Marriages Among Asian Americans in California, 1980," *Berkeley Journal of Sociology* 13 (1988), 95–114. Inter-Asian marriages are also high in Hawaii; see Morrison G. Wong, "A Look at Intermarriage Among the Chinese in the U.S. in 1980," *Sociological Perspectives* 32, no. 1 (1989), 87–107.

ages for all married Asian-American college graduates as a group were 51 percent for males and 59 percent for females.[9]

As might be deduced from the higher percentage of Asian-American college graduates marrying whites, there is a strong tendency for affluent immigrant minorities to marry affluent whites and for less affluent minorities, like Native Americans, Mexican Americans, and Puerto Ricans, to marry less affluent whites. The same pattern holds for marriages between African Americans and whites — the partners usually have similar education and occupational levels.[10]

Based on these findings, it seems likely to us that, over time, the overwhelming majority of the children and grandchildren of new immigrants to the United States will blend together with non-Hispanic whites into a common cultural pool and then sort themselves out along class and educational lines, using ethnic and racial identities for mostly symbolic and strategic purposes. This mix will include the 79 percent of self-identified American Indians who do not live on reservations (few of whom have pure Native American ancestry).[11] Such a sorting along class and educational lines would reinforce the tendency to class-and-values politics that we noted as a possibility in an earlier section of this chapter.

Put more strongly, class is going to be the factor most affecting the likelihood of reaching the highest levels of the institutional structure for all Americans except blacks and darker-skinned Latinos. Blacks, as Pettigrew has argued, have been treated very differently from all other minority groups. Pettigrew is fully aware that other groups "have suffered discrimination in many forms," and neither he nor we wish to diminish the depth of personal anguish that such discrimination has caused, but he also points out that the situation is different for blacks because they are "the only group to experience the confluence of

9. Jacobs and Labov, "Sex Differences in Intermarriage," 11.

10. On black-white marriages and socioeconomic similarities, see also James H. Gadberry and Richard A. Dodder, "Educational Homogamy in Interracial Marriages: An Update," *Journal of Social Behavior and Personality* 8, no. 6 (1993), 155–163; Matthijs Kalmijn, "Trends in Black/White Intermarriage," *Social Forces* 72, no. 1 (1993), 119–146; Kristyan M. Kouri and Marcia Lasswell, "Black-White Marriages: Social Change and Intergenerational Mobility," *Marriage and Family Review* 19, nos. 3–4 (1993), 241–255.

11. Stephen Steinberg, *The Ethnic Myth: Race, Ethnicity, and Class in America* (New York: Atheneum, 1981); Mary C. Waters, *Ethnic Options: Choosing Identities in America* (Berkeley: University of California Press, 1990).

In making this claim, we are aware that the Hmong, Laotians, Cambodians, and many Vietnamese are more accurately described as refugees fleeing war-ravaged countries and that they may be exceptions to our general statement.

race, slavery, and segregation."[12] They also have been by far the largest minority in the country for centuries, constituting 18.9 percent of the population in 1800, 11.6 percent in 1900, and 12.3 percent in 1990, and they have always been concentrated in specific areas, first in the rural South, then in large cities.

In our view, blacks are still seen as a subjugated minority that remains a potential threat to the white system of power relations, which is why many of the stigmas built into the culture over the course of U.S. history continue to be used by many white Americans, even if the communication of these stigmas is now more subtle.

Blacks have resisted this subjugation and its attendant indignities to self-esteem by developing a "resistance culture" that defies white culture and authority. In the past, when violence was so readily and easily used by whites on assertive blacks, this resistance most often manifested itself in a seeming conformity, passivity, and inarticulateness that slowed the pace of work.[13] Since the Civil Rights Movement the resistance has very often taken the form of an "oppositional culture" that challenges white culture and is communicated through such varied forms as rap music, style of walking, and use of language, although there are regional, class, and individual variations in the degree of acceptance of this culture. The oppositional culture, which is a response to white prejudices, is annoying and even frightening to many white adults, who in turn use it as evidence that blacks are "different," unemployable, and untrustworthy. Further complicating the picture, the oppositional culture is often attractive to privileged white adolescents, who pick up on its defiance of authority and use aspects of it for their own purposes in gaining independence from their parents.

For our purposes, the clash between the dominant and oppositional cultures expresses itself most pertinently in the school setting, leading young blacks to have great ambivalence about doing well in school. Historically, whites did everything they could to deprive blacks of adequate education, fearing that the

---

12. Pettigrew, "Integration and Pluralism," 24–26. For detailed evidence on the difficulties still faced by black Americans, including members of the middle class, see Lois Benjamin, *The Black Elite* (Chicago: Nelson Hall, 1991); Joe R. Feagin and Melvin P. Sikes, *Living with Racism* (Boston: Beacon, 1994).

13. See, for example, Signithia Fordham, *Blacked Out: Dilemmas of Race, Identity, and Success at Capital High* (Chicago: University of Chicago Press, 1996), chapter 1. See also Bonnie L. Mitchell and Joe R. Feagin, "America's Racial-Ethnic Cultures: Opposition Within a Mythical Melting Pot," in Benjamin P. Bowser, Terry Jones, and Gale Auletta Young, eds., *Toward the Multicultural University* (Westport, Conn.: Praeger, 1995), 65–86.

ability to read and write might aid them in their attempts to escape enslavement and segregation. Conversely, blacks put an enormous value on education for the same reason — as an avenue to liberation. More recently, however, as blacks have come to see that a good education does not necessarily lead to respect and occupational levels commensurate with their efforts, many lower-income blacks have begun to doubt its worth. Education came to be seen as a "white man's thing," and those who continued to work hard in school were accused of "acting white." Defying school authorities and refusing to do homework became part of the oppositional culture, and those who ignored the code became subject to rejection by their peers, a combination of social isolation and hazing that few adolescents of any group — or adults, for that matter — are able to endure. The result is that many black students who attend predominantly black public schools, including some children of middle-class parents, are underachievers.[14] Poor performance in school is then used by whites as further evidence for black inferiority, and the lack of proper educational credentials is used to disqualify blacks from job opportunities. The cycle of white and black separation is thereby perpetuated.[15]

To make matters more complex, the unique oppositional identity created by blacks to protect their dignity is not well understood by the immigrant minorities, who are often assumed to be potential allies of blacks because they too

14. John U. Ogbu, "Class Stratification, Racial Stratification, and Schooling," in L. Weis, ed., *Race, Class, and Schooling: Special Studies in Comparative Education* (Albany: State University of New York Press, 1988). For the story of a middle-class black male who developed an oppositional identity, served time in prison, and then became a reporter for the *Washington Post,* see Nathan McCall, *Makes Me Wanna Holler: A Young Black Man in America* (New York: Random House, 1994). For the story of a middle-class black female who developed an oppositional identity, served time in prison, and then became a reporter for the *Washington Post,* see Patrice Gaines, *Laughing in the Dark: From Colored Girl to Woman of Color — a Journey from Prison to Power* (New York: Crown, 1994).

15. We recognize that many children of the white working class also develop negative attitudes toward school and authority figures that lead to discouragement and under-achievement. We also recognize that low-income Latinos of the second and third generations may develop negative attitudes toward school as they come to see themselves less as immigrants and more as members of the working class (see Carola Suarez-Orozco and Marcelo Suarez-Orozco, *Transformations: Migration, Family Life, and Achievement Motivation Among Latino Adolescents* [Stanford: Stanford University Press, 1995]). But we are not focusing in this book on the way the educational system reproduces the class structure. For our views on this issue, see Richard L. Zweigenhaft and G. William Domhoff, *Blacks in the White Establishment? A Study of Race and Class in America* (New Haven: Yale University Press, 1981), 159–162.

are "people of color." In fact, most of these immigrants of color have a very different attitude toward the society than African Americans do and often are puzzled that African Americans do not see the "opportunities" that lie before them and therefore "work harder." Sometimes they are as bothered as whites by the boisterous expressive behaviors that are part of the oppositional culture. Thus most immigrants come to share the stereotypes and prejudices of the dominant white majority.

Perhaps the most painful evidence of this point is an interview study of second-generation West Indians and African Americans conducted by Mary Waters. Her Caribbean interviewees claimed that African Americans are lazy, loud, and impolite. Indeed, their views often sound like those of southern whites in the past, when open expression of prejudice was common. African Americans, in turn, told Waters of their contempt for what they saw as the obsequious behavior of many immigrant blacks, and their skepticism about the immigrants' self-respect and understanding of the obstacles in white American society. The result is a complex relationship between immigrant and native-born blacks, with the immigrants emphasizing their foreign origins to whites and masking their origins to African Americans.[16]

As the sociologist Philip Kasinitz notes, some West Indians in New York City have created ways to educate and socialize their children so as to protect them from adopting certain characteristics prevalent among their African-American peers. Earlier generations of West Indian immigrants sent their children back to the Caribbean to be educated. Shirley Chisholm, for example, who served in Congress from 1969 until 1983, wrote in her 1970 memoir:

> Years later I would know what an important gift my parents had given me by seeing to it that I had my early education in the strict, traditional, British-style schools of Barbados. If I speak and write easily now, that early education is the main reason. . . . It's an inescapable fact, but one I have never liked to discuss because of the bad feeling it can cause, that a surprising number of successful black politicians are of West Indian descent. . . . I think that blacks from the islands tend to have less fear of whites, and therefore less hatred of them. They can meet whites as equals; this is harder for American blacks who tend to overreact by jumping from the feeling that whites are superior to looking down on them as inferior.[17]

16. Mary C. Waters, "Ethnic and Racial Identities of Second-Generation Black Immigrants in New York City," *International Migration Review* 28, no. 4 (1994), 795–820.

17. Cited in Philip Kasinitz, *Caribbean New York: Black Immigrants and the Politics of Race* (Ithaca, N.Y.: Cornell University Press, 1992), 76, 220–221. Both Sidney Poitier, the actor, and Harry Belafonte, the singer, spent portions of their childhoods in the West Indies. As Poitier observed, "I firmly believe that we both had the opportunity to arrive at

More recently, West Indian New Yorkers have founded many private schools that provide "back home"–style education. These schools often emphasize that their teachers have been trained in the West Indies, the curricula are rigorous, the students wear British-style school uniforms, and there is strict discipline. Kasinitz notes that the demand for such schools "did not arise solely from cultural norms about what constitutes a 'good' education" but stemmed from the hope on the part of West Indian parents that they could help their children avoid feelings of inferiority.[18]

On the basis of this analysis, we can see why some of the most prominent black Americans are those who were able to bypass or overcome an oppositional identity. Some have done so because they were immigrants or the children of immigrants; some have done so by attending Catholic schools, where the stringent academic and social requirements provide an alternative identity, or by participating in special programs, like A Better Chance, that also provide new empowered identities; some have done so as a result of the rigorous resocialization provided by the military; and some have been raised in part by a white parent who did not share the oppositional identity of the black culture.[19] The African American who has reached the most powerful position in the power elite, Colin Powell, not only is light-skinned but is the son of Jamaican immigrants and moved up through (and was shaped by) the military, starting with his involvement in ROTC as a college student.[20]

This framework also explains the somewhat greater success of black women than of black men in school. Maintaining the subjugated state of a minority group involves constant vigilance against organized resistance by its male members, so whites have always had a greater fear of black men than of black

the formation of a sense of ourselves without having it fucked with by racism as it existed in the United States." Henry Louis Gates Jr., "Belafonte's Balancing Act," *New Yorker,* August 26–September 2, 1996, pp. 133–143. The quotation appears on p. 134.

18. Kasinitz, *Caribbean New York,* 75.

19. See, for example, James McBride, *The Color of Water: A Black Man's Tribute to his White Mother* (New York: Riverhead, 1996). As a teenager in the 1970s, McBride confronted the oppositional identity and resisted it, in no small part because of his white, Jewish mother. He and all eleven of his black siblings went to college, and eight of the twelve earned graduate or professional degrees. For another exceptionally fine book about the Jewish mother of two black sons educated at Brown and Columbia, see Jane Lazarre, *Beyond the Whiteness of Whiteness: Memoir of a White Mother of Black Sons* (Durham, N.C.: Duke University Press, 1996).

20. Charles C. Moskos and John Sibley Butler, *All That We Can Be: Black Leadership and Racial Integration the Army Way* (New York: Basic, 1996); Henry Louis Gates Jr., "Powell and the Black Elite," *New Yorker,* September 25, 1995, 63–80.

Table 7.2
*Median Annual Full-Time Earnings, 1994*

| | Men | | Women | |
| --- | --- | --- | --- | --- |
| | High School | College | High School | College |
| Black | $25,349 | $36,000 | $17,750 | $31,890 |
| White | 29,321 | 48,600 | 20,050 | 33,700 |
| B/Wa | 86% | 78% | 89% | 95% |

*Source:* Drawn from Ramon G. McLeod, "Elite Black Women Closing Income Gap," *San Francisco Chronicle,* June 11, 1996; see also *Black Population in the U.S.,* U.S. Bureau of the Census, January 1995.
aEarnings of blacks expressed as a percentage of earnings of whites in the same category.

women and have dealt with the slightest hint of organized resistance by them with deadly force. True enough, many black women have been abused physically and sexually by whites, and we are not minimizing the negative psychological consequences of such mistreatment, but it is nonetheless the case that whites have been far more likely to kill, maim, and exclude black men than black women. Most dramatically, less than 1 percent of known lynching victims were women. The legacies of this long historical power confrontation between white and black males are very great.

White fear of black males then interacts with the form of resistance to discrimination that is more often practiced everywhere by males than by females — opposition and defiance. Black males are more likely to defy school authorities and to be disciplined and suspended. They are more likely to come into conflict with their bosses at work and thus lose their jobs. Black women, on the other hand, are less likely to express open resistance because of the way most women are socialized in societies throughout the world. They therefore have fewer open conflicts with authority figures and are more likely to do well in school and hold onto a job.

A related factor reinforces these gender differences: the earnings gap is narrower between black women and white women than it is between black and white men. Because black women use gender as one of their reference points and realize that some of the discrimination against them is based on gender, they are more hopeful about their future and therefore more willing to put up with school. Information on black and white earning differences for men and women is presented in table 7.2. Among other things, it shows that the gap is even greater between college-educated black and white males than it is for men with less education, a fact not easily explained by conventional theories.

Support for this analysis can be found in a detailed attitudinal survey in Los Angeles high schools by sociologist Roslyn Mickelson, who showed that blacks were just as positive as whites in their abstract belief in the value and importance of education but far less likely to trust that education would have any practical value for people such as themselves. She also found that the gap between these abstract and concrete attitudes was smaller for middle-class black women than for either middle- or working-class black men. Concrete attitudes were better predictors of school achievement than abstract attitudes for all the students she studied, and being female was "much more important in achievement for blacks than for whites." These findings, Mickelson argues, reflect the different occupational realities that black men and women face, for "middle-class black women receive the best returns on higher education of any black cohort."[21]

If our overall analysis of the power relationship between whites and blacks is correct, then we are not hopeful that there will be a gradual integration of African Americans without the strong support of laws and programs at the federal level advocated by the sociologist Sharon Collins.[22] It is the need for such laws that is likely to keep African Americans of all income and educational levels as part of the liberal-labor coalition in the Democratic Party. Contrary to those who say that race is no longer important — by pointing to immigrant blacks or Asian Americans — we believe that the gap between African Americans and all others remains the sharpest divide in U.S. society. Indeed, as we argued in *Blacks in the White Establishment? A Study of Race and Class in America,* this divide is wider than all others, including class.

## The Ironies of Diversity

The impetus for greater diversity, as we have stressed, did not come from within the power elite but was the result of external pressures. Generally speaking, members of the power elite reluctantly accepted diversification as a goal for themselves only because they had little choice. This point is best demonstrated in the case of one aspect of diversity called affirmative action, a

21. Roslyn Arlin Mickelson, "The Attitude-Achievement Paradox Among Black Adolescents," *Sociology of Education* 63 (1990), 44–61. The quotations appear on pp. 56, 59.

22. See our discussion of Collins's work in Chapter 3. For a systematic empirical demonstration of the importance of such government policies using time series data, see Martin Carnoy, *Faded Dreams: The Politics and Economics of Race in America* (New York: Cambridge University Press, 1994).

set of programs originally designed to create more job opportunities for African Americans.

As John Skrentny argues, the idea of affirmative action as a policy was adopted by business and political elites very hurriedly in the face of the 290 serious urban disturbances that occurred between 1963 and 1968. These elites quickly legitimized what they saw as preferential hiring through a series of special commissions and government hearings, before the concept was widely discussed, because they feared that even greater unrest might develop. Job programs were seen not only as the quickest and surest way to restore domestic tranquility but as a means of avoiding larger government programs and expanded welfare benefits as well. Moreover, it was the Nixon administration that created the stringent guidelines later attacked as a "quota" system. Once the fear of urban unrest subsided, however, the elite origins of the plan were ignored, and conservatives began to attack affirmative action as unfair to whites and unconstitutional. In the first of many ironies, liberals and minorities ended up defending a plan endorsed by white male elites in a time of crisis.[23]

Moreover, the diversity forced upon the power elite may have helped to strengthen it, at least in the short run. Diversity has given the power elite buffers, ambassadors, tokens, and legitimacy. This is an unintended consequence that few insurgents or social scientists foresaw. One who did was the late E. Digby Baltzell, who argued in the early 1960s that the acceptance of successful Jews would strengthen what he called the establishment. Baltzell believed that the exclusion of successful newcomers, whatever their social origins, would cause the establishment to become castelike and hence vulnerable.[24] But even Baltzell missed the bigger picture. As the power elite diversified far beyond the inclusion of Jews, he joined the long parade of those who lamented the alleged death of the establishment. By the late 1980s and into the 1990s, rather than praising the establishment for taking in new members, Baltzell was bemoaning the "decline of traditional class authority."[25]

23. John David Skrentny, *The Ironies of Affirmative Action: Politics, Culture, and Justice in America* (Chicago: University of Chicago Press, 1996), 78–91. Although he concludes that affirmative action was an "elite" response to a possible loss of societal control, Skrentny abandons any consideration of class. For a critical analysis of the return to a classless paradigm in American social science, see G. William Domhoff, *State Autonomy or Class Dominance?* (Hawthorne, N.Y.: Aldine de Gruyter, 1996).

24. E. Digby Baltzell, *The Protestant Establishment: Aristocracy and Caste in America* (New York: Vintage, 1964; New Haven: Yale University Press, 1987).

25. E. Digby Baltzell, *Sporting Gentlemen: Men's Tennis from the Age of Honor to the Cult of the Superstar* (New York: Free Press, 1995), 388. At the time of his death, in August 1996, Baltzell was in the early stages of research for a book on what he called "the

The power elite has been strengthened because diversity has been achieved primarily by the selection of women and minorities who share the prevailing perspectives and values of those already in power. The power elite is not "multicultural" in any full sense of the concept, but only in terms of ethnic or racial origins. This process has been helped along by those who have called for the inclusion of women and minorities without any consideration of criteria other than sex, race, or ethnicity. Because the demand was strictly for a woman on the Supreme Court, President Reagan could comply by choosing a conservative upper-class corporate lawyer, Sandra Day O'Connor. When pressure mounted to have more black justices, President Bush could respond by appointing Clarence Thomas, a conservative black Republican with a law degree from Yale University. It is yet another irony that appointments like these served to undercut the liberal social movements that caused them to happen.[26]

It is not surprising, therefore, that when we look at the business practices of the women and minorities who have risen to the top of the corporate world, we find that their perspectives and values do not differ markedly from those of their white male counterparts. When Linda Wachner, one of the few women to become CEO of a *Fortune*-level company, the Warnaco Group, concluded that one of Warnaco's many holdings, the Hathaway Shirt Company, was unprofitable, she decided to stop making Hathaway shirts and to sell or close down the factory. It did not matter to Wachner that Hathaway, which started making shirts in 1837, was one of the oldest companies in Maine, that almost all of the five hundred employees at the factory were working-class women, or even that the workers had given up a pay raise to hire consultants to teach them to work more effectively and, as a result, had doubled their productivity. The bottom-line issue was that the company was considered unprofitable, and the average wage of the Hathaway workers, $7.50 an hour, was thought to be too high. (In 1995 Wachner was paid $10 million in salary and stock, and Warnaco had a

---

end of the Protestant establishment." See Eric Pace, "E. Digby Baltzell Dies at 80; Studied WASP's," *New York Times,* August 20, 1996.

26. In addition, evidence from experimental work in social psychology suggests that tokenism has the effect of undercutting the impetus for collective action by the excluded group. See, for example, Stephen C. Wright, Donald M. Taylor, and Fathali M. Moghaddam, "Responding to Membership in a Disadvantaged Group: From Acceptance to Collective Protest," *Journal of Personality and Social Psychology* 58, no. 6 (1990), 994–1003. See also Bruce R. Hare, "On the Desegregation of the Visible Elite; or, Beware of the Emperor's New Helpers: He or She May Look Like You or Me," *Sociological Forum* 10, no. 4 (1995), 673–678.

net income of $46.5 million.) "We did need to do the right thing for the company and the stockholders," explained Wachner.[27]

Nor did ethnic background matter to Thomas Fuentes, a senior vice president at a consulting firm in Orange County, California, a director of Fleetwood Enterprises, and chairman of the Orange County Republican Party. Fuentes targeted fellow Latinos who happened to be Democrats when he sent uniformed security guards to twenty polling places in 1988 "carrying signs in Spanish and English warning people not to vote if they were not U.S. citizens." The security firm ended up paying $60,000 in damages when it lost a lawsuit stemming from this intimidation.[28]

We also recall that the Fanjuls, the Cuban-American sugar barons, have had no problem ignoring labor laws in dealing with their migrant labor force, and that the Sakioka family illegally gave short-handled hoes to its migrant farm workers. These people were acting as employers, not as members of ethnic groups. That is, members of the power elite of both genders and all ethnicities have practiced class politics, making it possible for the power structure to weather the challenge created by the social movements that began in the 1960s.

Those who challenged Christian white male homogeneity in the power structure during the 1960s not only sought to create civil rights and new job opportunities for men and women who had previously been mistreated, important though these goals were. They also hoped that new perspectives in the boardrooms and the halls of government would bring greater openness throughout the society. The idea was both to diversify the power elite and to shift some of its power to previously excluded groups and social classes. The social movements of the 1960s were strikingly successful in increasing the individual rights and freedoms available to all Americans, especially African Americans. As we have shown, they also created pressures that led to openings at the top for individuals from groups that had previously been excluded.

But as the concerns of social movements, political leaders, and the courts came to focus more and more on individual rights, the emphasis on social class and "distributive justice" was lost. The age-old American commitment to

27. Sara Rimer, "Fall of a Shirtmaking Legend Shakes its Maine Hometown," *New York Times,* May 15, 1996. See also Floyd Norris, "Market Place," *New York Times,* June 7, 1996; Stephanie Strom, "Double Trouble at Linda Wachner's Twin Companies," *New York Times,* August 4, 1996. Strom's article reveals that Hathaway Shirts "got a reprieve" when an investor group stepped in to save it.

28. Claudia Luther and Steven Churm, "GOP Official Says He OK'd Observers at Polls," *Los Angeles Times,* November 12, 1988; Jeffrey Perlman, "Firm Will Pay $60,000 in Suit Over Guards at Polls," *Los Angeles Times,* May 31, 1989.

individualism, reinforced at every turn by members of the power elite, won out over the commitment to greater equality of income and wealth that had been one strand of New Deal liberalism and a major emphasis of left-wing activists in the 1960s.

We therefore have to conclude on the basis of our findings that the diversification of the power elite did not generate any changes in an underlying class system in which the top 1 percent have 45.6 percent of all financial wealth, the next 19 percent have 46.7 percent, and the bottom 80 percent have 7.8 percent.[29] The values of liberal individualism embedded in the Declaration of Independence, the Bill of Rights, and the civic culture were renewed by vigorous and courageous activists, but despite their efforts the class structure remains a major obstacle to individual fulfillment for the overwhelming majority of Americans. This fact is more than an irony. It is a dilemma. It combines with the dilemma of race to create a nation that celebrates equal opportunity but is, in reality, a bastion of class privilege and conservatism.

29. Edward N. Wolff, *Top Heavy* (New York: New press, 1996), 67.

# Index